Growing up with unemployment

The transition from school to work is recognised by developmental psychologists as a significant phase in the maturation of young people. The likelihood that the transition might be delayed by a period of prolonged unemployment is now greater than at any time since the 1930s. The psychological consequences of such a delay need to be understood because they may be damaging both to the individual and to society, particularly if they are long-lasting. Such an understanding is essential for the development of sound policy in relation to youth unemployment.

Growing Up with Unemployment describes a major longitudinal study of a large group of South Australian school leavers through the 1980s. It assesses the scale and context of the problem and reviews the methods and theories that have been developed to study the psychological impact of unemployment. It also looks at those factors which may contribute towards helping young people cope with it, such as financial security, social support and being involved in constructive activities with other people. The authors also examine how we might be able to predict future unemployment and understand the relationship between it and alcohol consumption, smoking and drug use.

Growing Up with Unemployment describes a major study with important implications for employment policy, as well as future theory and research. It will be valuable reading for students in social policy and psychology, policy makers and all those who deal with young people.

Anthony H. Winefield, **Helen R. Winefield** and **Robert D. Goldney** are at the University of Adelaide. **Marika Tiggemann** is at the Flinders University of South Australia.

Adolescence and Society

Series editor: John C. Coleman

The Trust for the Study of Adolescence

The general aim of the series is to make accessible to a wide readership the growing evidence relating to adolescent development. Much of this material is published in relatively inaccessible professional journals, and the goals of the books in this series will be to summarise, review, and place in context current work in the field so as to interest and engage both an undergraduate and professional audience.

The intention of the authors is to raise the profile of adolescent studies among professionals and in institutes of higher education. By publishing relatively short, readable books on interesting topics to do with youth and society, the series will make people more aware of the relevance of the subject of adolescence to a wide range of social concerns.

The books will not put forward any one theoretical viewpoint. The authors will outline the most prominent theories in the field, and will include a balanced and critical assessment of each of these. Whilst some of the books may have a clinical or applied slant, the majority will concentrate on normal development.

The readership will rest primarily in two major areas: the undergraduate market, particularly in the fields of psychology, sociology and education; and the professional training market, with particular emphasis on social work, clinical and educational psychology, counselling, youth work, nursing and teacher training.

Also available in this series

Identity in Adolescence
Jane Kroger

The Nature of Adolescence (second edition)
John C. Coleman and Leo Hendry

The Adolescent in the Family
Patricia Noller and Victor Callan

Young People's Understanding of Society
Adrian Furnham and Barrie Stacey

Growing up with unemployment

A longitudinal study of its
psychological impact

Anthony H. Winefield,
Marika Tiggemann, Helen R. Winefield
and Robert D. Goldney

London and New York

First published in 1993
by Routledge
11 New Fetter Lane, London EC4P 4EE

Simultaneously published in the USA and Canada
by Routledge
29 West 35th Street, New York, NY 10001

© 1993 Anthony H. Winefield, Marika Tiggemann,
Helen R. Winefield and Robert D. Goldney

Typeset in Times by
NWL Editorial Services, Langport, Somerset

Printed and bound in Great Britain by
Biddles Ltd, Guildford and King's Lynn

British Library Cataloguing in Publication Data
A catalogue record for this book is available from the British
Library.

Library of Congress Cataloging in Publication Data
Growing up with unemployment: A longitudinal study of its
  psychological impact / Anthony H. Winefield, Marika
  Tiggemann, Helen R. Winefield and Robert D. Goldney.
  p. cm. – (Adolescence and society)
Includes bibliographical references and indexes.
  1. Youth – Employment – Australia – Psychological aspects –
Longitudinal studies. 2. Young adults – Employment –
Australia – Psychological aspects – Longitudinal studies
  3. Unemployment – Australia – Psychological aspects –
Longitudinal studies.
  I. Winefield, Anthony H. (Anthony Harold), 1937–
  II. Series.

HD6276.A82G76   1993   92–28811
331.3′4137994 – dc20   CIP

ISBN 0–415–07454–1
      0–415–07455–X (pbk)

Contents

Illustrations

FIGURES

TABLES

Tables in the Appendix

1 Introduction

There are many reasons for studying the effects of unemployment on young people. In the first place, when the overall level of unemployment is high, as it is during the current recession, it is young people who are the most affected. Also, although the ongoing distress may be less severe in the young unemployed than it is in older people, the effects of unemployment may be more long lasting and produce not only psychological damage, but also negative attitudes to work or even negative attitudes to society.

In a famous review of the literature on the psychological effects of unemployment during the 1930s, Eisenberg and Lazarsfeld (1938) comment:

> The unemployment of youth is probably one of the most serious problems that has had to be faced in the present depression. Statistical data indicate that the age group under 20 was the hardest hit as far as employment was concerned. . . . In general, we obtain the same effects upon the personality of unemployed youth as upon that of unemployed adults, but because of the greater susceptibility of youth and because they are going through a transition period between childhood and maturity these effects are probably more lasting. Youth has in addition the problem of his *first* job. He has typically never worked before, and the job that he gets may very well determine his entire vocational future.
>
> (Eisenberg and Lazarsfeld, 1938: 383)

The transition from school to work is recognised by developmental psychologists as a significant phase in the maturation of young people. It represents their initiation into the adult world. For the vast majority, their first job means that they are no longer completely dependent on their parents financially. On the other hand, the new financial independence is contingent upon their performance on the job and thus carries with it responsibilities such as being punctual, industrious, competent and socially agreeable. It also replaces a peer group of adolescents (school mates) with a peer group of adults (fellow workers).

The likelihood that the normal transition from school to work might be delayed by a period of prolonged unemployment is now greater than at any time since the 1930s. The psychological consequences of such a delay need to be understood because they may be damaging both to the individual and to society, particularly if they are long lasting. Such an understanding must surely be essential for the development of a sound policy in relation to youth unemployment.

This book describes a longitudinal study of more than 3000 South Australian school leavers who left school from 1980–1982. They were surveyed annually throughout the 1980s, although by 1989 the number was reduced to about 450 through attrition. The main focus of the study was to examine the psychological impact of unemployment. However many other questions were asked relating to the important psycho-social transition from adolescence to maturity. Some of the questions were theoretically based, others addressed important practical issues, such as substance use and suicidal ideation. Most of the results have been published in some forty articles in a range of professional journals (all cited in the text and listed in the references) but this monograph, addressed to the non-specialist reader, brings them together and attempts to provide an overview, conclusions, policy implications and suggestions for further research.

The title of the book, *Growing Up with Unemployment*, refers to adolescent life in the decade from 1980 to 1989, when youth unemployment rates were very high in Australia, as in much of the rest of the industrialised world. A whole cohort of young people has grown up in a time of uncertainty and insecurity. Whether or not they themselves have experienced unemployment, they would have friends or relatives who were unemployed. Thus the possibility of unemployment would provide the context for all their early working lives, for their transition from adolescence to adulthood. While we initially thought our study was to be specifically about the psychological effects of unemployment, in the end our work is really about attaining an occupational identity, one of the clearest marks of entry into adult status in our society.

Who do we see as the reader of the book? We have written the book for anyone who has an interest in important social issues and the ways in which individuals cope with their worlds. We also hope the book will be useful to early undergraduate students of psychology, sociology and social work. Teachers, school-counsellors and anyone dealing with young people, might also gain some insight from our study. Fellow researchers will find detailed statistical information in the Tables contained in the Appendix. Finally, perhaps naively, we would like to think that our findings might be useful to those responsible for formulating and implementing policy.

THE CONTEXT: UNEMPLOYMENT IN OECD COUNTRIES SINCE 1980

Although the average unemployment rate in OECD (Organisation for Economic Co-operation and Development) countries was lower in 1990 (6.3 per cent) than it was during the 1980s (average 7.4 per cent), having fallen every year since 1983, by 1991 it had increased to 7.1 per cent and was projected to reach 7.4 per cent in 1992. Unemployment rates in all twenty-four OECD countries from 1989 to 1991, as well as projected rates for 1992 are shown in Table 1.1.

As can be seen, unemployment rates increased in most countries from 1990 to 1991. Of the twenty-four countries, no fewer than eighteen showed an increase. Moreover, in ten cases the increase exceeded 1 per cent. The increase was greatest in Finland (4.2 per cent), followed by the UK (2.8 per cent), Australia and New Zealand (2.6 per cent) Canada (2.2 per cent), Ireland (2.1 per cent), Sweden and the US (1.2 per cent) and Turkey (1.1 per cent). Even in Switzerland, the country enjoying the lowest unemployment rate of all, the rate doubled (from 0.6 per cent to 1.2 per cent). Moreover it was anticipated that the unemployment rate in seventeen of the countries would continue to increase from 1991 to 1992. In 1992, more than half (thirteen) of the OECD countries were expected to have unemployment rates of around 10 per cent or more, ranging from 9.6 per cent to 16.5 per cent.

Of course, the rates differ considerably from country to country, but based on the following arbitrary cut-offs, in 1991 five countries might be regarded as enjoying very low unemployment rates (1.2 per cent to 2.7 per cent): Iceland, Japan, Luxembourg, Sweden and Switzerland; four countries might be classified as low (3.4 per cent to 5.3 per cent): Austria, Germany, Norway and Portugal; three countries might be classified as moderate (6.1 per cent to 7.7 per cent): Finland, Netherlands and the US; ten countries might be classified as high (8.6 per cent to 11.5 per cent): Australia, Belgium, Canada, Denmark, France, Greece, Italy, New Zealand, Turkey and the UK; and two countries might be classified as very high (15.8 per cent to 15.9 per cent): Ireland and Spain.

The situation in Australia, by comparison with the other OECD countries, was worse in 1991 than at any time during the 1980s. In 1991 the unemployment rate in Australia (9.5 per cent) exceeded the OECD average (7.1 per cent) by 2.4 per cent. The largest difference during the 1980s was only 1.3 per cent in 1983 (9.8 per cent vs 8.5 per cent). In 1992, an even greater difference of 2.7 per cent was projected (10.1 per cent vs 7.4 per cent), when the unemployment rate in Australia was expected to be higher than at any time since the 1930s. The contrast is illustrated graphically in Figure 1.1 which compares the unemployment rates in Australia with the average OECD rates from 1980 to 1992.

Table 1.1 Unemployment rates (1980–1991) and projected rate (1992) in OECD countries

Country	1980	1981	1982	1983	1984	1985	1986	1987	1988	1989	1990	1991	1992
Australia	6.0	5.7	7.0	9.8	8.9	8.1	8.0	8.0	7.1	6.1	6.9	9.5	10.1
Austria	1.9	2.5	3.5	4.1	3.8	3.6	3.1	3.8	3.6	3.1	3.3	3.4	3.8
Belgium	7.9	10.2	11.9	13.2	13.2	12.3	11.6	11.3	10.3	9.3	8.8	9.4	9.7
Canada	7.4	7.5	10.9	11.8	11.2	10.4	9.5	8.8	7.7	7.5	8.1	10.3	10.2
Denmark	6.5	10.3	11.0	11.4	8.5	7.3	5.5	5.4	6.5	9.2	9.5	10.3	10.2
Finland	4.6	4.8	5.3	5.4	5.2	5.0	5.3	5.0	4.5	3.5	3.5	7.7	9.8
France	6.3	7.4	8.1	8.3	9.7	10.2	10.4	10.5	10.0	9.4	8.9	9.4	10.1
Germany	3.2	4.5	6.4	7.9	7.9	8.0	7.6	7.6	7.6	5.6	5.1	4.6	5.0
Greece	2.8	4.0	5.8	7.9	8.1	7.8	7.4	7.4	7.6	7.5	7.2	8.6	9.6
Iceland	0.0	0.0	0.9	0.9	0.8	0.8	0.8	0.8	0.7	1.1	1.7	1.6	2.0
Ireland	7.3	9.9	11.4	14.0	15.6	17.4	17.4	17.6	16.7	15.6	13.7	15.8	16.5
Italy	7.5	7.8	8.4	9.3	9.9	10.1	10.9	11.8	11.8	12.1	11.2	10.9	10.8
Japan	2.0	2.2	2.4	2.6	2.7	2.6	2.8	2.8	2.5	2.3	2.1	2.2	2.3
Luxembourg	0.6	1.3	1.3	1.9	1.9	1.8	1.2	1.7	1.7	1.3	1.3	1.4	1.4
Netherlands	6.0	8.5	11.3	11.8	11.9	10.9	10.3	9.6	9.2	7.4	6.5	6.1	6.4
New Zealand	2.2	3.6	3.5	5.6	5.7	4.1	4.0	4.1	5.6	7.1	7.8	10.4	11.5
Norway	1.6	2.0	2.6	3.4	3.1	2.6	2.0	2.1	3.2	4.9	5.2	5.3	5.1
Portugal	7.7	7.4	7.3	7.8	8.4	8.5	8.5	7.0	5.7	5.1	4.6	3.9	4.5
Spain	11.8	13.8	15.6	17.0	19.7	21.1	20.8	20.1	17.1	17.3	16.3	15.9	15.2
Sweden	2.0	2.5	3.1	3.5	3.1	2.8	2.7	1.9	1.6	1.4	1.5	2.7	4.1
Switzerland	0.2	0.2	0.4	0.9	1.1	0.9	0.8	0.7	0.6	0.6	0.6	1.2	1.6
Turkey	11.2	11.3	11.4	11.7	11.4	11.4	10.2	9.2	9.5	10.2	10.4	11.5	13.2
UK	5.6	9.0	10.4	11.2	11.1	11.5	11.6	10.4	8.3	6.2	5.9	8.7	9.9
US	7.0	7.5	9.5	9.5	7.4	7.1	6.9	6.1	5.4	5.3	5.5	6.7	6.7
Total	5.9	6.7	8.0	8.5	8.1	8.0	7.9	7.5	6.9	6.4	6.3	7.1	7.4

Source: OECD (1991a, 1991b)

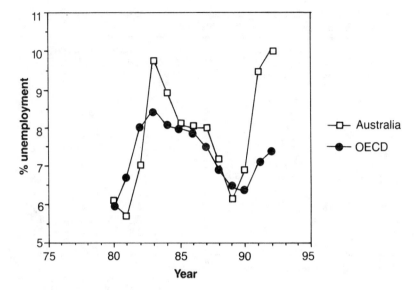

Figure 1.1 Unemployment rates in Australia and average rates in all OECD countries, 1980–1992
Source: OECD (1991a, 1991b)

As many political commentators have pointed out, national governments responsible for producing labour market statistics have a vested interest in minimising official unemployment rates, and frequently use strategies deliberately designed to conceal the real extent of the problem. Therefore, it is reasonable to conclude that the real levels of unemployment were higher than those shown in Table 1.1.

Amongst young people (defined as those aged from 15 to 24 years), the unemployment rates are much higher, usually around double the overall rate. Interestingly, there was a reduction in this ratio in Europe from 2.52 in 1979 to 2.07 in 1990. This reduction, according to the OECD *Economic Outlook* of December 1991:

> can be partly attributed to deliberate efforts by certain European countries to target a wide variety of labour market schemes specifically to young people. During the latter part of the 1980s, France, the United Kingdom and Denmark each spent around a quarter per cent of GDP on youth measures, Italy and Ireland twice as much, whereas outlays on similar measures in the United States were negligible.
>
> (OECD, 1991a: 41)

In Australia, there was a dramatic increase in the unemployment rate from 1.6 per cent in 1970, to 4.6 per cent in 1975 to 6.7 per cent in 1980. In South

Table 1.2 Overall and youth (15–19-year-old, 20–24-year-old) national and South Australian unemployment rates, 1980–1992

Year	National			South Australia		
	15–19	*20–24*	*Total*	*15–19*	*20–24*	*Total*
1980	18.6	9.6	6.7	22.2	11.1	8.1
1981	17.6	8.9	6.3	22.5	10.9	7.7
1982	19.1	9.9	7.1	20.7	10.7	8.3
1983	25.8	16.2	10.7	27.1	15.2	11.1
1984	26.0	14.7	10.4	25.3	15.0	10.5
1985	26.2	13.7	9.6	23.1	13.8	9.5
1986	22.6	11.9	8.9	23.8	11.9	8.8
1987	23.5	12.3	9.1	23.1	12.2	9.8
1988	20.8	11.2	8.2	21.0	14.4	9.8
1989	18.0	9.2	7.3	18.0	11.1	8.6
1990	16.8	10.3	7.1	18.3	12.2	8.2
1991	22.6	14.2	9.5	19.8	13.8	9.8
1992	26.4	15.7	11.5	29.5	18.6	12.5

Source: Australian Bureau of Statistics (February figures)

Australia, the unemployment rate has been somewhat higher than the national rate as can be seen from Table 1.2.

Table 1.2 shows the overall unemployment rates, as well as the unemployment rates for 15 to 19-year-olds and for 20 to 24-year-olds from 1980 to 1992. These are February figures obtained from the Australian Bureau of Statistics (ABS) which, unlike the OECD, publishes monthly, rather than annual figures. (This accounts for the discrepancies between the figures shown in Tables 1.1 and 1.2.) We chose to quote the February figures for purposes of illustration, because they seemed most relevant for portraying the employment prospects facing Australian school leavers. (In Australia, the school year ends in December and January is the month when most people are on holiday.)

Throughout our study (1980 to 1989), the unemployment rates for 15 to 19-year-olds in South Australia ranged from 21 per cent to 27 per cent (during the relevant years from 1980 to 1984) and the unemployment rate for 20 to 24-year-olds in South Australia ranged from 12 per cent to 15 per cent (during the relevant years from 1983 to 1989). Of course, the current (1992) rates of 29.5 per cent (for the 15 to 19-year-olds) and 18.6 per cent (for the 20 to 24-year-olds) show that the youth unemployment problem in South Australia (as in the rest of the country) is even worse than at any time during the 1980s.

In 1980, we had both practical and academic reasons for starting a major study of youth unemployment. Practically, the rate was high and the problem was causing much unease and a sense of lack of direction, in governments used to 'full employment' since the 1930s. In terms of psychological theories, unemployment represented a major life stress which was affecting substantial numbers of people in the community. Thus it provided an opportunity to study how people cope with stress and who copes best. We therefore initiated the longitudinal study which is described in this book, starting with more than 3000 young people. Our goals were multiple and included finding answers to questions such as:

1 What are the psychological and other effects of unemployment on young people? We followed a large group from school into the workforce, comparing the unemployed with the employed and students.
2 Who is most likely to become unemployed?
3 What helps people to cope with unemployment?
4 Are there policy implications from our results?

PREVIEW

The chapters of our book follow a logical progression but can also be read independently to cover a particular facet. This enables instructors to set a particular chapter for study if they so choose, and readers with particular interests to find the relevant material.

Chapter 2 begins by looking at the negative social attitudes towards unemployed people and considers whether this is likely to persist, given the likelihood that there may not be enough jobs to go round for the foreseeable future. It then compares the situation in the 1980s and 1990s with the earlier decade of economic recession and very high unemployment, the 1930s, and compares the research carried out in the 1930s with recent research. It goes on to discuss the costs of unemployment to the individual in terms of both psychological and physical health. Next, it briefly mentions different methods that have been used to study the psychological effects of unemployment, then it lists factors that have been shown to moderate the psychological consequences of unemployment. Finally, it outlines eight theories that have been proposed to help understand the psychological response to unemployment.

Chapter 3 looks in more detail at the different methods that have been used in unemployment research (aggregate studies, case studies, cross-sectional studies and longitudinal studies) and offers a critical analysis of their strengths and shortcomings. It goes on to describe in detail the methods used in our own prospective longitudinal study, including details of the sample (including information about attrition over the years), details of the measures we used, and the procedures of data collection. It concludes by presenting a profile of the young people in our sample, including data concerning their work attitudes and aspirations.

Chapter 4 presents the main longitudinal and cross-sectional data relating employment status to psychological well-being. Each year, different occupational groups were compared on a range of measures of psychological well-being. Some measures were incorporated into our questionnaire from the outset (1980), so that later scores could be compared with baseline (at-school) measures. Others were only introduced for the first time in 1984 so baseline measures were not available. In 1981 and 1982 the following occupational groups were compared: those still at school, those employed, those unemployed and those engaged in full-time tertiary study. In 1983 there were only three groups because all our respondents had left school. From 1984 to 1988 we distinguished between those employed youngsters who expressed overall satisfaction with their jobs and those who expressed overall dissatisfaction. These two groups were compared with the unemployed and the tertiary students. In 1989, the final year of the study, a shortened version of the questionnaire was distributed. By then, the number of unemployed was only eight, so they were combined with the dissatisfied employed.

Chapter 5 looks at moderating factors – those factors that might help unemployed youngsters cope with their unemployment. The factors examined were age, sex, ethnic origin, socio-economic status, academic potential (based on teacher ratings), educational level (defined by years of secondary schooling), financial hardship, social support, employment commitment, attributional style, reasons for unemployment, length of unemployment and time use.

Chapter 6 considers the theoretical implications of our findings in relation to the eight theories that were outlined in Chapter 2: first, four specific theories (stage theory, deprivation theory, agency theory and the vitamin model); and then four general theories (life-span developmental theory, learned helplessness theory, attribution theory and expectancy-value theory).

Chapter 7 looks at factors that might enable us to predict future unemployment, as well as future participation in tertiary study, based on information that was available while the young people were still at school. We looked at background characteristics such as sex, ethnic origin and socio-economic status, as well as a range of academic, personality and attitudinal variables.

Chapter 8 uses the data both from the questionnaires administered as well as from psychiatric interviews conducted in 1984, to examine the possible connection between unemployment and clinically significant psychological illness, and suicidal ideation.

Chapter 9 is concerned with the possible link between drug use, health, finances and employment status. In later versions of our questionnaire, administered after our respondents had left school, we included questions relating to the consumption of alcohol, tobacco, prescription drugs, non-prescription (over-the-counter) drugs and 'other' drugs, including the possible use of illegal substances such as marijuana, heroin and cocaine. We also included questions asking respondents about their physical health and about their financial status.

Chapter 10 summarises the findings and discusses them in terms of their theoretical implications, their practical implications, their implications for further research and their policy implications.

ACKNOWLEDGEMENTS

We would like to thank the following organisations and individuals who have helped us with our work. We are grateful to John Coleman, Sally McGregor, Joan Thompson and John Keeler for their constructive comments on an earlier version of the book and they are in no way responsible for any of its shortcomings. At various stages we have received financial support from the following Australian funding bodies: the Education Research and Development Committee, the Australian Research Grants Committee, the National Health and Medical Research Council, the Australian Research Council, the University of Adelaide, the Glenside Hospital Research Foundation and the Australian Wine Foundation.

Collaborators in the early stages of the project included Peter Tillett and Jane Delin from the South Australia Department of Education for whose contributions we are grateful. We are indebted to the following individuals who have provided assistance with data coding and statistical computing: Michael Correll, Queenie Inshaw, Adrian Barnett, Shirley Smith and Judith Saebel. We are grateful to Matthew Winefield for his help in formatting and preparation of the text and tables. We wish to thank the principals and staff of the twelve schools which participated in the project for their generous and enthusiastic help in the initial stages. Finally, and most of all, we want to thank the young people who gave up so much of their time to participate, particularly the 450 who stayed with it until the end.

2 Background

Unemployment since the early 1980s has come to be seen as a serious social problem in many industrialised societies. Whether it should be regarded as more or less serious than the widespread unemployment of the 1930s, however, is open to debate. On the one hand the level of unemployment has not yet reached the levels that were prevalent during the Great Depression. Moreover, the physical hardship endured by the unemployed today is no doubt less severe because of improved welfare benefits. On the other hand, some writers have argued that even so, the psychological distress experienced by the currently unemployed may be even greater than was the case during the earlier decade.

SOCIAL ATTITUDES TO THE UNEMPLOYED

The psychological distress suffered by the unemployed today appears to be compounded by their own pessimism and by the hostile attitude of society to them. It is by no means unrealistic for an unemployed person to be pessimistic about the future. Because of structural changes in the economy, particularly the shift from labour-intensive to capital-intensive industry, the future availability of jobs may well continue to decline throughout the 1990s. Moreover it is well known that an unemployed person's chances of getting a job decrease as the length of unemployment increases (Adams and Mangum, 1978; Casson, 1979).

On the other hand, the hostile attitude of society towards the unemployed does not appear to be justified. It usually takes the form that unemployed people could get work if they really wanted it. In other words, they choose to be unemployed. As Kelvin and Jarrett (1985) put it:

In effect, the unemployed individual always seems to be somehow suspect: at best he is seen as probably in part to blame for his unemployment; and even if he is 'genuine' it is thought that he should be kept short, so that he keeps looking for work – otherwise there is the suspicion that he might just sit back and do nothing.

(Kelvin and Jarrett, 1985: 95)

This attitude reflects a theory in neo-classical economics known as 'search theory'. The theory sees people as wealth maximisers who, when unemployed, choose to search for a better job than what is currently available (Lippman and McCall, 1976). While this may explain the behaviour of some unemployed people, it hardly seems applicable to the majority. Parnes (1982), on the basis of a ten-year longitudinal study conducted in the United States, concluded that there is very little support for the notion of 'voluntary unemployment'.

One factor which contributes to the feeling that the workless do not really want jobs is the fact that areas of very high unemployment tend to be localised. Thus in the United Kingdom, for example, unemployment is very much higher in the industrial north and Midlands than it is in the south. The unwillingness of many unemployed people to migrate south in order to obtain employment is seen as evidence that they prefer living on the dole to working. Of course, this conclusion overlooks the disruption to the family and friendship bonds that such migration entails, as well as the substantially higher cost of housing in the south of England (Sinfield, 1980).

Another factor which can contribute to hostile attitudes towards the un-employed is the policy of the government. This was illustrated in Australia, following a change of government in 1975. The new government sought to implement a policy of getting tough with the unemployed, many of whom it viewed as 'dole cheats' (or 'dole bludgers'). This view was widely dissemin-ated by the news media and public opinion polls taken in the late 1970s showed that, despite evidence to the contrary (Brewer, 1975), 40 to 50 per cent of Australians thought that the main cause of unemployment was that the unemployed did not want to work (Windschuttle, 1979). More recent surveys suggest that public attitudes in Australia show opposition to the payment of unemployment benefits.

A third factor that seems to be important is that some unemployed people, if only a small minority, do cheat the system either by deliberately avoiding work, or by taking unemployment benefits to which they are not entitled. Many people know of such instances, either directly or indirectly, and are likely to assume that such practices are more widespread than they really are.

Seabrook (1982) proposed three ways in which unemployment in the 1980s was worse than it was in the 1930s. First, because society was generally more affluent in the 1980s, the contrast in living standards between the unemployed and employed was much greater than in the 1930s. Second, because benefits have increased, the unemployed were more likely to be seen as lazy and choosing not to work. Third, there was a more widespread feeling that the situation was unlikely to improve than was the case in the 1930s.

Finally, social attitudes to unemployment are influenced by the fact that it is unevenly distributed throughout society. As Sinfield (1980) puts it:

> those who piously claim that unemployment is a burden which affects everyone are usually not affected by it themselves. It is mainly those who are already disadvantaged upon whom the main burden falls: people in low-paying and insecure jobs, the very young and the oldest in the labour force, people from ethnic or racial minorities, people from among the disabled and handicapped, and generally those with the least skills and living in the most depressed areas.
>
> (Sinfield, 1980: 18)

Kelvin (1980), in a prophetic piece, examined likely changes in social attitudes assuming that unemployment continues to increase until the end of the century. He argued that hostility to the unemployed stems from the Protestant ethic: the belief that individual salvation depends on hard work. As unemployment becomes more widespread almost everyone will be affected by it, directly or indirectly. Then it will no longer be possible to attribute it to individual laziness or lack of commitment. This, in turn, will lead to a decline in the Protestant ethic and a more tolerant attitude to the unemployed.

The view that unemployment is bound to increase is not shared by all who have written on the subject. For example, both Illich (1978) and Sinfield (1980) have argued that all citizens have a right to work and that it is the responsibility of the government to protect that right.

UNEMPLOYMENT AND POVERTY

At the end of the 1970s, Jahoda (1979) commented on the dearth of research into the psychological consequences of unemployment during that decade, in contrast to the extensive work in the 1930s (reviewed by Eisenberg and Lazarsfeld, 1938). A similar comment was made by Hyman (1979) who suggested also that the study of poverty is too often confused with the study of unemployment. Of course poverty is frequently associated with unemployment but not always. Many poor people have jobs and some very affluent people do not, but social scientists have not generally considered the latter group worthy of serious study.

The playwright Shaw once declared that the problem of the poor is poverty. Possibly the main reason for the relative neglect of the problem of the unemployed until recently has been the implicit assumption that the problem of the unemployed is poverty. The corollary, of course, is that people for whom unemployment is not accompanied by poverty do not have a problem. This assumption may well be justified in relation to the rich although even that is open to question. Anecdotal evidence about the emotional problems of the sons and daughters of very rich and successful people suggests that they may suffer from a lack of purpose and sense of personal identity as a result of not having a meaningful occupation. The sort of physical degradation suffered by many unemployed people in the 1930s described so graphically by George Orwell in *The Road To Wigan Pier* is less common today. Nevertheless many unemployed people are poor in the sense that they are unable to afford many of the basic comforts which most of us take for granted. This is well illustrated by the responses elicited from the unemployed people interviewed by Marsden (Marsden, 1982; Marsden and Duff, 1975).

Even in the 1930s, it was possible to disentangle the negative effects of unemployment from those of plain poverty. This can be illustrated from the classic *Marienthal* study (Jahoda, Lazarsfeld and Zeisel, 1933, translated 1971). Marienthal was a small industrial village in Austria consisting of only 478 families all of which relied for employment on a single textile firm until it closed down in 1929. The team of researchers lived in the village as part of the community for several months during which time they collected an enormous amount of data. Although the main object of the study was the unemployed community rather than the unemployed individual, many of the observations are relevant to the latter. The authors concluded that the effects of unemployment were not to increase anger and resentment but rather the reverse. It seemed to lead to an overall 'diminution of expectation and activity, a disrupted sense of time, and a steady decline into apathy through a variety of stages and attitudes' (Jahoda, Lazarsfeld and Zeisel 1933/1971: 2).

One of the most revealing observations concerned the decline in library usage. From 1929 to 1931 the number of loans dropped by 49 per cent even though the former borrowing charge had been abolished. This was accounted for both by a decline in the number of borrowers as well as by a decline in the number of books per borrower. This change in behaviour could be attributed to a growth in apathy due to unemployment rather than just to poverty.

Further evidence that not all of the negative effects of unemployment are a consequence of poverty has been gathered from studies of the relatively affluent unemployed. Hartley's (1980) study of unemployed managers in the United Kingdom and Kaufman's (1982) study of unemployed professional engineers in the United States both fall into this category. Kaufman maintained that although most studies of the psychological effects of unemployment have concentrated on blue-collar workers, professionals experience more severe psychological problems. Moreover, he suggested that among the highly educated, underemployment is an even greater problem than unemployment.

Another strategy for separating the effects of unemployment from the effects of poverty is to study youth unemployment. For a variety of reasons, such as what Casson (1979) calls the 'job-search' hypothesis, unemployment tends to be relatively high among young people even during times of prosperity. This is attributable to a number of factors. For example school leavers, because they still live at home and are provided for, can afford to explore the job market. Also, due to their inexperience of work, they are more inclined to want to try out different jobs. Finally, because they are often unskilled, the types of jobs that are open to them are likely to be boring and arduous so that they are tempted to seek something better. This hypothesis, as was pointed out earlier, is not applicable during periods when jobs are scarce, like the present. Other factors explain the very high levels of youth unemployment that are the source of so much concern currently.

The school leaver is especially vulnerable during periods of recession when there are not enough jobs. Most employers are not willing to dismiss older workers just to provide vacancies for the young. This unwillingness is likely to be based on a number of grounds. For example, there is the risk that the new employee may be less satisfactory; the new employee may require on-the-job training at the expense of the employer; and the older employee is more likely to be protected by a strong trade union which could initiate industrial action in the event of one of its members being dismissed without due cause. Another consideration is that the employer may feel that it is not humane to discard an older employee who may have family dependents, in order to take on a school leaver. Finally, even when young people are able to get jobs, they sometimes find themselves dismissed when they reach a certain age and become eligible for a higher (adult) rate of pay.

YOUTH UNEMPLOYMENT

Not only are young people the most likely to be affected when unemployment rates are high, but there is also the danger that the psychological effects of unemployment on young people may be more damaging, both to the individual and to society, than its effects on older people.

We need to distinguish the acute (short-term) and chronic (long-term) effects of unemployment. So far as the acute effects are concerned, it is generally found that young unemployed people suffer less ongoing distress than mature unemployed people, even after similar periods of continuous unemployment (Broomhall and Winefield, 1990; Rowley and Feather, 1987). On the other hand, it has been shown in many studies that unemployed youngsters show poorer psychological well-being than their employed counterparts (Banks and Jackson, 1982; Stokes, 1983; Tiggemann and Winefield, 1980).

Whether unemployment, particularly prolonged unemployment, after leaving school produces lasting psychological damage, remains to be seen. Unfortunately, there are good reasons, from a theoretical standpoint, to believe that it may. Two of the theories outlined later in this chapter, Erikson's (1959) life-span developmental theory and Seligman's (1975) learned helplessness theory, both suggest that unemployment may be particularly damaging for young people.

An additional cause for concern is the fear that unemployed young people may develop anti-social attitudes or behaviours. Certainly it is a widely held popular view that unemployed youngsters tend to become engaged in delinquent or criminal acts, although there is a lack of reliable evidence supporting such a view. Nevertheless, some incidental evidence was reported by Donovan, Oddy, Pardoe and Ades (1986) in a longitudinal study of 16-year-old school leavers:

> Thirty-seven % (16) of the unemployed group had either been formally cautioned or found guilty of a criminal offence . . . compared with 21% (9) of the YOPS group and 20% (9) of the employed. More important, over half of the unemployed (and only one individual from the other two groups) with a criminal record had committed offences since leaving school.
>
> (Donovan, Oddy, Pardoe and Ades 1986: 75)

Some writers have expressed the fear that unemployed young people, even if they do not commit criminal acts, may engage in various forms of rebellious activity. There seems to be little foundation for this fear, however. As Coleman and Hendry (1990) say, after reviewing the literature: 'In reality it seems that unemployed individuals are more likely to become isolated, apathetic, and helpless than to collude on some collective rebellion' (Coleman and Hendry, 1990: 197).

Perhaps a more realistic cause for concern is that unemployed youngsters will develop socially undesirable attitudes to work. For example, work commitment might be expected to decline as a result of prolonged unemployment. Several studies have shown that individuals whose commitment to work is low suffer less distress than those whose commitment is high (Banks and Ullah, 1988; Jackson, Stafford, Banks and Warr, 1983; Stokes, 1983). On the other hand, other studies have shown that unemployment does not seem to affect adolescent work values (Isralowitz and Singer, 1986, 1987; Tiggemann and Winefield, 1980).

INDIVIDUAL COSTS OF UNEMPLOYMENT

The psychological effects of failing to find employment on young school leavers may well be different from the effects of job loss on mature workers. Psychologists have devoted a great deal of attention to the emotional changes that usually occur in the individual following job loss. Hayes and Nutman (1981), for example, view job loss as a 'psycho-social transition', a notion proposed by Parkes (1971). Parkes defined psycho-social transitions as 'those major changes in life space which are lasting in their effects, which take place over a relatively short period of time and which affect large areas of the assumptive world' (Parkes, 1971: 103).

Following Bakke (1933), several authors have proposed a sequence of stages that characterise the response to job loss. Harrison (1976), for example, postulated four stages: shock, optimism, pessimism and fatalism. Changes in morale are assumed to accompany the transition through the four stages, in particular changes in self-respect or self-esteem.

Although many studies have explored the psychological effects of job loss, until recently there has been very little evidence relating to the consequences of failing to find a job. Researchers have understandably tended to view the problems of the redundant worker as more pressing than those of the young job seeker. Consequently the literature contains more reports of studies of job loss than studies of youth unemployment. Moreover many reported studies of youth unemployment have been carried out by economists whose interest has been to understand its economic, not its psychological, causes and consequences (Adams and Mangum, 1978; Casson, 1979).

As a result, the economic costs to the community of job loss are well documented. Its effects on both physical and mental health have been extensively studied. Brenner's work has established that downturns in the economy are associated with increases in heart disease mortality (Brenner, 1971), as well as various other measures of physical illness (Brenner and Mooney, 1983) and mental illness (Brenner, 1973). Similar findings have been reported by Catalano and Dooley (1983), Dumont (1989), Feather and Barber (1983), Iversen, Sabroe and Damsgaard (1989), Kasl and Cobb (1980), Kasl, Gore and Cobb (1975), Kemp and Mercer (1983), Smith (1987a, 1991), Warr (1987) and Warr and Jackson (1984).

Warr (1983) lists nine potentially negative features of unemployment based on findings from a number of recent empirical investigations. First, because unemployment usually implies reduced income, financial anxiety is frequently observed. Second, partly due to not having to leave the house, and partly due to reduced income, the variety of life tends to be restricted. Third, there are fewer goals or aims in the life of the unemployed person. Fourth, unemployment leads to a reduction in the scope of decision making. Of course, there is endless scope for decision making with respect to trivial matters such as when to get up, or whether to watch television, but not with respect to significant decisions that might have wide or long-term consequences. Fifth, the satisfaction derived from the practice of skill or expertise is denied. Sixth, unemployment frequently leads to an increase in psychologically threatening activities. Seeking unsuccessfully for jobs, and trying to borrow money, for example, are both likely to entail unpleasant rebuffs and interactions with others of a humiliating kind. A seventh, associated consequence is insecurity about the future.

The last two consequences affect social life and status. The number of social contacts for the unemployed person is clearly reduced, although this does not necessarily imply a reduction in the amount of social contact. Warr and Payne (1983), for example, found that unemployed men reported spending more time with friends and neighbours since they became unemployed. Finally, social status is generally related to employment status. Thus an unemployed person will have lost, or failed to acquire, an accepted social position. The unemployed status is widely regarded as inferior and this is likely to result in the unemployed person being held in low esteem by others, as well as experiencing low self-esteem.

Despite all these potentially negative consequences of unemployment, it has been found that not all unemployed people report being worse off in terms of psychological health. In a study of nearly 1000 unemployed men, Warr and Jackson (1984) found that although 20 per cent reported a deterioration, 8 per cent reported an improvement. Where an improvement was reported it was nearly always attributed to the removal of occupational pressures. Finally, Kagan (1987) has argued that it is misleading to say that unemployment causes ill health. According to him, ill health is caused by poverty and psycho-social stressors both of which may occur in either employment or unemployment.

SOCIAL COSTS OF UNEMPLOYMENT

Although beyond the scope of this book, it appears that there are also social costs of unemployment. Much has been written, much of it speculative, about the link between unemployment and crime as well as other forms of anti-social activity including increased hostility to minority groups. It is frequently assumed, for example, that increased unemployment is a cause of increased criminality but this is a contentious issue. In Britain, for example, research by Carr-Hill and Stern (1983) has questioned the assumption and similar reservations have been expressed based on American research (Little, Villemez and Smith, 1982) and Australian research (Blakers, 1984).

Statistical evidence of an association between increases in youth unemployment and increases in reports of juvenile delinquency does not demonstrate a causal connection. (The limitations of data based on aggregate studies is discussed further in the next chapter.) It is possible, for example, that poverty (or income inequality) rather than unemployment is responsible for increased delinquency. An Australian study by Braithwaite and Biles (1979) showed that the unemployed experienced a higher victimisation rate than the employed in areas such as theft, breaking and entering, robbery with violence and assault. Although this study did not identify the employment status of those responsible for these crimes, it suggests that the unemployed are more likely to be victims of crime than are the employed.

THE PSYCHOLOGY OF UNEMPLOYMENT

The study of unemployment may be of interest to the psychologist for a number of reasons. During periods of prosperity when there are plenty of jobs available, the main question of interest may be why some people nevertheless remain unemployed. The psychologist may wish to develop a psychological profile of the 'work-shy' individual. This was one of the main aims of Tiffany, Cowan and Tiffany (1970). They saw the problem of unemployment as a failure of the individual to adjust to a specific, i.e. work, social environment. Using the Tennessee Self-Concept Scale developed by Fitts (1965), to compare employed with unemployed, or 'work-inhibited', individuals, they arrived at a social-psychological portrait of the unemployed. They concluded that the unemployed see themselves as 'undesirable, doubt their own worth, often feel anxious, depressed, and unhappy, and have little faith or confidence in themselves' (Tiffany, Cowan and Tiffany, 1970: 92).

Since the 1960s when the Tiffany research was carried out, there has been a shift of focus. Psychologists now are more interested in the psychological effects of unemployment than in the psychological characteristics of the 'work-shy'. This interest has both practical and theoretical implications. From a practical point of view, it is clear that if unemployment produces a deterioration in the psychological well-being of the unemployed then this is likely to have further repercussions. It will have fairly immediate consequences, for example, on marital harmony. This has been demonstrated in every recent study in which unemployed people and their spouses have been studied (e.g. Aubrey, Tefft and Kingsbury, 1990; Liem and Liem, 1988; Marsden, 1982; Seabrook, 1982; Sinfield, 1980), as well as similar studies carried out in the 1930s (e.g. Jahoda, Lazarsfeld and Zeisel, 1933/1971).

In cases where the effects are more severe, perhaps following prolonged periods of unemployment, there may be effects that require some sort of intervention. The effects may range from emotional disorders such as anxiety or depression to psychosomatic disorders requiring physical treatment. The emotional problems, if not treated, may lead to various forms of anti-social behaviour. These are likely to include wife and child abuse, alcoholism or other forms of drug abuse, as well as criminal activities such as house-breaking and shop-lifting.

Psychosomatic disorders are physical symptoms that arise primarily as a result of exposure to psychological stress. Typical examples include hypertension, headaches, ulcers and dermatitis. Many other, if not all, physical illnesses are believed to be aggravated by exposure to psychological stress. Given that unemployment is frequently a major source of psychological stress, it can be assumed to be a contributory factor, at least, to physical illness.

Of course, as pointed out earlier, work can also be a source of stress, both physical and psychological. The field of occupational health is concerned with health hazards in the work place. Certain occupations have always been recognised as dangerous, either because of the risk of accident, or because of regular exposure to toxic substances, or both. Other occupations, particularly those involving the making of difficult decisions where the cost of an error is high, are likewise regarded as psychologically stressful. Such occupations are often more highly paid as compensation.

In attempting to evaluate the psychological effects of unemployment it is necessary to examine the role of work and its significance to the individual. The difficulty, of course, in discussing the significance of work is that its significance depends a great deal on what the work is. Jobs vary enormously with respect to how socially useful they are deemed to be, how interesting they are to perform, how much freedom or autonomy they allow, how much opportunity they provide for social interaction, how much power and prestige is associated with them and, of course, how well paid and secure they are. Most people evaluate jobs in terms of how they rate on the basis of these criteria. Moreover many employed people are unhappy because they are not able to work in their chosen occupation and have to settle for something less desirable. Such job dissatisfaction is also a potential source of stress and complicates the task of assessing the psychological effects of unemployment.

FACTORS MODERATING THE PSYCHOLOGICAL IMPACT OF UNEMPLOYMENT

It is not surprising that no longer being employed in a psychologically stressful occupation should lead to an improvement in psychological health. Similar results were obtained by Warr and Jackson (1984) with respect to physical health. The levels of psychological stress and physical stress associated with one's former job may be regarded then as two factors that moderate the potentially damaging effects of unemployment, although, of course they relate only to job loss, not to failure to find a job. Psychologists have studied a number of other possible moderating factors. These moderating, or mediating, factors may explain the considerable individual variation in response to unemployment. It is important to identify such factors for a number of good reasons. For example, if there are individual characteristics that make a person particularly vulnerable to the stress of unemployment, it may be possible to provide counselling at an early stage and thereby offset the negative effects.

The value attached to being in paid employment, termed 'work involvement' or 'employment commitment', has been shown to moderate the effects of unemployment (Jackson, Stafford, Banks and Warr, 1983; Shamir, 1986b). People with a strong employment commitment are more likely to suffer psychological distress if they are unemployed.

Age is another factor which has been shown to mediate the effects of unemployment, at least in men. In general there appears to be a curvilinear relationship between age and the negative effects of unemployment with middle-aged men experiencing greater distress than those who are older or younger (Broomhall and Winefield, 1990; Hepworth, 1980; Rowley and Feather, 1987; Warr and Jackson, 1984). This greater distress is, in turn, related to financial strain arising from more demanding family responsibilities in the middle-aged.

Length of unemployment is another variable that seems to mediate the effects of unemployment, in middle-aged, although not apparently in young or old, men. Psychological health shows a gradual decline followed by stabilisation during the first few months of unemployment, at least in mature people (Warr and Jackson, 1984, 1987).

Two further variables that moderate the psychological stress induced by unemployment are financial resources and activity level. Finlay-Jones and Eckhardt (1981), for example, in their study of young people, found that unemployed men who were unable to borrow $100 readily were more prone to psychiatric disorder than those who could. This relationship was not observed, however, in the women. Other studies have shown that a low level of activity is associated with psychological ill health during unemployment (Feather and Bond, 1983; Hepworth, 1980).

The last two factors are both related to social class in that lower class people have greater financial problems and are also less skilled at using free time (Warr and Payne, 1983). On the other hand, they are also likely to be less committed to work. Social class, then, is perhaps not to be regarded as a single mediating factor, but rather one which combines several.

Other mediating variables that have been studied include sex, ethnic origin, personality differences, availability of social support, local unemployment levels and access to constructive and stimulating leisure activity. Finally, the attitude which the unemployed individual adopts may make it easier (or more difficult) to cope or adjust.

This latter possibility was demonstrated by Stokes (1983) on the basis of a study of youth unemployment carried out in the English Midlands. He found that as a result of redefining their attitudes towards the value of work, the youngsters no longer experienced unemployment as a significant personal crisis. Nevertheless, they had also become 'lethargic, apathetic, disinclined to participate in constructive leisure activities and had little commitment to a society that seemed to be offering no worthwhile future' (Stokes, 1983: 271).

To redefine one's attitude to the value of work may well be an adaptive response in the face of the unavailability of jobs. Certainly it would be predicted from the theory of cognitive dissonance (Festinger, 1957) according to which beliefs are modified so as to remove conflicting cognitions. On the other hand, such a response may be highly undesirable from the point of view of society. Such an attitude, formed at an early age, may persist throughout life resulting in social alienation, and a refusal to become a useful member of the community. This sort of attitude change might be less likely to occur in an older person, particularly where previous employment experience is associated with positive feelings.

Warr and Jackson (1987) in their longitudinal study of long-term unemployed men reported that those who had been continuously unemployed for an average of 25 months were better off than when they had been unemployed for an average of only 15 months (although their financial situation had not improved). They proposed three sorts of response: constructive adaptation, resigned adaptation and despair. Both forms of adaptation evidently involved some change in attitude about the value of employment.

Factors influencing how well young people are able to cope with unemployment and unsatisfactory employment are discussed further in Chapter 5.

THEORIES OF THE PSYCHOLOGICAL SIGNIFICANCE OF EMPLOYMENT AND UNEMPLOYMENT

Much of the research on unemployment has been atheoretical, and some influential commentators, such as Jahoda, have suggested that this is a good thing:

Most studies on unemployment are purely descriptive in the sense that they are not guided by a formal theory, but by hunches. That is as it ought to be. As long as the *explicandum* is left to guesswork and ideologically biased opinions, formal explanations are, to say the least, premature.

(Jahoda, 1988: 16)

Nevertheless, several theories have been proposed to explain the psychological significance of employment and other, more general, theories have been seen as relevant. We will briefly outline four theories in each category. They are discussed in greater detail in Chapter 6.

FOUR SPECIFIC THEORIES

Stage theory

Several writers have suggested that the response to unemployment (or, more precisely, job loss) can be described in terms of several discrete stages. Eisenberg and Lazarsfeld (1938) following their review of the 1930s literature, were the first to suggest such a theory, and more recent versions have been proposed by Harrison (1976) and by Hayes and Nutman (1981).

Deprivation theory

Jahoda herself, notwithstanding her recent disclaimer, is responsible for one of the most influential theories concerning the psychological significance of employment (Jahoda, 1981, 1982). According to her, employment (even bad employment) has five latent functions that are psychologically beneficial: it imposes a time structure on the waking day; it provides social contact; it involves us in shared goals; it gives us an identity; and it enforces activity.

Agency theory

As an alternative to deprivation theory, Fryer (1986) has proposed what he calls an agency theory. His main objection to the former is that he believes that for many people the five supposed benefits of employment are all too often costs rather than benefits. Compared with deprivation theory, which Fryer sees as dehumanising and implying a passive and reactive view of human nature, agency theory stresses the proactive and enterprising aspect of human nature, as well as people's desire and ability to plan for themselves, rather than having their lives planned and regulated for them by others.

The vitamin model

Warr (1987) has suggested nine features of the environment that seem to have a curvilinear effect on mental health, just as certain vitamins seem to affect physical health. Without suggesting that employment is necessarily better than unemployment in terms of these nine features, most good jobs provide them. Unlike deprivation theory then, the vitamin model clearly distinguishes between good and bad employment (as well as good and bad unemployment).

FOUR GENERAL THEORIES

Life-span developmental theory

A number of writers such as Tiffany, Cowan and Tiffany (1970) and Taylor and Gurney (1984) have suggested that Erikson's (1959) developmental theory is relevant to an understanding of the consequences of youth unemployment. The theory assumes eight developmental stages throughout the life span. The main task of the fifth of these stages, adolescence, is supposed to be the development of identity (both sexual and occupational). Failure to negotiate successfully each developmental stage is believed to lead to later psychological problems.

The theory of learned helplessness

A further reason to suppose that the lack of previous, successful employment experience may influence a young person's response to unemployment is suggested by the theory of learned helplessness (Abramson, Seligman and Teasdale, 1978; Seligman, 1975). This theory assumes that prolonged failure to control important outcomes will result eventually in the generalised expectation that such outcomes are uncontrollable. This expectation will produce three behavioural deficits: cognitive, motivational and affective (or emotional). First, the cognitive deficit is displayed in interference with new learning. The expectation that outcomes are generally uncontrollable will reduce the ability to recognise those that are controllable, and hence impair problem solving. Second, the expectation that outcomes are uncontrollable will result in a reduced desire or motivation to try to control them. Third, where the failure to control important outcomes is painful, such failure will produce anxiety, and eventually, depressed affect.

The theory of learned helplessness was originally developed to explain findings from animal experiments, in which mongrel dogs were exposed to uncontrollable electric shocks. This exposure led to helpless behaviour in a new situation where shocks could easily be escaped. On the other hand, prior experience of successful shock avoidance seemed to immunise them against the learned helplessness.

The inability to find a job might be seen as failure to control an important outcome. Moreover such failure is usually very painful. Therefore it is reasonable to apply the theory of learned helplessness to the unemployment situation. The theory would make the following three predictions. First, unemployed people should tend to become helpless, showing all three of the associated behavioural deficits (cognitive, motivational and affective). Second, young people, because they lack previous experience of successful employment, will not be immunised against the effect, and should thus be at greater risk than others. Third, young unemployed people who characteristically attribute bad outcomes to internal, stable causes and good outcomes to external, unstable causes, should be those most likely to suffer from depression (Abramson, Seligman and Teasdale, 1978; Peterson and Seligman, 1984).

Attribution theory

Weiner (1985) has proposed an attributional analysis of motivation and emotion that attempts to explain how people will react to good and bad outcomes depending on the causal attributions they make. Unlike learned helplessness theory, attribution theory is concerned with causal attributions for specific events, rather than causal attributions for good and bad events in general (attributional style).

Insofar as being unemployed is regarded as a bad outcome, Weiner's theory can be applied to it, and makes predictions as to how unemployed individuals should react, depending on the causal attributions that they make for their unemployment.

Expectancy-value theory

The theory of mathematical decision making defines rational decision making as maximising the mathematical expectation of success. Assuming that values and probabilities associated with the possible choices or decisions are known, then the best choice can be determined algebraically. In order to make the theory descriptive of actual human behaviour (as opposed to merely prescriptive), Edwards (1954) proposed that objective values be replaced with subjective values (utilities) and objective probabilities be replaced with subjective probabilities.

The theory, known as expectancy-value (or expectancy-valence) theory as been applied to the youth unemployment situation by Feather and his associates (Feather and Barber, 1983; Feather and Davenport, 1981).

Assuming that school leavers' expectations about getting a job, as well as the utility to them of getting a job, can be measured, predictions can be made both about their job seeking behaviour and about their affective reactions to later employment or unemployment.

Chapter 6 describes these eight theories in greater detail and considers how well they are able to account for the results of our prospective longitudinal study. The details of this study are given in Chapter 3.

3 Methods used to study the psychological effects of unemployment

OVERVIEW

This chapter sets out some of the methodological issues and pitfalls involved in assessing the effects of unemployment in general. Within this context, we then give details of the method used in our own longitudinal study and then present a profile of the young people in our sample that includes data on their work attitudes and expectations.

INTRODUCTION

There are many different ways to study the effects of unemployment. The most direct way is just to ask an unemployed person about their experience. They might tell us about their lack of money and resultant curtailment of social activities, their feelings of frustration and powerlessness, their feelings of boredom and having nothing to do. However the notion of 'just' asking someone is more complicated than it seems. It in fact involves many hidden decisions: *who* to ask? Another person may describe to us a different set of circumstances and experiences. Both will be equally valid, but we need to make a choice. *How* do we ask our questions? Do we ask our questions in a face-to-face interview, in which the person may be embarrassed in expressing their real feelings? Or do we ask in a written questionnaire which is anonymous, but which they may not bother to post back to us? Then we have the question about *what* to ask them. Do we just let them talk in a free manner, or do we pose specific questions that we are interested in for them. The answers to these questions of who, how and what will determine not only how we conduct our study, but also the nature and generalisability of the information we obtain. The *method* is an important, integral part of any study.

In the last decade or so, a number of different general methodologies have been adopted in the study of the effects of unemployment. Each has its strengths and weaknesses, but all contribute to an emerging picture of the experience of unemployment. Dooley and Catalano (1980) divide the research concerning the relationship between economic variables such as unemployment and psychological and behavioural effects into four categories on the basis of two orthogonal (i.e. independent) dimensions: (1) aggregate versus individual measures; and (2) cross-sectional versus longitudinal collections of measures.

AGGREGATE STUDIES

Aggregate studies examine aggregated or overall data that are collected from a large number of people in a community or nation over a long period of time, and then carry out complicated time–series analysis. In this way the relationship between economic indicators and physical or mental health can be determined. The results of some such studies have been reviewed by O'Brien (1986), Warr (1987) and Feather (1990).

Probably the best-known study of this kind was published by Harvey Brenner in 1973 in a book entitled *Mental Illness and the Economy*. Brenner studied admission to psychiatric hospitals in New York State between 1910 and 1967. He found a strong relationship between the employment rate in manufacturing industries and the number of people admitted to mental hospitals. As unemployment increased, for example during the Depression, so did the incidence of mental illness dramatically increase.

O'Brien (1986) points out that there could be at least two explanations for this relationship. First, unemployment might cause or precipitate mental illness. Second, mental illness itself may not increase, but tolerance of it might decrease during periods of economic hardship. Families that might have been able to support marginally mentally ill members during good economic times, might find it too burdensome when financial resources are reduced. Brenner (1979a, 1979b), however, presents some results of subsequent studies investigating the incidence of other disorders which are unlikely to be explained in terms of family or social tolerance. He found that the rate of unemployment was positively related to heart disease, cirrhosis of the liver and mortality. These diseases did not appear immediately, but about two years after the increase in unemployment. Further studies showed a delayed effect of changes in unemployment rate for suicide rates, homicide and crimes against people and property.

More recently Brenner (1984, in Dooley and Catalano, 1988) reported to the Joint Economic Committee of the US Congress on the impact of the rise in unemployment during the 1973–1974 recession in the United States. Associated with this 'moderate' recession were estimated increases of 2.3 per cent in total mortality, 1 per cent in suicide, 6 per cent in mental hospital admissions and 6 per cent in total arrests. So aggregate studies show us that the social costs of unemployment are considerable.

The method used in aggregate studies, however, is not without technical problems. Warr (1984) among others suggests: (1) 'optimum lag' procedures increase the probability of statistical significance; (2) confounding with e.g. change in diet, medical care; (3) mis-specification of variables based on available statistics.

A fourth difficulty is known as the 'ecological fallacy'. The results of aggregate studies cannot be generalised to individual processes. Dooley and Catalano (1988) explain that if unemployment and suicide rates are observed to increase together, it does not necessarily mean that an unemployed individual is more likely to commit suicide. It might be, for example, that it is the non-working dependents of the unemployed who commit suicide, or that a more pessimistic climate pervades which makes it more likely for anyone (employed or unemployed) to commit suicide. There has been some evidence to support the association between aggregate and individual effects of unemployment (Catalano and Dooley, 1977), and some showing aggregate unemployment to affect workers across the board (Dooley, Catalano and Rook, 1988). Following a recent review of the aggregate time–series data on unemployment and suicide rates, Dooley, Catalano, Rook and Serxner (1989) concluded that any effect on suicide is complex and dependent on individual factors.

Whatever the difficulties in interpretation, aggregate studies are important in viewing unemployment at a macro-level and showing us its social costs. Although they do not look at effects on specific groups, e.g. unemployed adolescents, they do complement the micro approach of studies investigating the effects on individuals, to which we now turn.

STUDIES FOCUSING ON THE INDIVIDUAL

Studies which are interested in specifically psychological effects of unemployment focus on the experience of the individual. They are interested in the effects on actual people, not in the costs to society at large. Here again there are several different research strategies which can all contribute to the picture and all have problems. Whatever the method used, however, it appears that overall the impact of unemployment at the individual level is negative.

Research into the psychological consequences of unemployment increased rapidly in the 1970s and 1980s, and continues in the 1990s, with the high unemployment rates, particularly among young people, in most Western countries at these times. One can chart the progress of the resulting research enterprise according to the methodology employed. The progression from simple descriptive accounts to more sophisticated and theoretical accounts is the natural process for any developing area of research.

Case studies

Just asking someone about their experience, as in the introduction to the chapter, is an example of a case study. Case studies provide us with a wealth of descriptive material, often providing a detailed narrative of the psychological deterioration accompanying unemployment. Marsden and Duff's (1975) *Workless* or Hayes and Nutman's (1981) *Understanding the Unemployed* provide accounts that are very disturbing, and describe the loss of morale and feelings of powerlessness and rejection very powerfully. Typically they adopt the strategy of studying one group of unemployed, for example those attending a particular job centre. Thus we have problems of self-selection and non-representativeness, and we cannot be confident that our results will generalise to other groups of unemployed individuals.

However, case studies can give us a very rich and meaningful picture of what it is like to be unemployed, in a way that other methods cannot. For example, Turner (1983) describes the case of 19-year-old Jeremy who walks around the streets all day getting depressed because there's nothing to do, or the spiral of social problems (drugs, unwanted pregnancy, attempted suicide, etc.) experienced by 18-year-old Eva since she ran away from home aged 14. Young unemployed people describe their lack of money, sometimes not enough to eat properly (Wendy has half a sausage or a cup of coffee for dinner), their family tensions, their decreasing confidence and the stigma of being unemployed. The actual experience of the individual, which is the focus and of foremost importance in case studies, can get lost in other methodologies. Turner's 1983 Penguin book *Stuck!* is aptly subtitled *Living Without Work – the Stories that Statistics Can't Tell.*

Cross-sectional studies

Although very powerful, it is clear that anecdotal reports of the unemployment experience must be substantiated with more *quantitative* evidence if we wish to effect any political or educational change. There are a number of studies which show that a variety of societal ills, such as crime, drug-taking, health problems, occur disproportionately among the unemployed. Less spectacular perhaps, are studies which employ psychological inventories or rating scales of some sort. The General Health Questionnaire (GHQ) of Goldberg (1972, 1978), for example, is a questionnaire measure used to detect minor psychiatric disorders in the general population, an index of potential psychiatric illness, which can be easily administered and scores compared in different groups.

In fact, studies using psychological measures typically use statistical techniques to compare a selected group of unemployed with a matched control group, usually consisting of employed people. If there is any difference then, in psychological well-being, this difference is attributed to unemployment. Clearly the groups need to be comparable in order to come to definite conclusions. It would not make sense, for example, to compare a group of young unemployed adolescents from a working-class suburb with a group of employed managers of big city companies. These groups differ in many important ways other than unemployment.

A large number of such cross-sectional studies have been carried out in a number of different countries, including Europe, North America and Australia. They have shown that, on a range of measures of psychological well-being, young unemployed people are worse off than their employed counterparts (Donovan and Oddy, 1982; Finlay-Jones and Eckhardt, 1981, 1984; Maizels, 1970; Murray, 1978; Stokes, 1983; Warr, Banks and Ullah, 1985). For example, Banks and Jackson (1982) reported greater minor psychiatric disorder among unemployed British adolescents.

The major problem with cross-sectional studies, however, is that they are only able to establish correlates, not causes. The fact that unemployed youngsters may be less well adjusted psychologically than those who are employed does not imply that this difference is a consequence of being unemployed. It is possible that poorly adjusted youngsters are less likely to get offered jobs in the first place. A further possibility is that a third factor, such as a prolonged illness, may be responsible for both the psychological maladjustment and the unemployment.

Retrospective and longitudinal studies

In order to establish whether or not an observed correlate of unemployment can be regarded as a consequence it is necessary to obtain repeated observations over time. This may be achieved in either one of two ways. First retrospective data may be collected. For example an unemployed person, or someone who knows him or her well, may be able to report on his/her state of health, mood, morale and the like before the loss of job occurred. Comparing such observations with those currently taken may shed light on what changes, if any, have occurred in the unemployed person's health and/or psychological well-being since the job loss. Such changes may be regarded as consequences rather than antecedents or concomitants of job loss.

Of course retrospective studies are methodologically suspect because they rely on recall data. Such data are likely to be unreliable because an individual's memory is known to be influenced by a variety of factors which tend to produce selective omissions as well as distortions. Events perceived as important are more likely to be recalled than those perceived as trivial. Also, events that are inconsistent with the individual's attitudes and expectations are likely to be forgotten or distorted to bring them into line. Bartlett (1933) and Nisbett and Wilson (1977) cite numerous examples of these processes based on observations from psychological experiments.

A better method of analysing changes occurring over time is the longitudinal approach. Longitudinal studies involve carrying out two or more observations on the same subjects at different times. Such studies tend to be both time consuming and costly, however. Where it is considered necessary to study changes over a lengthy period, such as several years, there will inevitably be a considerable loss of data. Some of the people who agreed to participate initially will drop out for a variety of reasons before the study is complete. They may move and no longer be contactable. They may die, or be too ill to take part. Or they may simply lose interest in the research and refuse to maintain their participation, even if offered a financial inducement.

It is necessary to begin any long-term longitudinal study with a large sample of participants in order to ensure that a reasonable number remain by the end. For example, assume that a three-year longitudinal survey is planned with four 'waves' of observations: one initially, and one at the end of each year. Assume also that 25 per cent drop out each year. In that case the initial sample will have shrunk to less than half its original size by the conclusion of the study. (If the original sample was 1000, for example, it will be reduced to 750 after one year, to 563 after two years and to 422 after three years.)

Apart from the cost involved in selecting a very large initial sample so as to guard against drop outs over time (sample attrition), there is a further problem with longitudinal studies: the problem of attrition bias. This would not be a problem if it could be assumed that the drop outs were random. In that case those who dropped out would not differ in any systematic way from those who stayed in. On the other hand, it is possible that they do differ. For example, the drop outs might tend to be less intelligent, less mature, less healthy, more emotionally unstable or more independent, than those who stay in. Any such difference could, of course, result in a final sample that was biased, or unrepresentative of the population from which the original sample was selected. A discussion of some of the advantages and disadvantages of both retrospective and longitudinal approaches for studying the labour market is given by Kalachek (1980).

Prospective longitudinal studies

A subcategory of longitudinal designs is known as prospective designs, in which measures are taken before and then again after an event. In the unemployment context, this involves obtaining measures on people before they become unemployed or employed, and then again afterwards. If there are no differences between the groups initially, then subsequent differences can be attributed to the (un)employment experience. If, on the other hand, there are initial differences between the groups, then these differences are likely to reflect predisposing factors.

Apart from the problem of attrition referred to above, there are other potential difficulties associated with longitudinal studies. Feather and O'Brien (1986b), for example, identify two further problems: the effects of repeated testing and societal/historical factors. In repeated testing, if the same people are asked the same questions several times, they may feel compelled either to change, or alternatively stay consistent with, their previous answers. Societal or historical factors have their influence because over any reasonable time period, there are likely to be environmental changes which affect all members of a given population regardless of their group membership.

In their own study of adolescents conducted over three years, however, Feather and O'Brien (1986b) found little evidence of effects that might be attributed to either repeated testing or to societal/historical effects. In a follow-up of our own initial sample, we found that high school students in 1986 displayed greater optimism about their prospects of obtaining satisfactory employment than their 1980 counterparts, despite no decline in the official youth unemployment statistics between 1980 and 1986 (Winefield, Tiggemann and Winefield, 1989; Winefield and Winefield, 1987).

Despite their difficulties, however, prospective longitudinal studies present us with the most useful research strategy, and now quite a number have been conducted. There are two major types. Studies of adult unemployment have tended to investigate retrenchment and have followed people who worked in places that were about to be shut down. This strategy, however, suffers because even at initial testing people usually know that they are about to be retrenched, and some studies have suggested that the anticipation of losing one's job can be as distressing as the eventuality (Kasl and Cobb, 1979). For adolescents, however, unemployment comes about usually because they fail to gain a job, rather than because they have lost one. Thus, in studying the effects of unemployment in young people, the major strategy is to investigate school leavers, beginning before they have left school and before they have experienced either employment or unemployment. Both these types of investigation have shown unemployment to have negative consequences. Some studies of school leavers have also demonstrated the existence of predisposing factors.

WHAT NEXT?

Once the comparisons made cross-sectionally have demonstrated clearly that the unemployed are worse off than their employed counterparts, and longitudinal studies have verified that the effects are attributable to unemployment, what then? Typically the realisation dawns that the unemployed are not a homogeneous group, but have many different characteristics. The effects on young people may be different from the effects on older adults, people who have money or social support may react differently from those who do not, etc. There are many possible variables which may moderate the relationship between unemployment and psychological distress. Some which have been identified include age, sex and financial resources.

Allied to this search for moderator variables, comes a closer look at what employment and unemployment mean, and which aspects in particular are important. Is it, for example, the lack of money or lack of a socially-defined role, or lack of things to do with one's time, that results in the observed psychological deficits? A number of theories have been put forward to explain the effects of unemployment which were outlined in Chapter 2, although Feather (1985) points out we have not really got very far.

And so we move through this pathway to increasing sophistication in our thinking about unemployment, usually accompanied by increasing methodological rigour and increasingly difficult statistical analytic procedures. As we do so, it becomes increasingly apparent that there are no simple answers. The psychological effects of unemployment turn out to be quite complex, and some of these complexities will be demonstrated in the subsequent chapters.

Methods used to study the psychological effects of unemployment vary in their level of sophistication. At the lowest level we find descriptive, anecdotal accounts of the unemployment experience. At the next level, there are well designed studies using quantitative and standardised measures and incorporating control groups such as the employed. Finally, at the highest level there are studies aimed to demonstrate causality using longitudinal designs, to differentiate subgroups of unemployed people, to identify moderator variables and coping strategies, and through closer analysis, to refine the underlying mechanisms and test between different theories.

METHOD IN THIS STUDY

Design

The present study follows a prospective longitudinal design, which takes measures at different points in time. In 1980 more than 3000 upper level high school students were surveyed. They were then annually surveyed through the 1980s.

The sample

The research strategy was to study three cohorts of school leavers over a ten-year period. School leavers were chosen as subjects because they have no history of successful previous employment. Adolescence is an important time for establishing independence and consolidating a sense of personal identity, and one way of achieving this is through employment. As Windschuttle (1979) noted, the first job is the capitalist equivalent of initiation rites in primitive society. The young are, of course, the most likely to become unemployed as we pointed out in Chapter 1.

An initial sample of more than 3000 young people was surveyed at schools in August of 1980. The sample was chosen from twelve high schools in metropolitan Adelaide, randomly selected by the South Australian State Education Department. Adelaide, a city of approximately one million people, is the capital of the Australian state of South Australia. It is the centre of the Australian 'white goods' industry and an important centre for automobile production, precisely the kind of manufacturing industries which are among the first to suffer during periods of economic recession. South Australia is the poorest of the mainland states in terms of natural resources, and has suffered levels of unemployment which are among the highest of the Australian states during recent years.

The sample was restricted to students attending metropolitan high schools, excluding those attending private schools. The decision to confine the study to the metropolitan area was based on the high urban concentration in South Australia, as well as logistic considerations. Private schools were excluded, although they are attended by approximately 25 per cent of the secondary school population, as it was assumed that the unemployment rate would be relatively low in this population.

In South Australia, the minimum age at which a child can leave school is 15 years. This age is normally attained during Year 10 of high school, and although some children leave as soon as they reach their fifteenth birthday, the majority wait until the end of the school year. In 1980, somewhat less than 50 per cent continued on to two additional years, Years 11 and 12. (This percentage increased steadily throughout the course of the study.) At the end of Year 12, students could sit for the public matriculation examination. Entrance to universities and other tertiary institutions depended on performance in this examination. (The situation has changed in recent years with some matriculation subjects being school assessed rather than publicly examined.) An initial sample of 3000 was aimed for, comprising 1000 from each of Years 10, 11 and 12. Within each selected school, all the Year 12 students were chosen. Then a corresponding number of Year 11 and Year 10 students were obtained by random selection of classes. This selection was necessary because within a school the number of students decreases from Year 10 to Year 12. Students in Years 10 and 11 were randomly selected by class rather than individually, so as to minimise disruption to normal school routine. All students in a class were tested simultaneously, and asked to complete a questionnaire which was designed to require no longer than a normal lesson period of 40 minutes. In the end, the sample comprised 1092 Year 10 students, 1104 Year 11 students and 934 Year 12 students, totalling 3130 students in all.

In conducting such longitudinal research it is important to have more than a single cohort. Essentially the interest lies in observing changes occurring in individuals over time based on repeated observations. In a sample of adolescents, it is important to distinguish between changes arising because of developmental or maturational factors, and those that can be attributed to environmental events. By choosing three cohorts of adolescents of different ages all of whom were at school when first observed, it was hoped to be able to distinguish between these different kinds of change.

One of the difficulties associated with longitudinal research mentioned in the previous section is illustrated by the falling numbers over the years. From 1986 we succeeded in increasing the retention rate by using Dillman's 'Total Design Method' (Dillman, 1978) and over the duration of the study, the average annual response rate (nearly 80 per cent) was impressively high. However, over a period as long as ten years the attrition rate also becomes quite large. Of the 3130 students in the initial sample, 2260 (72 per cent) responded in the following year, 1981. Of those, 1713 (76 per cent) responded in 1982; of those, 1392 (81 per cent) in 1983; 1029 (74 per cent) in 1984; 759 (74 per cent) in 1985; 652 (86 per cent) in 1986; 603 (81 per cent) in 1987; and 483 (80 per cent) in 1988. Thus, despite an average annual retention rate of just under 80 per cent, by 1988 there were fewer than 500 remaining in the sample.

More serious than just a loss in numbers, is the possibility that there may be sources of bias in the attrition. Those who drop out may differ systematically from those who stay in, resulting in an increasingly biased sample. For example, it may be the more depressed people who tend to drop out of the study. Where such sources of attrition bias exist, the eventual sample might differ significantly from the original sample and not be representative of the overall population, even though the original sample was representative. Attrition analyses of the present study have been reported in Winefield, Winefield and Tiggemann (1990) and Winefield, Tiggemann and Winefield (1991a). Although most of the differences were small, there was evidence of some selective bias in attrition. During the early years, those dropping out tended to be of lower academic ability, lower socio-economic status and from non-English-speaking backgrounds. In later years the unemployed and dissatisfied employed were the most likely to drop out, although these status-related differences in attrition did not seem to be related either to demographic characteristics, or to pre-test scores on the dependent variables. Nevertheless, some caution needs to be exercised in the interpretation of results of the study.

It must further be recognised that the initial sample selected in this study is unrepresentative in a number of ways, which must limit the generalisations that can be drawn. First, we were concerned with only young urban people; second, because no students from private schools were included, more affluent groups were under-represented; and third, the selection of equal numbers of students from each of Years 10, 11 and 12, meant that less scholastically able, or less ambitious students, were probably under-represented.

Measures (1980–1983)

Ratings of academic potential for each student were obtained from the schools in 1980. These were provided by the teacher judged by the contact person best able to provide the assessment. The contact person was generally the Principal, Deputy Principal or Student Counsellor at the school. Judgements were made on whether the student was thought to be 'definitely capable', 'possibly capable' or 'definitely not capable' of tertiary study. We felt that such judgements would be relatively easy to give and would therefore be offered readily.

All other information gathered was supplied by the students themselves. They completed the initial questionnaire during school hours. A member of the research team would address the group of assembled students, briefly explaining the aims of the research, emphasising its ongoing nature, the fact that none of the answers required were 'right' or 'wrong', the fact that all replies would be treated as strictly confidential and the fact that participation was voluntary. Students were given the opportunity to ask questions before beginning to complete the questionnaire, and were offered assistance individually whenever they experienced difficulty with any of the items.

Section A of the initial questionnaire asked for biographical information, including age, school, ethnic origin and socio-economic status. Socio-economic status, based on father's occupation, was measured using the 19–point scale proposed by Broom and Jones (1969). Subsequently the scores were collapsed resulting in three categories (1 = professional and managerial, 2 = clerical and skilled, 3 = labourers and unskilled). Section B was concerned with attributional style, perceived social supports and leisure activities. Section C was concerned with scholastic and career aspirations.

The main interest of the study, however, concerned the psychological impact of unemployment. Sections D to H contained the various psychological measures. Section D comprised questions concerned with mood. These asked how often the students felt bored, lonely, angry with themselves, angry with society, happy, helpless and depressed. They were answered on a 4–point scale (from 1 = 'almost never', to 4 = 'almost always'). Subsequently these scores were totalled (reversing 'happy') to form a Negative Mood Scale.

Section E contained Rosenberg's (1965) Self-Esteem Scale designed specifically for adolescents. High self-esteem is taken to mean that the individual has self-respect and considers himself or herself worthy. Low self-esteem, on the other hand, implies self-rejection, self-dissatisfaction or self-contempt. Depression was likewise measured by Rosenberg's (1965) Depressive Affect Scale (Section G). This 5-item scale purports to measure depressive affect rather than clinical depression. It was chosen for its brevity, and also for lack of items dealing with physiological functioning such as sleep patterns or bowel movements which commonly appear in other depression scales. We did not wish to embarrass respondents or to have the questionnaire ridiculed.

Section F was the Nowicki-Strickland Internal-External Control Scale for Adults (ANS-IE) devised by Nowicki and Duke (1974). It is a scale designed to measure locus of control, a personality dimension proposed by Rotter (1966) that refers to a generalised expectancy for internal or external control of reinforcements. Thus internals are people who perceive events to be within their control, while externals believe events to be outside their control, e.g. determined by fate or luck. The scale is scored in the external direction. It was designed specifically for use with non-college as well as college adults and requires as little as fifth grade reading ability.

The last psychological scale, contained in Section H, was Smith's (1973) short measure of achievement motivation. Resultant achievement motivation derives from two competing tendencies: the need for success and the fear of failure. Individuals high in achievement motivation are those with a strong need for success relative to their motivation to avoid failure.

The concept of achievement motivation was first developed by

McClelland, Atkinson, Clark and Lowell (1953) to explain individual differences in motivation. It assumes that there are two competing tendencies of varying strength within all individuals: the need for success and the fear of failure. Traditionally these opposing tendencies have been measured independently. The need for success is most often measured by Murray's Thematic Apperception Test (Murray, 1938). This is a projective test that takes a long time to administer and score. The fear of failure is usually measured by the Mandler-Sarason Test Anxiety Questionnaire (Mandler and Sarason, 1952). Resultant achievement motivation is derived by subtracting the fear of failure score from the need for success score.

Because of the difficulties associated with the administration of projective tests, a number of questionnaire tests have been proposed for assessing the strength of achievement tendencies. Some have attempted to measure resultant achievement motivation directly, rather than assessing the need for success and the fear of failure separately. Some include separate forms for males and females (e.g. Mehrabian, 1968), and many are rather long. For convenience, the test we chose was the short one proposed by Smith (1973). It is very quick and easy to administer, and has been shown to correlate quite highly ($r = 0.53$) with the Mehrabian test in a sample of more than 200 young people (Jardine and Winefield, 1981).

The final section of the questionnaire, Section I, consisted of three general questions. The last one was open-ended, allowing students to express their views concerning the specific problem of obtaining employment faced by young people.

Apart from non-repetition of the biographical information, the subsequent questionnaires in 1981, 1982 and 1983 were identical to the original for students who were still at school. For students who had left school, Section C now included questions directed specifically at the employed, the unemployed or those engaged in further full-time study, and asked about their experiences.

A much shorter pilot study conducted over seven months enabled us to check the usefulness of some of the psychological measures as well as the general procedure (Tiggemann and Winefield, 1980).

Measures (1984–1987)

Because the initial questionnaire was administered at school, during a 40-minute class period, temporal constraints governed the selection of items. After 1984, however, when all respondents had left school, a number of additional scales were incorporated.

In particular, subjects were asked to complete the General Health Questionnaire (GHQ) (Goldberg, 1972, 1978), which has been used widely in studies concerned with the psychological impact of unemployment in England and Australia. The GHQ asks subjects about their general health and medical complaints over the past few weeks, for example, 'Have you recently lost much sleep over worry?' The scale was designed to detect non-psychotic psychiatric symptomatology in normal adults. Psychometric data for Australian populations for this scale have been published in Winefield, Goldney, Winefield and Tiggemann (1989).

Also included was the Hopelessness Scale of Beck, Weisman, Lester and Trexler (1974) which consists of 20 true–false items, e.g. 'I look forward to the future with hope and enthusiasm.' Hopelessness has been implicated in a number of different cognitive accounts of the development of depression.

Srole's (1956) 5-item scale for measuring anomia (anomie), or social alienation, was included because it has frequently been suggested that unemployment leads to an increase in social alienation, anti-social attitudes and anti-social behaviour (Winefield, Tiggemann, Winefield and Goldney, 1991).

For the employed subjects, a 16-item measure of job satisfaction (Warr, Cook and Wall, 1979) was also administered, in order to see whether subjects' perceptions of the quality of their jobs had any impact. On the basis of their replies to the final, global item, 'Now, taking everything into consideration, how do you feel about your job as a whole?', subjects were subsequently classified into satisfied or dissatisfied employed.

Interviews (1984)

In order to obtain a richer picture of our respondents' experiences, a subsample of the 1984 respondents were selected to undergo more intensive study and were invited to attend an interview. The members of the subsample were those respondents who scored more than 4 on the binary scoring criterion of the 28-item form of the GHQ (GHQ-positive cases), plus a group of matched controls. Of the 291 GHQ-positive cases, 118 were interviewed on the basis of availability. The controls were chosen by selecting the next GHQ-negative case subject of the same sex, age and school. The total subsample comprised 221 subjects with a mean age of 19.6 years.

Members of the subsample were interviewed individually by one of five experienced clinical psychiatrists and some of the information obtained is presented in Chapter 8. In addition to the psychiatric interviews a Global Assessment Scale was administered (Endicott, Spitzer, Fleiss and Cohen, 1976). Interviewed subjects also completed the EMBU (Perris, Jacobsson, Lindström, von Knorring and Perris, 1980; Ross, Campbell and Clayer, 1982), a self-report measure of parental rearing patterns. The short form (Winefield, Goldney, Tiggemann and Winefield, 1989) yields scores on three factors for each parent: *supportive*, referring to affectionate, accepting and encouraging behaviours on the parent's part towards the child; *rejecting*, referring to rejecting and depriving behaviours; and *over-involved*, to describe over-involved and over-protective behaviours.

Measures (1988)

The 1988 version of the questionnaire also included some questions on general health, some on financial resources as well as some additional scales. The additional scales were Srole's 9-item Anomia Scale (Dodder and Astle, 1980) to detect general disaffection (the original five items from the scale used from 1984 to 1987, plus four additional items), a 16-item scale for measuring life satisfaction (Warr, Cook and Wall, 1979), and a modified version of the Multi-Dimensional Support Scale (MDSS) used by Neuling and Winefield (1988) with a sample of breast cancer patients. Three sources of support were chosen: family and close friends, peer group (other people of about your age) and people in authority. Subjects rated the frequency and their satisfaction with the potentially supportive behaviours over the past month on the part of the three categories of source (Winefield, Winefield and Tiggemann, 1992a).

Measures (1989)

In 1989, the final year of the study, a shorter questionnaire was administered. It included the Depressive Affect Scale, the GHQ and the final items from the Job Satisfaction and Life Satisfaction scales. It further asked for a categorisation of what subjects mainly did in each of the ten years of the study: employed full-time, employed part-time, looking for work, student or not looking for work. In this way it was hoped to be able to chart work paths across the decade.

A PROFILE OF OUR SAMPLE: 1980

Background characteristics

Of the total sample, 52 per cent were boys and 48 per cent girls. The average age was 15.6 years. In terms of teacher-rated academic potential, 31 per cent were rated as definitely capable of tertiary study, 33 per cent as possibly capable and 36 per cent as not capable of tertiary study. In terms of socio-economic status, as defined by father's occupation, 34 per cent were classified as high (professional or managerial), 37 per cent as middle (clerical or skilled) and 29 per cent as low (unskilled).

With respect to ethnic origin, a language other than English was spoken regularly in 20 per cent of homes. There were 32 languages spoken overall, of which the most common were Italian (spoken in 33 per cent of the non-English speaking homes), followed by Greek (for which the corresponding figure was 23 per cent), followed by German (11 per cent), Dutch (8 per cent) and Serbian (4 per cent).

Work attitudes and expectations

Overall, 70 per cent of the respondents expected to leave school at the end of Year 12, 25 per cent at the end of Year 11, and 4 per cent at the end of Year 10. When they left, 42 per cent intended to go on to tertiary study, 48 per cent intended to look for a job and 9 per cent intended to start a job that was already arranged.

Students rated getting a job when they finished studying as important to very important (4.6 on a scale of importance from 1 = not important at all, to 5 = very important) for themselves, and for their parents (4.4). Most of them (79 per cent) had a particular job in mind, of which 46 per cent were in the top category (professional or managerial), 50 per cent in the middle (clerical or skilled) and only 4 per cent in the bottom category (unskilled).

Although they rated getting an acceptable job after finishing studying as moderately hard (3.4 on a scale from 1 = not hard at all, to 5 = very hard), 85 per cent expected to have a job within six months and 41 per cent within three months. Only 29 per cent said they would not go on the dole if unable to find a job.

From this, we conclude that our respondents were positive in their attitudes to work, as well as reasonably optimistic (indeed over-optimistic) in their expectations and aspirations.

Relations between background characteristics and work attitudes and expectations

Sex

There were some sex differences in work attitudes and expectations. Although they expected to leave school at the same time, relatively more girls than boys were intending to continue with further study (47 per cent vs 38 per cent). More girls also had a particular job in mind (82 per cent vs 77 per cent), perhaps reflecting slightly greater stereotypy in female vocational choice.

Boys were more confident about obtaining a job, in that 48 per cent of boys expected to have a job within three months of leaving school, compared to 30 per cent of girls. Perhaps correspondingly, or perhaps because not having a job is considered more acceptable for females, more girls than boys said that they would go on the dole if unable to obtain a job (73 per cent vs 68 per cent).

Boys tended to attribute the getting of jobs more to abilities and intelligence (39 per cent vs 33 per cent) and less to trying hard (45 per cent vs 57 per cent) than girls. They endorsed more the options of asking where not advertised (91 per cent vs 85 per cent), and taking any available job (73 per cent vs 66 per cent). Inability to get a job, on the other hand, was attributed more to luck, an external unstable cause (21 per cent vs 14 per cent), and less to the situation the person is in, an external stable cause (24 per cent vs 29 per cent) by boys than by girls.

Socio-economic status

There were also differences associated with socio-economic status (SES). More high SES students intended to leave school at the end of Year 12 (79 per cent) compared with medium and low SES students (both 67 per cent), and more intended to continue with further study (53 per cent vs 37 per cent, 39 per cent). More high SES students tended to attribute the getting of jobs to abilities (40 per cent vs 35 per cent, 34 per cent) and less to effort (48 per cent vs 52 per cent, 51 per cent). It was the medium SES, on the other hand, who were more likely to have a particular job in mind (high 77 per cent, medium 83 per cent, low 78 per cent).

Perhaps somewhat surprisingly, socio-economic groups did not differ on the perceived importance or difficulty of getting jobs, nor on whether they would accept the dole. The only real difference appears to be in educational aspirations.

Family unemployment

Having an unemployed member of the immediate family also affected the students' attitudes to work. More of those whose immediate family contained an unemployed member expected to take longer than six months to obtain a job (20 per cent vs 14 per cent). Fewer students who had an unemployed family member also said that they would not go on the dole (21 per cent vs 31 per cent). It is difficult to know whether to view such a pattern of responses as an unfortunate lowering of expectations, or rather more positively, as reflecting a more realistic appraisal of the actual situation forced upon them by personal experience.

Ethnic origin

Students from non-English speaking backgrounds were more inclined to continue at school until Year 12 (76 per cent vs 70 per cent) and, correspondingly, to go on to further study (51 per cent vs 40 per cent). More of them expected to take longer than six months to obtain a job (19 per cent vs 14 per cent). On the other hand, fewer said that they would go on the dole should they be unable to obtain a job (66 per cent vs 72 per cent).

Year at school

One would expect different perceptions and expectations by students as they move through the school years, in that someone who has completed Year 12 does have a higher probability of obtaining a good job than someone who has completed only Year 10. There are also likely to be maturational changes, and changes due to the educational process.

Not surprisingly, a greater proportion of Year 12 students were planning to go on to tertiary education (58 per cent vs 38 per cent for both Years 10 and 11). More also expected to have a job within three months of leaving (47 per cent vs 40 per cent Year 11, 34 per cent Year 10), and correspondingly perceived less difficulty in doing so. They tended to attribute the getting of jobs more to abilities and intelligence (39 per cent vs 35 per cent, 36 per cent) and less to effort (47 per cent vs 50 per cent, 54 per cent) than the other years. They endorsed more the option of asking where jobs were not advertised (93 per cent vs 90 per cent, 82 per cent). The inability to get a job was attributed more to the external situation (31 per cent vs 26 per cent, 23 per cent) and less to lack of abilities (14 per cent vs 19 per cent, 19 per cent).

Perhaps somewhat surprisingly, with increased school year, more students said they would go on the dole if unable to find a job (76 per cent Year 12, 71 per cent Year 11, 65 per cent Year 10). The getting of jobs was rated by Year 12s as less important both for themselves (mean rating = 4.59 vs 4.65, 4.69) and for their parents (4.28 vs 4.36, 4.39). Perceived control over the getting of jobs also decreased with increasing school year (3.41 for Year 10, 3.32 for Year 11, 3.19 for Year 12). Perhaps the possibility of unemployment looms larger and more real as one approaches the end of one's school life. The correlational nature of the above findings can not determine whether students' attitudes actually change as they progress through their education, or whether it is only those with particular attitudes in Year 10 who continue on to Year 12, while the remainder drop out from school.

Academic potential

Not surprisingly, the more academically capable intended to leave at the end of Year 12 (92 per cent vs 73 per cent, 46 per cent), and to continue on to further study (66 per cent vs 42 per cent, 20 per cent). They also rated the getting of a job as less important to their parents (4.26 vs 4.37, 4.40). The academically able also rated themselves as having more control over getting a job (3.38 vs 3.31, 3.28), and attributed such success more to abilities and intelligence (51 per cent vs 37 per cent, 22 per cent).

Summary: background characteristics and work attitudes and expectations

It appears that accepted work values of society were well entrenched in our sample of students. Jobs were considered important and worthwhile, and available providing applicants try hard enough. The vast majority of students expected to obtain employment within six months of leaving school. Unemployment and the reception of the dole were correspondingly devalued.

These positive attitudes to work tended to be shared uniformly across the group. Perhaps contrary to expectation, there were very few differences arising from differences in backgrounds, and where these occurred they were relatively small. The girls tended to be less confident than the boys about getting jobs, as were those students who had experienced some unemployment in their immediate families, perhaps resulting in a general lowering of expectations. The effects of socio-economic status and ethnicity appeared to be confined primarily to educational aspirations, although other Australian studies have shown that occupational aspirations are influenced by different factors in middle-class and working-class adolescents (Marjoribanks, 1986).

The greatest differences, and these were still minor, occurred between the different school years. It seems that as students move up through the levels of school, they (correctly) perceive themselves as more likely to get a job, but also perceive themselves as having less control in this arena. Their expressed greater willingness to go on the dole perhaps reflects a more realistic appraisal of their future, in contrast to responses at the lower levels of school which may be more ideologically based, or may reflect the kind of negative attitudes to welfare recipients discussed in Chapter 2.

Overall, we have found no evidence whatsoever to support the suggestion of some authors that there has been a decline in the work ethic among young people. From a societal view, this seems a reassuring result, one that supports societal structures as they stand. On the other hand, one must acknowledge that the perceptions offered by the young here may be somewhat idealistic.

Unfortunately, many of them would experience a period of unemployment, for which they might be inadequately prepared.

To the extent that individuals have high unrealistic expectations, unemployment may prove a more crushing blow and any negative consequences may be exacerbated. The assumption that jobs are available to those who try hard enough may serve to maintain motivation. It also, however, implies that an individual who is unable to get a job is likely to hold him or herself responsible, a view often reinforced by the media and others. This kind of internal attribution for failure is precisely what some psychological theories predict will lead to loss of self-esteem and depression.

4 The psychological impact of unemployment and unsatisfactory employment on young people

Longitudinal and cross-sectional data

Our prospective longitudinal study, described in Chapter 3, is one of several to have been reported in recent years looking at the transition from school to work. For example, Banks and Jackson (1982) in Sheffield, Gurney (1980a, 1980b, 1981) in Melbourne, Patton and Noller (1984, 1990) in Brisbane and Feather and O'Brien (1986a, 1986b) in Adelaide have all examined the psychological impact of unemployment on school leavers.

Banks and Jackson (1982) studied two cohorts of school leavers, both of which left school at the minimum age (16 years). The first cohort (Cohort A) was studied initially only after leaving school, consequently no baseline (at-school) measures were available for them. The second cohort (Cohort B) was studied initially in the final year of school (in 1978), then again in 1979 and 1980. The number was reduced from 1096 in the first year to 780 (71 per cent) in the second and to 496 (63.6 per cent) in the third, so that after two years the sample was less than half of its original size. (The authors report that this was due mainly to non-contacts rather than to refusals.)

Only academic under-achievers were included (those passing no more than one O level subject) and, in addition, all eligible non-white people were included but only about 30 per cent of the white young people. All participants were from the North Yorkshire city of Leeds. The single measure of psychological well-being was the GHQ-12 (see Chapter 3).

The authors showed that the unemployed group and the employed group (which included those engaged on the Youth Opportunities Programme and in further education as well as those in jobs) did not differ initially on the GHQ while at school. On the other hand, at both later times the unemployed showed a significant deterioration and the employed a significant improvement. The authors conclude that their results imply that unemployment causes an increase in psychological distress (as measured by the GHQ), and employment a decrease.

The study by Gurney (1980a, 1980b, 1981) was carried out in the

Australian city of Melbourne. His sample comprised 688 pupils from eighteen secondary schools, which included both state-controlled and private schools. All pupils were drawn from Years 10 and 11 only (none from Year 12, the final year during which university entrance examinations are undertaken). The participants were studied initially while at school (November 1978), then again about four months after school had concluded (April 1979). Unfortunately only 412 responded (to the postal questionnaire) on the second occasion, a retention rate of 60 per cent.

Gurney compared three groups: the employed (220), the unemployed (53) and those who had either returned to school or who had moved straight into some post-school training course (139). His measures included an adaptation of Rosenberg's (1965) Self-Esteem Scale (see Chapter 3), a causal attribution questionnaire (devised by the author) asking participants to give reasons for unemployment and a scale for measuring Eriksonian psycho-social development which was a modification of that described by Constantinople (1969).

Gurney was able to show that the groups did not differ significantly while at school, although there was a sex difference with the girls showing lower self-esteem, and being more internal than the boys on the last two items of the attribution questionnaire concerned with the importance of knowing people and having been to the right school in getting a job. (The girls placed less emphasis on these factors than the boys.) On the other hand, Gurney reported later differences between the groups, in each case arising through changes observed in the employed group, but in neither of the others. The employed girls (although not the boys) showed increased self-esteem, the employed had become more internal in their causal ascriptions for unemployment and the employed, particularly the girls, showed significant psycho-social development.

The two studies by Patton and Noller (1984, 1990) were both conducted in the Australian city of Brisbane. In the first, they studied 113 children in their final year of compulsory schooling (Year 10) in November 1982, and then again five months later. Three groups were compared: the employed (24), the unemployed (21) and those who had returned to school or full-time study elsewhere (68). Their measures comprised the same adaptation of Rosenberg's (1965) Self-Esteem Scale as used by Gurney, the Nowicki-Strickland Locus of Control Scale (Nowicki and Duke, 1974) (see Chapter 3) and the Beck Depression Inventory (Beck, Ward, Mendelson, Mock and Erbaugh, 1961).

The authors found that the three groups did not differ significantly at Time 1, but differed significantly at Time 2. On the other hand, there were sex differences at Time 1, with the girls showing lower self-esteem and higher depression than the boys. In the case of self-esteem and depressive affect, the unemployed were the only group to show a significant change: a decline in self-esteem and an increase in depression. In the case of locus of control, the unemployed showed a significant increase in externality and the school returners showed a significant decrease in externality. Again, the employed showed no significant change.

The second study by Patton and Noller (1990) had a larger initial sample (363) selected from three secondary schools in an unidentified Australian capital city, one state-controlled, the other two denominational private schools. Participants were tested initially in Year 10, then again in yearly intervals for two years. The retention rate was 70.2 per cent after one year and 84.7 per cent from Time 2 to Time 3. Only those 216 subjects responding at all three times were included in the data analysis (59.5 per cent of the initial sample). The Offer Self-Image Questionnaire (Offer, Ostrov and Howard, 1982) and a Children's Depression Scale (Lang and Tisher, 1978) were the measuring instruments.

The three comparison groups were those subjects who had left school and were employed at both times (47), those who had left school and were unemployed at both times (40) and those who had returned to school and were present at both times. (Only a small number had changed their status from Time 2 to Time 3 and they were excluded.) There were few differences between the groups at Time 1, but at both later times the unemployed were worse off than the other groups. From Time 1 to Time 2 the changes all involved changes for the worse observed in the unemployed, but from Time 1 to Time 3 there were also changes for the better in the employed.

The study by Feather and O'Brien (1986a, 1986b) was carried out in the Australian city of Adelaide. Samples of pupils were selected from Years 10, 11 and 12 from 15 state-controlled metropolitan high schools. More than 3000 took part, and the study was conducted over the period 1980 to 1982 with testing taking place in 1980 (Time 1), and again in 1981 (Time 2) and 1982 (Time 3). In order to check on possible effects of repeated testing and for societal or historical effects (see Chapter 3), additional groups were included that were tested initially in 1981 or 1982. The authors reported little evidence of effects from either repeated testing or from societal/historical factors.

The measures used included many that related to the theoretical interests of the authors:

> expectancy-valence theory ... attribution theory and the analysis of beliefs, attitudes and values ... function and need theories ... and a theoretical framework that emphasizes work values, feelings of control and the actual content of the task to be performed in terms of its positive and negative characteristics. ... These theoretical interests had a significant impact on the variables that were included.
>
> (Feather and O'Brien, 1986a: 463)

The authors confined their analyses to those who were employed or unemployed in 1981 and 1982. They reported several ongoing differences between the employed and unemployed groups, but some of these differences were also present while the groups were still at school. Overall, they found that most of the observed changes were changes for the worse in the unemployed, but these were observed largely from Time 1 to Time 3 and were often contaminated by at-school differences. They also looked at changed status but reported: 'There was little evidence from longitudinal analyses of change scores that a shift from employment to unemployment or the reverse transition had significant effects on psychological well being' (Feather and O'Brien, 1986a: 459). This is the only study to incorporate important methodological checks for possible effects due to repeated testing and to societal/historical factors.

The five studies described above were conducted for different purposes, using different samples, over different time spans and used different measures. This makes any direct comparisons between them difficult.

Some studies, like those of Banks and Jackson and Patton and Noller focused on academic under-achievers. In addition, Banks and Jackson included a disproportionate number of under-privileged ethnic minority group members. On the other hand, the studies by Gurney and by Feather and O'Brien employed more broadly based samples from high schools. The sample size also varied from study to study, ranging from 113 (Patton and Noller, 1984) to more than 3000 (Feather and O'Brien, 1986a and 1986b). Both the size and nature of the sample must influence the generalisability of the results.

The generalisability of the results will also be limited by response rates. Banks and Jackson reported response rates of 71 per cent (in the first year) and 63.6 per cent (in the second year); Gurney reported a rate of 60 per cent; Patton and Noller did not report the rate in their first study, but reported rates of 70.2 per cent (in the first year) and 84.7 per cent (in the second year) in their second study; Feather and O'Brien reported rates of 74 per cent (in the first year) and 90 per cent (in the second year). An important issue in any longitudinal study is the potential problem of attrition bias (see Chapter 3). If those who drop out differ systematically from those who stay in, the results may be distorted. As Hansen, Collins, Malotte, Johnson and Fielding (1985) argue, attrition bias may compromise both the external and internal validity of a longitudinal study. For example, Banks and Jackson reported that in their study subject attrition was due to non-contacts rather than to refusals. A possible reason for the unemployed not being contactable could have been that they were busily engaged in social activities and therefore were rarely at home when the interviewer called. If this were so, it could be that their final sample included a disproportionate number of the unemployed who were coping least well: those with few or no friends, for example. Because none of the five studies described above reported results of attrition analyses, it is impossible to assess the extent of any such biases.

Another factor that could affect the results of a longitudinal study of school leavers is the time interval between observations. A few months may be insufficient for important differences between the employed and unemployed to emerge, especially since school leavers may consider the first few months after leaving school as a holiday. Gurney's subjects were surveyed just once after an interval of only four months. Similarly in the first of the studies by Patton and Noller, data were collected on a single occasion after an interval of only five months. On the other hand, in the studies by Banks and Jackson, by Feather and O'Brien, and in the second study of Patton and Noller, data were collected on two subsequent occasions after intervals of one and two years respectively.

Another difficulty in comparing results from the different studies arises because they sometimes used different measures. As we have said, Banks and Jackson used the GHQ-12; Gurney used Rosenberg's Self-Esteem Scale, a causal attribution questionnaire (devised by himself) and a scale for measuring Eriksonian psycho-social development; Patton and Noller used Rosenberg's Self-Esteem Scale, the Nowicki-Strickland Locus of Control Scale, and the Beck Depression Inventory in the first study, and the Offer Self-Image Questionnaire and Lang and Tisher's Children's Depression Scale in their second study; Feather and O'Brien used four bipolar adjective scales for measuring depression, nine items selected from Rotter's (1966) Locus of Control Scale and a set of self-concept measures devised by themselves based on a factor analytic study.

In some cases the measures used proved unsatisfactory in terms of their psychometric properties. For example, the causal attribution questionnaire used by Gurney lacked reliability with reported internal reliability coefficients of only 0.51 (on the first testing occasion) and 0.54 (on the second testing occasion). Likewise, the shortened version of Rotter's Locus of Control Scale used by Feather and O'Brien was unreliable, with internal reliability coefficients of only 0.44 for the employed sample and 0.48 for the unemployed sample.

Finally, a problem that can obscure the results of any longitudinal study of school leavers is that the comparison groups might have differed while at school, either on background characteristics or on the dependent measures. Any such initial difference makes it very difficult to attribute later differences to employment status, although if the later differences are similar in magnitude to the initial differences it may be reasonable to conclude that they were *not* due to employment status.

In four of the five longitudinal studies under discussion the employed and unemployed groups were well matched while at school. The exception was the study by Feather and O'Brien:

> Those respondents who subsequently became unemployed were less confident about finding a job when they were at school and they obtained lower ratings of academic potential from their teachers. The unemployed group also contained a higher proportion of those who left school early and who were female respondents when compared with the employed group.
>
> (Feather and O'Brien, 1986a: 462)

In addition to these differences in background characteristics and attitudes, there were also at school differences between the employed and unemployed groups on some of the self-concept measures, some of which became more pronounced over time. Unfortunately, it is impossible to know whether the later differences, even when more pronounced, would have occurred in the absence of the initial differences.

Feather and O'Brien did not report results from those who stayed at school. Such data could have provided valuable information showing either that some observed changes in the school leavers were due to age or maturation (because similar changes were observed in the school returners), or, that some changes that occurred in both the employed and unemployed groups might have been due to leaving school (because no such changes were observed in the school returners).

Despite the differences in sampling, procedures and measures, all of the above studies have shown superior psychological well-being (or less psychological distress) in those school leavers who have become employed. Nevertheless, there is considerable disagreement as to how the difference arose. Figure 4.1 illustrates five possible scenarios. In each case, ongoing differences (Time 2) are compared with baseline, at-school differences (Time 1).

The first scenario shows a difference that is apparently unrelated to employment status because a similar difference was present while the groups were still at school. Such a situation would suggest that some individuals are predisposed to becoming unemployed, perhaps because their low self-esteem and depressed mood is expressed in behaviour which makes them unattractive to potential employers. In fact, none of the published prospective longitudinal studies has reported this kind of finding.

The second scenario shows no difference at Time 1 (at school) but a later difference evidently due both to an improvement by those gaining jobs as well as to a deterioration by those failing to gain jobs. The longitudinal findings reported by Banks and Jackson (1982) conform to this scenario.

The third scenario shows a difference at Time 1 and a larger difference at Time 2, evidently due to a deterioration on the part of those failing to gain

Scenario 1 No effect (no one)

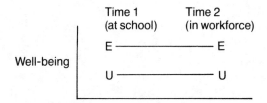

Scenario 2 Double effect (Banks and Jackson, 1982)

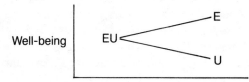

Scenario 3 Deterioration in unemployed, groups not matched initially
(Feather and O'Brien, 1986a)

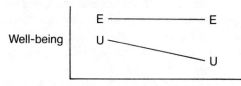

Scenario 4 Deterioration in unemployed, groups matched initially
(Patton and Noller, 1990)

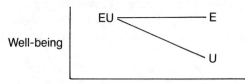

Scenario 5 Improvement in employed (Winefield, Winefield, Tiggemann
and Goldney, 1991)

Figure 4.1   Some possible scenarios

employment, but no change on the part of those gaining employment. The longitudinal data reported by Feather and O'Brien (1986a, 1986b) conform to this scenario.

The fourth scenario shows no difference at school, but a later difference due to deterioration by those failing to gain jobs. This scenario describes the findings reported by Patton and Noller (1984, 1990).

Finally, the fifth scenario shows no difference at Time 1, but a later difference due to an improvement on the part of those gaining jobs. This scenario was illustrated by the findings reported by Gurney (1980a, 1980b, 1981) as well as the findings from our own study to be described below. Some of these findings have been reported in the following publications: Tiggemann and Winefield, (1984), Winefield and Tiggemann (1985), Winefield, Tiggemann and Smith (1987), Winefield, Tiggemann and Goldney (1988), Winefield (1989), Winefield, Tiggemann and Winefield (1991b), Winefield, Winefield, Tiggemann and Goldney (1991).

How can such seemingly conflicting findings be explained? First, it should be pointed out that the studies by Banks and Jackson (1982) and Patton and Noller (1984, 1990) looked only at academic under-achievers. Consequently it may not be legitimate to generalise to the wider population of school leavers. Second, where the groups differed while still at school, it cannot be inferred that the later employment status-related differences would necessarily have been observed. This was a problem in the studies reported by Feather and O'Brien (1986a, 1986b), for example.

Only those longitudinal studies reported by Gurney (1980a, 1980b, 1981) and those based on our study were able to present data from a broad cross-section of school leavers in which later differences were not subject to possible contamination by earlier, at-school differences. These studies consistently showed marked improvements on the part of the employed (or the satisfied employed) but little change on the part of the unemployed (or the dissatisfied employed).

RESULTS OF THE UNIVERSITY OF ADELAIDE LONGITUDINAL STUDY

The rest of this chapter will be devoted to a complete account of the longitudinal and cross-sectional data which looked at various measures of psychological well-being (self-esteem, depressive affect, locus of control and negative mood) in relation to differences in employment status. First we present longitudinal data from the first phase (1981–1983), then longitudinal data from the second phase (1984–1989), and finally cross-sectional data on the additional measures introduced from 1984 (GHQ, hopelessness and anomie).

For each of the nine waves, means and standard deviations are presented both for males and females separately, and for the two combined. For each wave, there were baseline (1980) differences between the sexes, and for some of the waves there were also significant interaction effects between sex and group, or between sex, group and time, or both. An interaction between sex and group could mean, for example, that for the boys the employed were better off than the unemployed, whereas for the girls the employed were worse off than the unemployed. Or, it could mean that a difference between the employed and unemployed groups was apparent in one sex but not in the other. An interaction between group, sex and time might have arisen say, because the unemployed boys showed a deterioration over time whereas the unemployed girls showed no change. (In years where there were no such interactions, the results were analysed for the combined sexes, but in years where there was an interaction, the results were analysed separately for the boys and girls.)

In the first two waves (1981 and 1982) there were four comparison groups: those still at school, those employed, those unemployed and those engaged in full-time tertiary study. In 1983 there were only three comparison groups, because all our respondents had left school.

In using 1980 baseline measures we did not distinguish between different year levels, nor between those intending to leave school at the end of the current year and those intending to stay on. A recent study of Australian high school students has shown higher stress and anxiety levels in those in higher years, as well as in those intending to leave at the end of the current year (Ullah and Osborn, 1991). The authors have suggested that some longitudinal studies (including our own) might have used inappropriate baseline measures. We therefore analysed our data in order to check on this possibility (Winefield and Tiggemann, 1993). We found that later year students, and students intending to stay on at school, showed greater achievement motivation and less externality, but there were no differences on our three main measures of psychological well-being: self-esteem, depressive affect and negative mood. We concluded that the differences reported by Ullah and Osborn in 1990 were probably the result of a decade of very high youth unemployment in Australia (see Table 1.2). The analyses of our own data collected a decade earlier vindicated our use of the 1980 measures as appropriate baselines.

From 1984 to 1988 there were four comparison groups: the satisfied employed, the dissatisfied employed, the unemployed and the full-time tertiary students. From 1984, we introduced a job-satisfaction scale (Warr, Cook and Wall, 1979), the final item of which asks people to rate their overall job satisfaction on a 7-point scale from extremely satisfied to extremely dissatisfied. Except for the very few who were unsure, the remainder could be classified as expressing overall satisfaction or overall dissatisfaction with their jobs. In general, of these roughly 90 per cent expressed satisfaction and 10 per cent dissatisfaction each year.

In 1989, the number in the unemployed category was so low (8) that we combined them with the dissatisfied employed. The reason for this was that these two groups differed consistently from the satisfied employed and tertiary students but not from each other, so that it seemed reasonable to combine them rather than, for example, discard the unemployed respondents altogether.

As well as those unsure about their overall job satisfaction, other respondents who were discarded included those who did not fit into any of the above categories, either because they described themselves as married and engaged in home duties, or because they omitted to answer the relevant question. In fact, very few people were discarded. The percentage fluctuated from year to year within the range 4–9 per cent of the total.

Because this complete data set has not been published elsewhere (only parts of it have), it is given in full in the Appendix. The longitudinal data are contained in Tables 4.1 to 4.9, and the cross-sectional data are contained in Table 4.10 to 4.12. In reading what follows, it is not necessary to refer to these Tables. They are presented in the Appendix for the sake of fellow researchers who may wish to compare our findings with theirs. Indeed, readers who are *not* fellow researchers (or who have a low tolerance of boredom) may well wish to skip (or skim through) the following sections that present the detailed longitudinal findings, and go straight to the section headed: 'Summary of longitudinal findings' (p. 66).

In presenting the longitudinal findings for each year, ongoing differences between the groups will be compared with the at-school baseline measures. The reader is reminded that each year membership of the various occupational groups differed, partly through attrition and partly through individuals changing from one category to another from year to year. The baseline measures also differed of course, because they related to the individuals comprising the different occupational groups for a given year. (Statistically significant effects are those associated with a probability of .05 or less.)

BACKGROUND CHARACTERISTICS

In the first phase (1981–1983), the employed and unemployed groups did not differ on any of the background characteristics such as age, socio-economic status, ethnic origin and rated academic potential. However the at-school group tended to be younger, and the tertiary students tended to be older, than the other groups. Also, the tertiary students were rated higher on academic potential than the other groups.

In the second phase (1984–1989), the three groups in the workforce (satisfied employed, dissatisfied employed, unemployed) were generally well matched in terms of background characteristics, but (except for 1988 and 1989), the tertiary students were rated as higher in academic potential than the other groups. By 1988 and 1989, of course, the other groups included people who had received tertiary training. Also, during the second phase the groups differed somewhat in terms of marital status, with the satisfied employed most likely to be married, followed by the dissatisfied employed, then the unemployed, and finally the tertiary students.

LONGITUDINAL FINDINGS: FIRST PHASE (1981–1983)

Self-esteem

1981

The groups differed in 1980 with the employed and unemployed groups each showing lower self-esteem than the at-school and tertiary student groups. Also, the boys had higher overall self-esteem than the girls. This sex difference was still present in 1981 for the at-school group, but not for the other three groups that had left school. In each case the girls showed greater increases in self-esteem than the boys. In 1981, the unemployed group showed lower self-esteem than each of the other groups. Although there was an overall increase in self-esteem, the increase was greater for the employed group than for the others.

1982

The groups differed in 1980, with the at-school and tertiary student groups showing higher self-esteem than the unemployed group. There was also a sex difference, with the boys showing higher self-esteem than the girls. In 1982 there was still a sex difference although there was an overall increase in self-esteem. There was also a group difference in 1982, although this time it arose because the at-school group showed lower self-esteem than the employed and tertiary student groups. In fact, the employed and unemployed groups showed greater increases in self-esteem than the other two groups, but of course this could have been due to the initial difference.

1983

In 1980, there was a group difference, with the tertiary students showing higher self-esteem than the other two groups. There was also a sex difference, with the boys showing higher self-esteem than the girls. In 1983 there was no longer a sex difference, with the girls showing a greater increase in self-esteem than the boys. There was still a difference between the groups, however, but this time it arose because the unemployed group showed lower self-esteem than the other two groups. This was because the employed showed a significant increase in self-esteem whereas the unemployed and tertiary student groups each showed only a small, statistically insignificant, increase.

Depressive affect

1981

The groups did not differ in 1980, but the girls were higher than the boys. The sex difference was no longer present in 1981, with the girls showing a greater decrease in depressive affect than the boys. In 1981 the groups differed, with the unemployed group showing greater depressive affect than each of the other groups. There was a decrease in depressive affect for all groups except the unemployed, who showed no change.

1982

There was no difference between the groups in 1980, but a sex difference, with the girls showing greater depressive affect than the boys. In 1982, there was no longer a sex difference with the girls showing a greater decrease than the boys, but a difference between the groups. The at-school and unemployed groups showed greater depressive affect than the other two groups. Although there was an overall decrease in depressive affect, it was statistically significant only for the employed and tertiary student groups.

1983

There was no difference between the groups in 1980, but there was a sex difference with the girls showing greater depressive affect than the boys. In 1983, there was no longer a sex difference, but there was a group difference, with the unemployed showing greater depressive affect than the other groups, and the employed showing less depressive affect than the other groups. Both the employed and tertiary students showed decreases in depressive affect, but the unemployed group showed no change.

Locus of control

1981

The groups differed in 1980 with the tertiary students showing less externality than each of the other groups. There was also a sex difference in 1980 with the girls showing greater externality than the boys. In 1981, there was no longer a sex difference, with the girls showing a greater decline in externality than the boys, but there was a similar group difference as before, with the tertiary students showing less externality than each of the other groups. But the at-school group showed a somewhat smaller decrease than the other groups.

1982

The groups differed in 1980 with the unemployed group showing greater externality, and the tertiary students less externality than the other two groups. There was also a sex difference, with the girls showing greater externality than the boys. In 1982, there was still a sex difference with the girls showing greater externality than the boys although there was a large decrease in externality for both sexes. Again there was a difference between the groups with the tertiary students showing less externality than the other three groups. The earlier difference between the unemployed group and the at-school and employed groups was no longer statistically significant.

1983

In 1980 there was a group difference, with the tertiary students showing less externality than the other two groups. Also, the girls showed greater externality than the boys. In 1983, there was no longer a sex difference because the girls showed a greater decrease in externality than the boys. However there was still a difference between the groups, although this time it arose not only because the tertiary students showed less externality than the other groups (as in 1980), but also because the unemployed showed greater externality than the employed.

Negative mood

1981

The groups did not differ in 1980, but the girls were higher than the boys. The girls were still higher in 1981, although the difference was much less than before with the girls showing a greater decrease than the boys. In 1981 there was a difference between the groups, with the unemployed scoring higher than each of the other groups, and the at-school group scoring higher than the employed and tertiary students. In fact the latter two groups each showed a decrease in negative mood, whereas the at-school group showed no change, and the unemployed a slight increase.

1982

The groups differed in 1980 with the at-school group showing less negative mood than the other three groups. There was also a sex difference, with the girls showing greater negative mood than the boys. In 1982, there was no longer a sex difference, but there was a difference between the groups, with the at-school and unemployed groups both showing greater negative mood than the employed and tertiary student groups. The employed and tertiary student groups both showed significant decreases in negative mood whereas the other two groups showed no change.

1983

In 1980, there was no group difference, but the girls showed greater negative mood than the boys. In 1983, however, there was no longer a sex difference, but there was a group difference with the unemployed showing greater negative mood than each of the other groups. This arose because the employed and tertiary student groups each showed a decrease in negative mood, whereas the unemployed showed no change (a slight, but statistically insignificant increase).

LONGITUDINAL FINDINGS: SECOND PHASE (1984–1989)

Self-esteem

1984

There was a group difference in 1980, with the tertiary students showing higher self-esteem than the other three groups. There was also a sex difference, with the boys showing higher self-esteem than the girls. In 1984, there was no longer a sex difference, but there was a group difference as well as a group/sex interaction. The group difference arose because the satisfied employed and tertiary student groups both showed higher self-esteem than the other two groups. Separate analyses showed that the interaction arose because in the boys, the satisfied employed had higher self-esteem than each of the other groups, whereas for the girls, the tertiary students had higher self-esteem than each of the others, although the satisfied employed were higher than each of the other groups. There was an overall increase in self-esteem, but it was a larger increase for the satisfied employed and the tertiary students than for the other two groups.

1985

There was a group difference in 1980, with the unemployed showing lower self-esteem than each of the other groups. There was also a sex difference, with the girls showing lower self-esteem than the boys. In 1985, there was again a group difference, but only between the satisfied employed and the unemployed (the former showing higher self-esteem than the latter). There was also a group/sex interaction. Separate analyses for the boys and girls revealed that for the boys, the satisfied employed showed higher self-esteem than each of the other groups but for the girls, the tertiary students showed higher self-esteem than the unemployed. As well as an overall increase in self-esteem over time, there was also a significant sex/time interaction with the girls showing a greater increase than the boys. Finally, there was a significant group/sex/time interaction. Again, separate analyses for the sexes showed that for the boys, only the satisfied employed showed a statistically significant increase, whereas for the girls, the increase occurred uniformly over all the groups.

1986

There was no group difference in 1980 but the boys showed higher self-esteem than the girls. In 1986, there was no longer a sex difference with the girls showing a greater increase in self-esteem than the boys. However there was now a group difference, with the satisfied employed and the tertiary students both showing higher self-esteem than the dissatisfied employed and the unemployed.

1987

In 1980 there was no group difference, but the boys showed greater self-esteem than the girls. By 1987, there was no longer a sex difference and again there was no group difference. There was an overall increase over time from 1980 to 1987.

1988

There was no group difference in 1980, but the boys showed higher self-esteem than the girls. In 1988, there was no longer a sex difference, but there was a group difference, with the satisfied employed and the tertiary students showing higher self-esteem than the dissatisfied employed and the unemployed. There was an overall increase in self-esteem from 1980 to 1988.

Depressive affect

1984

In 1980, there were no differences associated with either group or sex. In 1984 however, there was a group difference, with the satisfied employed showing less depressive affect than each of the other groups and the tertiary students showing less depressive affect than the dissatisfied employed and unemployed groups. The satisfied employed and tertiary student groups both showed a decline in depressive affect (much greater for the satisfied employed) whereas the other groups showed no change.

1985

There was only a sex difference in 1980, with the girls showing greater depressive affect than the boys. In 1985, however, there was no longer a sex difference because the girls showed a greater decrease than the boys. On the other hand there was a group difference. The satisfied employed showed less depressive affect than each of the other groups, moreover the satisfied employed group was the only group to show a significant decrease in depressive affect.

1986

There was no group difference in 1980, but the girls showed greater depressive affect than the boys. In 1986, there was no longer a sex difference; however, there was now a group difference, with the satisfied employed showing less depressive affect than the dissatisfied employed and the unemployed. There was an overall decrease in depressive affect over time.

1987

There were no differences associated with either group or sex in 1980. In 1987 however, there was a group difference with the satisfied employed showing less depressive affect than either the dissatisfied employed or the unemployed. There was also a group/sex interaction. Separate analyses revealed that for the boys, the unemployed showed more depressive affect than each of the other groups, whereas for the girls, it was the dissatisfied employed who showed most depressive affect (significantly more than the satisfied employed and the tertiary students). Finally, there was a group/sex/time interaction. Separate analyses revealed that this arose because for the boys there was a decrease in depressive affect for both the satisfied employed and dissatisfied employed groups, but not for the other two groups, whereas for the girls a significant decrease occurred only in the satisfied employed and the unemployed. (The dissatisfied employed actually showed an increase, although it did not approach statistical significance.)

1988

Again there was no group difference in 1980, but the girls were more depressed than the boys. In 1988, there was no longer a sex difference because the girls (but not the boys) showed a decrease over time, but there was a group difference, with the satisfied employed being less depressed than the dissatisfied employed and unemployed, and with the tertiary students being less depressed than the dissatisfied employed. There was also a group/time interaction arising because the satisfied employed and tertiary students (but neither of the other groups) showed decreased depressive affect from 1980 to 1988.

1989

In the abridged questionnaire that was distributed in 1989, depressive affect was the only one of the four measures to be included. Because there were only 8 in the unemployed group (5 boys and 3 girls), the unemployed group was combined with the dissatisfied employed group. There were no group or sex differences between the three groups in 1980, but there was a group/sex interaction.

Separate analyses showed that for the boys, the dissatisfied employed/ unemployed group was more depressed initially than each of the other groups, whereas for the girls, the groups did not differ initially. In 1989, there was a group difference, with the satisfied employed being less depressed than each of the other groups. For the boys, the satisfied employed group was less depressed than the dissatisfied employed/unemployed group but for the girls, the satisfied employed group was less depressed than each of the other two groups. It should be noted, however, that because of the initial group difference observed in the boys, the later difference is difficult to interpret.

On the other hand, for the girls, who showed no initial group difference, the later difference may be attributed to the satisfied employed showing a greater decrease than the other two groups.

Finally, there was also an overall decrease in depressive affect from 1980 to 1989.

Locus of control

1984

There was a group difference in 1980, with the tertiary students showing less externality than each of the other groups. The girls also showed greater externality than the boys. In 1984, there was again a group difference, only this time not only were the tertiary students less external than each of the other groups, but the satisfied employed were also less external than the unemployed. The girls again showed greater externality than the boys. Although all groups showed a decrease in externality, the decrease was least for the unemployed group and greatest for the satisfied employed and tertiary students.

1985

There was a group difference in 1980, with the tertiary students showing less externality than each of the other groups, and the satisfied employed showing less externality than the unemployed. There was also a sex difference, with the girls showing greater externality than the boys. In 1985, there were also group and sex differences with the girls continuing to show greater externality. In the case of the group difference, the unemployed showed greater externality than each of the other groups, and the tertiary students showed less externality than each of the others. There was an overall decline in externality over time, but no interactions with group or sex.

1986

In 1980, there was a group difference with the tertiary students showing less externality than the other groups. Also, the girls showed greater externality than the boys. In 1986, the girls continued to show greater externality than the boys and there was again a group difference, although this time the effect was due to the unemployed showing greater externality than the satisfied employed and tertiary student groups. There was a large overall decline in externality observed in all groups.

1987

In 1980 there was no group difference, but a sex difference (the girls showing greater externality) and a group/sex interaction. Separate analyses revealed that for the boys there were no group differences, but for the girls, the tertiary students were less external than the dissatisfied employed and unemployed groups. In 1987 there was a group difference, with the unemployed showing greater externality than both the satisfied employed and tertiary student groups. Separate analyses revealed that for the boys, the group difference was not significant, but for the girls it was, with the tertiary students being less external than the dissatisfied employed and unemployed groups. Because the later group difference was evident only for the girls, for whom there was a similar difference initially, the later difference cannot be interpreted unambiguously.

There was also a sex difference, with the girls showing greater externality than the boys. Finally, there was an overall decline in externality from 1980 to 1987.

1988

There was no group difference in 1980, but the girls showed greater externality than the boys. In 1988, there was no longer a sex difference, but there was a group difference, with the unemployed showing greater externality than each of the other three groups. There was also a group/time interaction, arising because all of the groups, except for the unemployed, showed a significant decrease in externality. Finally, there was a group/sex/time interaction. Separate analyses revealed no significant group/time interaction for the boys, who showed a decrease in externality that occurred in all four groups. However there was a significant group/time interaction for the girls, arising because the satisfied employed and the tertiary student groups both showed significant decreases in externality, whereas the dissatisfied employed group showed a decrease that was not statistically significant, and the unemployed showed a (non-significant) increase.

Negative mood

1984

There was a group difference in 1980, with the dissatisfied employed showing greater negative mood than each of the other groups. There was a sex difference, with the girls showing greater negative mood than the boys.

In 1984, the sex difference was no longer present because the girls showed a greater decrease in negative mood than the boys. However, there was still a group difference, with the satisfied employed and tertiary students each showing less negative mood than each of the other groups. This difference was due to a decrease in negative mood in the satisfied employed and tertiary student groups but no change in the dissatisfied employed and unemployed groups (the latter showing an insignificant increase).

1985

There was no group difference in 1980, but the girls showed greater negative mood than the boys. In 1985, there was no longer a sex difference with the girls showing a greater decrease in negative mood than the boys. However, there was a group difference, with the unemployed showing greater negative mood than the satisfied employed and tertiary students, and with the dissatisfied employed showing greater negative mood than the satisfied employed.

1986

There was no group difference in 1980, but the girls showed greater negative mood than the boys. In 1986, there was no longer a sex difference, but now there was a group difference, with the satisfied employed and tertiary student groups both showing less negative mood than each of the other groups. Both the satisfied employed and the tertiary students showed a significant decrease in negative mood, whereas the dissatisfied employed and the unemployed showed no change.

1987

There was no group difference in 1980, but the girls showed greater negative mood than the boys. In 1987, there was no longer a sex difference but there was a significant group difference, with the satisfied employed showing less negative mood than both the dissatisfied employed and unemployed groups, and the tertiary students showing less negative mood than the unemployed. There was also a group/sex interaction. Separate analyses revealed that for the boys, the unemployed showed greater negative mood than each of the other groups, whereas for the girls, the dissatisfied employed showed greater negative mood than each of the other groups. Finally, there was a group/time interaction, arising because only the satisfied employed group showed a statistically significant decrease in negative mood from 1980 to 1987.

1988

There was no group difference in 1980, but the girls showed greater negative mood than the boys. In 1988, there was no longer a sex difference, but there was a group difference, with the satisfied employed showing less negative mood than each of the other groups. There was also a group/time interaction, with the satisfied employed and the tertiary student groups each showing a significant decrease in negative mood from 1980 to 1988, but the other two groups showing no change.

SUMMARY OF LONGITUDINAL FINDINGS

Group differences

During the first phase (1981–1983) most of the initial (1980) group differences arose either because the tertiary students or the at-school group differed from the employed and unemployed groups. For example, in each year the tertiary students initially showed higher self-esteem than the employed and unemployed groups, and in 1981 and 1982 (the only years where they were represented), so did the at-school students. These initial differences were no longer present at the later times. The tertiary students initially also showed less externality than the other groups in each year, and these initial differences were still present at the later times.

Of course, the tertiary students and the at-school students also differed from the other groups on some of the demographic variables. For example, the at-school students were younger and the tertiary students older (during the first phase) as well as higher in rated academic potential, than the other groups.

In terms of the main focus of the study – the psychological impact of unemployment – it was important that the employed and unemployed groups should have been well matched initially, both on the demographic variables and on the measures of well-being. Moreover, it was desirable that the groups be matched for both sexes separately as well as combined. Such matching required not merely that there should be no group differences present in 1980 on any of the four variables, but also that there should be no statistically significant group/sex interaction effects in 1980.

Fortunately, there were no initial group/sex interaction effects and only one case where there was an initial difference between the groups: in 1982 when the unemployed group was initially more external than the employed group. With this one exception, the employed and unemployed groups were matched initially on all four measures in each of the three years, yet with one or two exceptions, in each year they differed in self-esteem, depressive affect, locus of control and negative mood. In every case, the ongoing difference came about because the employed showed an improvement: increased self-esteem, less depression, less externality and decreased negative mood. These later differences were often associated with statistically significant group/time interactions.

The relevance of the comparison with the at-school group is that any change observed in that group would have to be attributed to age (say) rather than to a change in employment status. In fact, the at-school group showed little change in self-esteem, depressive affect and negative mood, but a substantial decrease in externality (both in 1981 and in 1982), so locus of control seems to be age-related in this population.

During the second phase (1984–1989), again initial (1980) differences were mostly due to the tertiary students differing from the other three groups. For example, in 1984 they were initially higher in self-esteem and less external than the other three groups. They were also initially less external than the other three groups in both 1985 and 1986.

On the other hand, the three workforce groups – the satisfied employed, the dissatisfied employed and the unemployed – were well matched initially except in three instances. In 1984, the dissatisfied employed were initially higher in negative mood than the other groups, and in 1985 the unemployed were initially both lower in self-esteem than the other three groups as well as more external than the satisfied employed. Except in these three cases then, later, ongoing employment status-related differences could not be attributed to initial differences. (As in the first phase, the workforce groups were generally well matched on the demographic variables.)

In only two years, 1987 and 1989, were there initial group/sex interaction effects that partially confounded later differences. In 1987, although for the boys the groups were matched initially, this was not true for the girls. For the girls, there were initial differences that mirrored the later differences. In 1989, for the girls but not the boys, the groups were matched initially. Consequently the later difference observed in the girls may be attributed to employment status; for the boys it is not easy to interpret.

In every year except one, there were differences between the workforce groups, with the satisfied employed (and often the tertiary students too) being better off than the dissatisfied employed and the unemployed. As during the first phase, the later differences generally arose because the satisfied employed and the tertiary students showed significant improvements whereas the dissatisfied employed and the unemployed showed no change. Again, these later differences were often associated with significant group/time interactions.

Data from 1986 were fairly typical of the years from 1984–1988 and are illustrated in Figure 4.2.

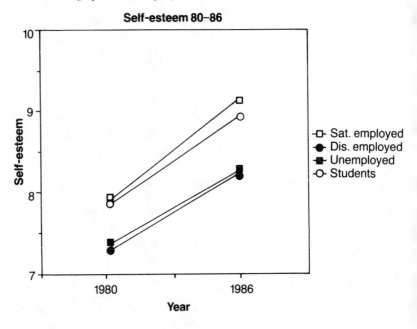

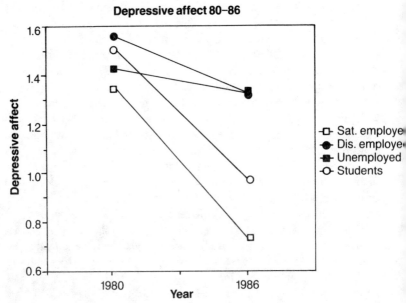

Figure 4.2 Differences on psychological scales, 1980–1986

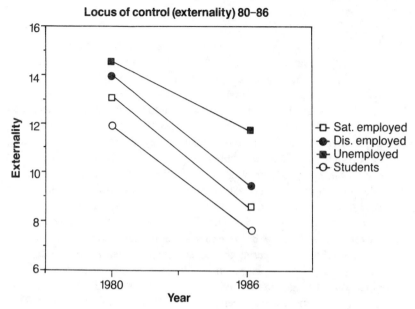

Locus of control (externality) 80–86

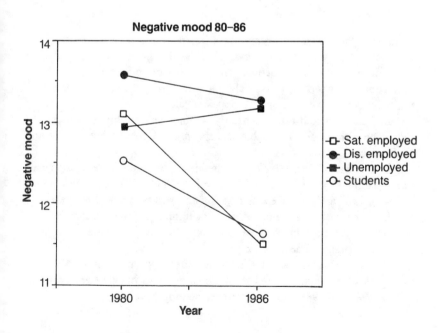

Negative mood 80–86

Conclusions

Taken together, the results best exemplify the fifth scenario depicted in Figure 4.1. The initial matching of the employed and unemployed groups (first phase) and the satisfied employed, dissatisfied employed and unemployed groups (second phase) makes it easier to interpret the later differences than is the case in other similar prospective longitudinal studies where the groups have differed initially (while at school). Our results suggest that young people who are employed in jobs that they regard as satisfactory are better off in terms of their psychological well-being than other members of the workforce because they gain a positive advantage through their employment status. By contrast, those young people who are either employed in jobs they regard as unsatisfactory, or who are unemployed, are relatively disadvantaged by comparison. Their relative disadvantage, however, comes about not because they suffer a deterioration in well-being on leaving school and entering the workforce, but because they are denied the benefits of satisfactory employment. We have also shown in longitudinal comparisons of transition into and out of jobs, that gaining a job leads to a marked improvement in well-being, whereas losing a job has little effect (Winefield and Tiggemann, 1990a).

Sex differences

Although there were consistent sex differences at school, on most of the variables they were no longer evident later. This gave rise to a number of significant sex/time interactions. In the cases of self-esteem, depressive affect and negative mood, typically the girls were worse off than the boys initially but the difference had disappeared later.

In the case of self-esteem, the boys initially showed higher self-esteem than the girls in every year but, except in 1982, there were no ongoing differences.

In the case of depressive affect, the girls were initially more depressed than the boys in 1981, 1982, 1983, 1985, 1986 and 1988 but not in 1984, 1987 or 1989 and there were no ongoing differences in any of the years.

In the case of negative mood, the girls initially showed greater negative mood than the boys in every year, but only in 1981 was there an ongoing difference (in the same direction).

Only for locus of control was there a different pattern of results. Although the girls were initially more external than the boys in every year, only in 1981, 1983 and 1988 was the difference no longer present.

CROSS-SECTIONAL DATA

From 1984, several additional measures of psychological well-being were used: the 12-item version of Goldberg's (1972) General Health Questionnaire (GHQ) which measures minor psychiatric symptomatology or psychological distress, a measure of hopelessness (Beck, Weisman, Lester and Trexler, 1974) and a measure of social alienation or anomie (Srole, 1956; Dodder and Astle, 1980). From 1984 to 1987 Srole's original 5-item scale was used, but in 1988, the 9-item version (incorporating four additional items) was used. Of these three measures only the GHQ was administered in 1989. (On each of the measures, a higher score implies poorer psychological well-being than a lower score.)

The General Health Questionnaire

There was a significant difference between the groups in every year, although in 1987 and in 1988 there was also a significant group/sex interaction. Separate analyses revealed a significant group difference in both the boys and the girls, but whereas in the boys, the unemployed and tertiary students scored higher than the other groups, in the girls it was the dissatisfied employed who scored highest.

In 1988, separate analyses revealed a significant group difference for the boys but not for the girls. In the boys, the dissatisfied employed scored higher than each of the other groups.

In every other year, the satisfied employed scored lowest, followed by the tertiary students. In some years the difference between them was significant, in others it was not. Similarly in some years, the differences between the tertiary students and the dissatisfied employed and unemployed groups were statistically significant. The dissatisfied employed never differed significantly from the unemployed overall (although in 1987 the dissatisfied employed boys scored higher than the unemployed boys, and in 1988 the dissatisfied employed girls scored higher than the unemployed girls).

There was an overall sex difference only in 1986, when the girls scored significantly higher than the boys.

Hopelessness

As for GHQ, there was a significant group difference in every year, although in 1985 it was confounded by a group/sex interaction. In that year, the group difference was significant only for the boys, with the unemployed and dissatisfied employed scoring higher than the satisfied employed and the tertiary students.

The overall pattern of results was very similar to that observed for GHQ. In each year, the satisfied employed scored lowest, followed by the tertiary students. In some years the dissatisfied employed scored lower than the unemployed and in other years higher, but the differences were never statistically significant. The most consistent difference was between the satisfied employed and dissatisfied employed groups which was statistically significant in every year (although, as pointed out earlier, in 1985 the difference was confined to the boys).

Anomie

Although there was a significant group difference in every year, it was not confounded with any group/sex interaction, nor were there any significant sex differences.

The overall pattern was somewhat different for this variable. In every year except 1988, it was the tertiary students rather than the satisfied employed who scored lowest. They were followed by the satisfied employed, but the difference between these two groups was significant in both 1984 and in 1987. The unemployed scored highest in every year except 1987, although they differed from the dissatisfied employed only in 1988.

The different pattern of results observed in 1988 was almost certainly due to the fact that four additional items were included in the scale. Dodder and Astle (1980) factor analysed national survey data using the nine items and found that although the original 5-item scale was reasonably unidimensional, the 9-item scale was more complex and included additional subdimensions which they labelled 'Valuelessness' and 'Cynicism'. They also found that the longer version correlated more strongly than the shorter version with 31 variables traditionally associated with anomie (or social alienation). They concluded that the 9-item version measures more reliably than the 5-item version a general dimension of despair.

OVERALL CONCLUSIONS

The main conclusion arising from both the cross-sectional and longitudinal data is that young people employed in jobs that they regard as satisfactory and young people engaged in full-time tertiary study enjoy superior psychological well-being to those employed in unsatisfactory jobs and those who are unemployed. The former two groups displayed superior well-being on all seven measures and there were no differences between the latter two. On the other hand, although the satisfied employed and the tertiary students did not differ with respect to three of the measures, self-esteem, locus of control and anomie, the satisfied employed were better off than the students in terms of depression, negative mood, GHQ and hopelessness. These differences are discussed further in Chapter 7.

The longitudinal data, in addition, permit the reasonable inference that the differences between the satisfied employed group on the one hand, and the dissatisfied employed and unemployed groups on the other, can be attributed to workforce experience rather than to other, predisposing factors. This was because these three groups were generally well matched not only on the 1980 at-school baseline measures, but also on demographic variables such as age, socio-economic status and rated academic potential. Prior to 1984, when the satisfied and dissatisfied employed were not differentiated, it can be assumed that the employed group would have comprised around 90 per cent who were satisfied with their jobs and only around 10 per cent who were dissatisfied (based on the later distributions).

The longitudinal comparisons also permit the reasonable inference that, by and large, the later differences were due to improvements shown by the satisfied employed and tertiary students, rather than to deteriorations shown by the dissatisfied employed and unemployed.

During the first two years, it is interesting to compare the changes in those leaving school with those who stayed on (bearing in mind the age difference). Those staying on showed little change on three of the four measures (locus of control being the exception), whereas the employed and tertiary students generally showed improvements. In 1982, surprisingly, the unemployed (both boys and girls) showed a large improvement in self-esteem that exceeded the relatively small increase shown by those still at school. For the employed and tertiary students, the girls showed greater improvements than the boys, but this could have been due to the fact that they were worse off initially.

The fact that the at-school group showed no change is important, because it rules out the possibility that the differences observed in the other groups might have been due to age, rather than the change in occupational status.

In general, the girls were worse off than the boys while they were at school, but not after leaving school. Whether this is typical of co-educational state schools, or of all schools is an interesting question. Some educationists have argued recently that girls, but not boys, perform better academically in segregated schools. Unfortunately until recently, segregated schools tended also to be fee-paying schools, whereas co-educational schools tend to be free, so the two factors were usually confounded. Now that more fee-paying schools are becoming co-educational, it will be interesting to see whether girls are similarly disadvantaged academically. Our results suggest that the co-educational school environment could be a factor in producing lower self-esteem, more depression and more negative mood in girls than in boys. This conclusion is based on the fact that on these three measures, the initial sex difference was not present after leaving school. With respect to locus of control, however, the girls tended to be more external than the boys after leaving, as well as while they were at school.

Of the four longitudinal measures, depressive affect proved to be the most satisfactory in the sense that it was not only sensitive to employment status-related differences in every year, but also there were never baseline differences between the groups. For the other three measures, there were occasional baseline differences (particularly in the case of locus of control) that made it difficult to interpret later differences. Self-esteem proved to be the least sensitive to employment status. In 1987 for example, the occupational groups did not differ in self-esteem (Winefield, Tiggemann and Winefield, 1991b) and in 1988 the differences in self-esteem were less reliable than the differences on the other three measures (Winefield, Winefield, Tiggemann and Goldney, 1991).

The three variables on which only cross-sectional comparisons could be made produced slightly different patterns of results. Although they confirmed the main findings that the satisfied employed and tertiary students were better off than the dissatisfied employed and unemployed groups, the ordering varied somewhat depending on the measure. With GHQ and hopelessness, the satisfied employed were slightly better off than the tertiary students, and the dissatisfied employed and unemployed were worse off, but did not differ. With anomie different patterns of results were observed in the years 1984–1987 when the 5-item scale was used, and 1988 when the 9-item scale (incorporating four additional items) was used. Whereas in the earlier years, the dissatisfied employed and the unemployed groups both scored higher than the other two, in 1988 the unemployed scored higher than each of the other groups. Assuming that the 9-item version is a more reliable and valid measure as Dodder and Astle (1980) have claimed, perhaps we should pay more attention to the 1988 data.

Finally, we feel able to maintain that our results provide a more valid account of the psychological impact of employment and unemployment than other, similar prospective longitudinal studies of school leavers that have been reported. First, our study was continued over a much longer period than any other, and spans the important developmental phase from adolescence to young adulthood. Second, unlike the studies by Banks and Jackson (1982) and Patton and Noller (1984, 1990), our sample was not restricted to academic under-achievers. Third, unlike the study by Feather and O'Brien (1986a, 1986b), our occupational groups were well matched on initial, baseline measures as well as on demographic variables. Fourth, by separating the satisfied and dissatisfied employed, we were able to demonstrate that the latter subgroup were just as badly off as the unemployed. The theoretical implications of these results are discussed in Chapter 6, following the discussion of coping in Chapter 5.

5 Coping with unemployment

Various factors appear to moderate the potentially harmful effects of unemployment, that is, influence how well (or badly) unemployed individuals manage to cope with their lot. In this chapter we discuss our results in terms of this very important question.

Hepworth (1980) suggested a number of such factors, and, in a study of unemployed men, she showed that length of unemployment was negatively correlated with mental health and psychological well-being, and that the semi-skilled and unskilled had poorer psychological well-being than those of higher occupational status.

These findings have not always been replicated however. Feather (1985) for example, after reviewing the literature, concluded, 'The evidence typically fails to show that longer durations of unemployment are associated with lower psychological well-being' (Feather, 1985: 270). Hepworth's (1980) finding concerning skill levels has not always been replicated either. Kaufman (1982), in a study of unemployed professionals, found that the more highly skilled suffered more than the less highly skilled.

A range of other variables has been shown to moderate the negative effects of unemployment including age (Broomhall and Winefield, 1990; Rowley and Feather, 1987), sex (Ensminger and Celentano, 1990; Warr and Parry, 1982), ethnic origin (Warr, Banks and Ullah, 1985), socio-economic status (Little, 1976; Payne, Warr and Hartley, 1984), financial strain (Finlay-Jones and Eckhardt, 1981, 1984; Kessler, Turner and House, 1987; Payne and Hartley, 1987), social support (Bolton and Oatley, 1987; Gore, 1978; Halford and Learner, 1984; Ullah, Banks and Warr, 1985), employment commitment (Jackson, Stafford, Banks and Warr, 1983; Ostell and Divers, 1987; Shamir, 1986a); time use (Feather and Bond, 1983; Kilpatrick and Trew, 1985) and attributional style (Ostell and Divers, 1987). One complication in studying the effects of moderating variables is that they are likely to interact. In other words, their combined effects may not be the same as the effects of each added together. For example, Hartley and

Fryer (1984) suggest that the effects of unemployment duration may affect the middle-aged more than the young or old, and may also affect men more than women. An additional complication that has not been widely recognised, is that moderating variables may operate differentially with respect to different aspects of psychological well-being. Hepworth (1980) for example, found that different moderating variables affected subjective well-being (as measured by a Present Life Satisfaction Scale) from those that affected mental health (as measured by Goldberg's General Health Questionnaire). Moreover, Shamir (1986a) has shown that the effects of unemployment on self-esteem, although not on depressive affect, may be related to both age and educational level.

THE EFFECTS OF POTENTIAL MODERATING VARIABLES AT TWO DIFFERENT AGES

The two major analyses that follow were based on data from our longitudinal study collected in 1984 and in 1987. These two years were chosen for comparison for a number of reasons. First, in 1984 we introduced a range of measures that enabled us to measure job satisfaction, as well as psychological distress (the GHQ) and hopelessness (for details, see Chapter 3). Prior to that, the only established measures of well-being that we used were Rosenberg's (1965) self-esteem and depressive affect scales. Although the number of unemployed in our sample declined over the years, it was still reasonably high in both 1984 (78) and in 1987 (40), having remained fairly constant over the years 1985–1987, but dropped to only 22 in 1988 and to 8 in 1989. In both years, we looked at the effects of twelve different moderator variables in each of three subgroups: the satisfied employed, the dissatisfied employed and the unemployed (defined as in Chapter 4) on four measures of psychological well-being: self-esteem, depressive affect, GHQ-12 and hopelessness.

In 1984, there were 586 in the satisfied employed group (263 boys and 323 girls), 75 in the dissatisfied employed group (36 boys and 39 girls) and 78 in the unemployed group (41 boys and 37 girls). The numbers in the employed groups were slightly lower than those shown in Table 4.4 (see Appendix) due to missing values. In 1987, there were 417 in the satisfied employed group (202 boys and 215 girls), 45 in the dissatisfied employed group (27 boys and 18 girls) and 40 in the unemployed group (23 boys and 17 girls). In 1984, the age range was roughly 19–21 years and in 1987 it was roughly 22–24 years. Thus there was an age range at both times, so that age could be entered into the regression analyses as a potential predictor at both times.

In addition to age and sex, there were four other background variables entered: socio-economic status, ethnic origin, academic potential and educational level (years of secondary schooling). The way in which these variables were measured was described in Chapter 3.

The remaining predictor variables included two on financial resources: one concerned with financial hardship (measured on a 5-point scale from 'very comfortable' to 'desperately hard up') and one on borrowing ability which asked 'If you needed money urgently for an emergency, how much money would you be able to borrow at a day's notice?' Five possible answers were $0–$50, $50–$200, $200–$500, $500–$1000 and more than $1000.

There were two questions on social supports, one concerned with the availability of people in whom one would confide a serious problem (confidants) and the other with number of friends.

Employment commitment was another potential predictor variable, as was attributional style (for negative outcomes). The latter was measured by the question: 'When bad things happen to you, is it mostly because of (a) lack of ability, (b) the fact that you didn't try hard enough, (c) the situation you're in, (d) bad luck?' These four answers may be classified as internal/stable (lack of ability), internal/unstable (lack of effort), external/stable (the situation) and external/unstable (bad luck). It has been shown that stable (and to a lesser degree internal) causal attributions for bad outcomes are associated with poorer psychological health (greater depressive affect) than unstable (and external) attributions (Peterson and Seligman, 1984). Consequently, responses to the attributional question were scored as follows: 1 = bad luck, 2 = the fact that you didn't try hard enough, 3 = the situation you're in, 4 = lack of ability. This scoring, although somewhat arbitrary, reflects the theoretical assumption that a high score represents a psychologically unhealthy response.

We did not include any potential moderator variables that were not applicable to all three occupational groups (such as unemployment duration). Moderator variables that applied only to the unemployed are considered in a later section.

Regression analyses

The younger sample

The full results of the regression analyses are presented for the younger (1984) sample and older sample (1987) separately. Table 5.1 in the Appendix shows the results for the younger sample.

Only those multiple correlation coefficients that account for at least 15 per cent of the variance (R^2) as well as being statistically significant (beyond the 0.05 level) will be regarded as psychologically meaningful. This is because with extremely large samples (such as the satisfied employed in both years), very small correlations can be statistically significant. We selected the double criterion of statistical significance plus effect size using the conventional level of statistical significance as well as the criterion for effect size suggested by Cohen (1977) as defining a 'large' effect in the behavioural and social sciences. In assessing the relative importance of the various predictor variables we will refer to their beta weights. (In regression analysis a beta weight refers to the standardised partial regression coefficient. The size of its beta weight reflects the relative importance of a predictor variable.)

None of the multiple correlations even approached psychological significance in the satisfied employed group. Only 4 per cent of the variance in self-esteem was accounted for, 9 per cent in the case of depressive affect, 8 per cent in the case of GHQ and 7 per cent in the case of hopelessness. Statistically significant, but very low (0.22 being the largest) beta values were obtained and these are shown.

In the dissatisfied employed and unemployed groups, the effects were much stronger, with large effects being shown on self-esteem, depressive affect and hopelessness. In the case of GHQ none of the beta values was statistically significant. The percentage of explained variance varied from 17 per cent to 36 per cent.

For these two groups, the social support measures (number of friends and confidants) seemed to be the best overall predictors, along with one of the measures of financial resources (borrowing ability). One or other of the social support measures featured as a significant predictor of psychological well-being in all six analyses (number of friends for both self-esteem and depressive affect, confidants in the case of hopelessness). Borrowing ability, on the other hand, seemed to be relatively more important for the dissatisfied employed, for whom it predicted self-esteem, low depressive affect and low hopelessness, than for the unemployed, for whom it predicted only low hopelessness.

The only other predictor variables to be included were employment commitment (which predicted depressive affect in the dissatisfied employed), academic potential (which predicted self-esteem in the unemployed), socio-economic status and years of schooling (both of which predicted depressive affect in the unemployed). The beta weights for all these predictor variables ranged from 0.27 to 0.41.

Looking at the significant predictors of well-being in the satisfied employed group, we see that the beta values were much lower (ranging from 0.09 to 0.22). The largest ones, however (those with beta weights of 0.15 or more), were a measure of social support (number of friends predicting depressive affect) and a measure of financial resources (borrowing ability, predicting both GHQ and hopelessness).

The older sample

Table 5.2 in the Appendix shows the results for the older (1987) sample. As with the younger sample, the amount of explained variance in the satisfied employed in no case reached 15 per cent. On the other hand, in the dissatisfied employed and the unemployed groups, the multiple correlations accounted for percentages of variance ranging from 16 per cent (for self-esteem in the dissatisified employed) to 58 per cent (for hopelessness in the unemployed). In the dissatisfied employed group, there were statistically significant predictors of self-esteem (financial hardship), depressive affect (financial hardship and number of friends) and GHQ (confidants and number of friends), but not for hopelessness.

In the unemployed group, there were statistically significant predictors of self-esteem (ethnic origin) and hopelessness (number of friends, unhealthy attributional style and academic potential), but not of depressive affect or GHQ. Those of English-speaking backgrounds showed higher self-esteem. Greater academic potential was associated with less hopelessness, but paradoxically, so was a more 'unhealthy' attributional style.

Looking at the statistically significant predictors of psychological well-being in the satisfied employed group, as with the younger sample, they are less useful (in terms of their contribution as measured by their beta values) than those in the dissatisfied and unemployed groups. Whereas the beta weights for the significant predictor variables in the latter groups ranged from 0.33 to 0.56, the range in the satisfied employed group ranged from 0.11 to 0.29. The best predictors (those with beta weights of 0.15 or more) were number of friends (predicting depressive affect, GHQ and hopelessness), and unhealthy attributional style (predicting GHQ and hopelessness in the expected manner).

Summary of findings

The regression analyses are interesting for several reasons. First, they show that psychological well-being in unemployed young people and in those who are employed but dissatisfied with their jobs, can be predicted much more accurately than it can in employed young people who are satisfied with their jobs.

Second, the measure of well-being that was best predicted in the dissatisfied employed and unemployed groups was self-esteem (predicted in both groups at both times) and the measure that was least well predicted was GHQ (predicted only in the dissatisfied employed at the later time).

Third, the best predictors of well-being were the two measures of social support (confidants, number of friends) and the two measures of financial resources (financial hardship, borrowing ability). This was true for both the dissatisfied employed and the unemployed groups, although financial resources seemed to be more important for the dissatisfied employed than for the unemployed. For the dissatisfied employed, borrowing ability was the better predictor at the earlier time, and financial hardship was the better predictor at the later time.

OVERVIEW

Social support has been widely studied as a moderating factor in relation to stress generally, and several studies have looked at its possible role in alleviating the stress of unemployment (Bolton and Oatley, 1987; Gore, 1978). Bolton and Oatley (1987) in their study of unemployed men, found that low social interaction was associated with greater depression, and interpreted their results in accordance with Cohen and Wills' (1985) buffering hypothesis, according to which social support only operates in the presence of a specific, independent source of stress. Similar findings have been reported by Kessler, Turner and House (1988). However other studies have shown that although social support enhances psychological well-being, it does so directly and not indirectly, as the buffering hypothesis implies (e.g. Dooley, Rook and Catalano, 1987).

Insofar as social support was more strongly associated with psychological well-being in the dissatisfied employed and the unemployed, than in the satisfied employed, our results may also be seen as supporting the buffering hypothesis. Indeed, it could be argued on similar grounds that financial resources operate in a similar fashion.

Payne and Hartley (1987), in testing their stress model of unemployment, also found that financial worry was an important moderating variable, although, somewhat surprisingly, they did not find social support was important. A possible explanation for this is that they used a support scale 'developed to measure the degree to which people perceive that individuals and organizations help or hinder them in coping with the problems of being unemployed' (Payne and Hartley, 1987: 35).

Perhaps the highly specific nature of what the scale attempted to measure vitiated its usefulness. It may be that the importance of social support in alleviating psychological distress in the unemployed has more to do with providing general emotional support than with helping them to solve a specific problem.

Other studies of the unemployed, like this one, have suggested that social support is an important moderator of the negative effects of unemployment. Broomhall and Winefield (1990), for example, in comparing young and middle-aged samples of unemployed men showed that the single best predictor of psychological well-being was a measure of social support, although it was a different measure for each group. In the young group it was 'perceived adequacy of social support' and in the middle-aged group it was 'participation in leisure activities involving other people'.

Surprisingly, some variables that have been shown to moderate the effects of unemployment in other studies, did not do so here. Employment commitment, for example, did not predict psychological well-being in either the younger or the older unemployed sample, on any of the four measures, although it did moderate depressive affect in the younger group of dissatisfied employed: greater commitment was associated with less depressive affect. Interestingly, this is the reverse of what has been found in the unemployed. Jackson, Stafford, Banks and Warr (1983), for example, found that greater commitment was associated with greater psychological distress. In fact, this was the only instance of a variable other than one measuring either social support or financial resources, predicting psychological well-being in the dissatisfied employed.

In the unemployed, sometimes different variables moderated psychological well-being in the younger and older samples. For example, socio-economic status and years of schooling both predicted depressive affect in the younger, but not the older, sample. On the other hand, ethnic origin (predicting self-esteem) and unhealthy attributional style (predicting hopelessness) were significant only in the older sample.

Perhaps the most surprising finding was that unhealthy attributional style was negatively, rather than positively, correlated with hopelessness. This finding is contrary to learned helplessness theory predictions (Abramson, Metalsky and Alloy, 1989; Peterson and Seligman, 1984) as well as being inconsistent with findings reported by Ostell and Divers (1987) and by Winefield, Tiggemann and Smith (1987). Ostell and Divers (1987) found the predicted relationship between unhealthy attributional style for negative outcomes and GHQ scores in a sample of middle-aged managers, and Winefield, Tiggemann and Smith (1987) found the predicted relationship with depressive affect in an earlier wave (1983) of this study, when the unemployed sample was considerably larger. There seems to be no obvious explanation for these discrepant findings.

Interestingly, the GHQ-12, widely used as a measure of psychological distress in many studies of unemployment, proved to be less amenable to potential moderator variables than were the measures of self-esteem, depressive affect and hopelessness.

TIME USE AS A MODERATING FACTOR

Another variable that has been shown to moderate the negative effects of unemployment is how unemployed people spend their time. Kilpatrick and

Trew (1985) showed that mental health in a group of 121 unemployed men was affected by how they spent their time. They distinguished four groups using cluster analysis: the first group (passive) spent most of their time watching TV or doing nothing. They showed the poorest psychological well-being. The next group (domestic) also spent most of their time at home, but, unlike the first, assisted with household tasks. They showed only slightly better mental health than the first group. The third group (social) spent much of their time with people outside their immediate family. They exhibited superior mental health to the first two groups. Finally, the fourth group (active) not only spent much of their time in active leisure pursuits outside the home, but also spent more time on work-related activities. They were the least affected by unemployment.

Feather and Bond (1983), in a study of unemployed university graduates, found that structured and purposeful use of time was positively correlated with self-esteem and negatively correlated with depressive symptoms.

Other studies have also tended to show that unemployed people who cope best are those who are engaged in purposeful activity and who maintain regular contact with people outside the nuclear family (McKenna and Fryer, 1984; Warr and Jackson, 1985).

In our own study (see Winefield, Tiggemann and Winefield, 1992b) we asked our respondents each year the following question: 'How much of your spare time do you spend engaged in each of the following: (1) doing nothing in particular; (2) watching TV; (3) an activity by yourself, e.g. stamp collecting, cooking, reading, fiddling with cars; (4) an activity with other people, e.g. sport, disco?' The four possible answers were: 1 = none or very little of the time, 2 = some of the time, 3 = a lot of the time, 4 = most of the time.

From 1981 to 1983 (first phase) we correlated time use with the following three measures of psychological well-being: self-esteem, depressive affect and negative mood for the employed and unemployed groups. From 1984 to 1988 (second phase) we correlated time use with the following six measures of psychological well-being: self-esteem, depressive affect, negative mood, hopelessness, anomie and GHQ. Only statistically significant correlations (at the 0.05 level) that were equal to or greater than 0.39 were regarded as psychologically significant, using Cohen's (1977) suggested criterion for a 'large' effect in the behavioural and social sciences (an effect that accounts for at least 15 per cent of the variance).

Unemployed group: first phase (1981–1983)

The results from the first phase (1981–1983) for the unemployed boys and girls are shown in Table 5.3 (see Appendix). There were no (psychologically) significant correlations involving self-esteem or solitary activities and only one involving watching TV. However, there were several correlations between both doing nothing and gregarious activities, and the other two measures of well-being (depressive affect and negative mood).

Employed group: first phase (1981–1983)

There were no significant correlations between any of the activities and any of the measures of psychological well-being for the employed group.

Unemployed group: second phase (1984–1988)

The results for each of the years in the second phase (1984–1988) for the unemployed group are given in Table 5.4 (see Appendix). Altogether there were 81 significant correlations between the four different categories of activity and the various measures of psychological well-being, all of which were in the predicted direction. The first two activity categories ('doing nothing', 'watching TV') were seen as aimless and would therefore be expected to be positively correlated with psychological distress (i.e. with depressive affect, negative mood, hopelessness, anomie and GHQ) and negatively correlated with self-esteem.

The other two activity categories ('solitary activities' and 'gregarious activities') were both seen as purposeful and would therefore be expected to be positively correlated with self-esteem and negatively correlated with the other five measures (depressive affect, negative mood, hopelessness, anomie and GHQ). Although in 1984 only two of the measures of well-being (self-esteem and negative mood) were involved, and in 1985 only four were involved (negative mood, hopelessness, anomie and GHQ), in each of the remaining years all six were involved to some extent. Of the activity categories, 'doing nothing' was involved in every year, 'watching TV' was involved in every year except for 1984, 'solitary activities' was involved in 1986 and 1988 but not in 1984, 1985 or 1987, and 'gregarious activities' was involved in 1986, 1987 and 1988, but not in 1984 or 1985. There was no clear difference between the men and women, although there was a tendency for 'watching TV' and 'solitary activities' to be correlated with well-being more often for the women than for the men.

Dissatisfied employed group: second phase (1984–1988)

For the dissatisfied employed, there were 70 significant correlations over the years 1984–1988 as shown in Table 5.5 (see Appendix). Of these, 66 were in the predicted direction. The first three measures (self-esteem, depressive affect and negative mood) were involved in every year, hopelessness was involved in every year except for 1988, anomie was involved in every year except for 1986, but GHQ was involved in only 1985 and 1988. As with the unemployed, 'doing nothing' was involved in all years. The same was true for 'gregarious activities', but 'watching TV' and 'solitary activities' were not involved in either 1984 or 1985. Except for 'solitary activities', all the correlations were in the predicted direction. In the case of 'solitary activities' there were eight significant correlations of which four were in the unpredicted direction: it was negatively correlated with self-esteem for both men and women in 1985 and for women in 1986; also, it was positively correlated with hopelessness for men in 1987.

Satisfied employed group: second phase (1984–1988)

For the satisfied employed group there were only two significant correlations. In 1986 and 1988 there were positive correlations between 'doing nothing' and negative mood for the men only: 0.41 and 0.43, respectively.

Conclusion

The fact that time use was highly correlated with measures of psychological well-being for both the unemployed and dissatisfied employed groups, but not for the satisfied employed group, has two clear implications. First, it shows again that psychologically the dissatisfied employed are much more similar to the unemployed than they are to the satisfied employed. Second, it suggests that time use, like social support, may have a buffering role in coping with stress.

OTHER MODERATING FACTORS

The remaining factors to be considered are those that are specific to the unemployed: reason for being unemployed (i.e. through job loss or failure to find a job), reason for job loss (dismissal or other), causal attribution for unemployment and unemployment duration.

Intuitively, it might be supposed that there would be a difference in how well unemployed young people cope, depending on whether they had had a job and lost it, or never had a job since leaving school. In fact, analyses of the first phase of our longitudinal study (1981–1983) showed no differences on any of our measures of well-being (Winefield and Tiggemann, 1989a). Moreover, the groups were well matched, both on demographic variables as well as baseline measures.

Another possibility that we considered, was that young unemployed people who have left their last job voluntarily, might cope better than those who had left their last job involuntarily (e.g. through having been dismissed). Again, we were able to look at this in relation to those unemployed from 1984, and found (in 1984, the only year when there were sufficient numbers in the two subgroups to allow a reasonable comparison) no difference in well-being (Winefield, Tiggemann and Winefield, 1992b).

Finally, it might be supposed that the reasons, or causal attributions, given by unemployed youngsters for their unemployment might affect how well they cope. We examined this possibility in relation to the third wave of our longitudinal study (1983) when we had the highest number of unemployed (138) as well as the fourth wave when the number of unemployed was still reasonably high (78). The question we asked was: 'What is the main reason you do not have a job now: (a) lack of abilities or skills, (b) you didn't try hard enough, (c) the situation you're in, (d) bad luck?'

In 1983, the question was answered by all but three of the respondents. Of the 135 responding, 46 gave internal stable attributions (lack of abilities or skills), 22 gave internal unstable attributions (lack of effort), 46 gave external stable attributions (the situation), and 21 gave external unstable attributions (bad luck). The pattern was similar for both boys and girls. Type of causal attribution was not related to psychological well-being.

In 1984, the question was answered by all but five of the respondents. Of the 73 responding, 22 gave internal stable attributions, 9 gave internal unstable attributions, 29 gave external stable attributions and 13 gave external unstable attributions. External attributions were associated with better well-being than internal attributions, but stability of attributions was not associated with psychological well-being. (These findings are discussed further in Chapter 6.)

UNEMPLOYMENT DURATION

Several studies have examined psychological distress in unemployed people in relation to how long they have been unemployed. Eisenberg and Lazarsfeld (1938) and several writers since then have proposed stage models to describe the time course of psychological reactions to job loss (see Chapter 2). Such models generally assume a curvilinear relation between length of unemployment and distress so that, following the assumed shock reaction, there is renewed optimism (stage one) which eventually gives way to pessimism, anxiety and active distress (stage two) and the final stage (stage three) is assumed to be fatalism and resignation. Stage two is assumed to be associated with the highest level of distress.

Some support for the stages model was reported from a longitudinal study of unemployed men by Warr and Jackson (1984, 1985, 1987) who showed some improvement in the long-term unemployed after extended periods of unemployment. They concluded that the negative mental health consequences of unemployment occur within the first three to six months and may show some improvement from 15 to 25 months, even where there is no improvement in financial situation.

We studied the effects of unemployment duration, first over the first phase of our longitudinal investigation, from 1981–1983 (Winefield and Tiggemann, 1989b), and second over the second phase, from 1984–1987 (Winefield and Tiggemann, 1990b).

In the first phase, we compared the employed, the unemployed and full-time tertiary students. The unemployed were subdivided into the following five subgroups reflecting how long they had been unemployed: (a) less than one month, (b) 1–3 months, (c) 3–6 months, (d) 6–12 months and (e) more than 12 months. Inevitably there was some overlapping in the categories from one year to another and, of course, some individuals featured in different categories from one year to another. This precluded any sort of meaningful statistical analysis. Nevertheless, we combined the three years, and derived a mean improvement score (from the 1980 baseline) for self-esteem, depressive affect and negative mood. (Improvement was defined as an increase in self-esteem, and decreases in depressive affect and negative mood.)

The improvement scores are illustrated in Figure 5.1. (A bar graph below the zero line shows a deterioration.) As can be seen from Figure 5.1, although all seven groups displayed an increase in self-esteem, the improvement was greatest for the employed and least for the 3–6 months and 6–12 months unemployed groups. For the other three unemployed groups, the improvement was at least equal to that shown by the tertiary students.

In the case of both depressive affect and negative mood, the 3–6 months and the 6–12 months groups were the only ones not to show an improvement. Not only did the other unemployed groups show an improvement, but in the case of depressive affect the other two (the less than one month and the more than 12 months groups) showed a greater improvement than the tertiary students, and in the case of negative mood one of them (the less than one month group) showed a greater improvement than both the employed and the tertiary student groups. Moreover, the longest unemployed group (more than 12 months) showed greater improvement in depressive affect than the tertiary students, as well as greater improvement in negative mood than the 1–3 months unemployed group.

In summary, the data seem to suggest that the maximum psychological impact of unemployment in young people probably occurs after about six months and declines thereafter.

In the second phase, we compared those unemployed over the years 1984

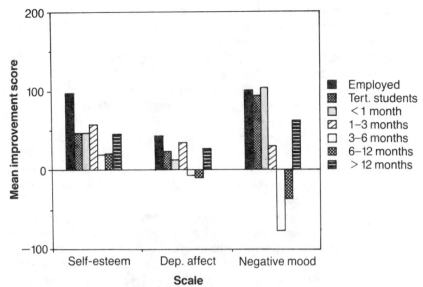

Figure 5.1 Mean improvement scores
Source: Winefield and Tiggemann (1989b)

to 1987. We divided them into three subgroups, based on their responses to the question: 'Roughly how many months have you been unemployed?' The three categories were (a) 3 months or less, (b) 4–8 months and (c) 9 months or more. These three categories were selected because they best satisfied the following two criteria: to provide reasonable and roughly equivalent numbers in each group; and to provide the best test of the curvilinear hypothesis suggested by the results of the first phase. We anticipated, in the light of the earlier results, that the 4–8 months unemployed group would be worse off than either of the others.

The three groups were compared on the following eight measures: self-esteem, depressive affect, negative mood and locus of control (on all of which 1980 baseline measures were available), work involvement, social alienation (anomie), hopelessness and GHQ (on none of which 1980 baseline measures were available).

In order to permit meaningful statistical analyses to be performed, it was necessary to remove overlapping members (individuals who featured in more than one group). Some individuals for example, had been unemployed for 3 months or less both in 1984 and in 1985, with an intervening period of employment. It would have been undesirable to allow the same individuals to feature in more than one of the groups both because this could have biased the results and because it would have violated the assumption of independence underlying the statistical analyses. The way in which such overlaps were removed was decided in advance and always involved removing observations from the larger, rather than the smaller, group. The reason for adopting this procedure was to keep the smallest group as large as possible as well as to avoid any suggestion of bias. It also tended to produce groups which were comparable in size, a desirable attribute when making statistical comparisons.

When the four years were combined and the overlaps removed in the manner described above, there were 47 in the first group, 53 in the second group and 45 in the third group, giving a total of 145. The overall total, including overlaps, was 184. (In practice, the pattern of results was virtually unaffected by removing the overlaps.)

The three groups were compared on each of the four measures on which pre-test measures were available. The groups differed initially, although not later, on self-esteem. However, with the other three measures, there were no initial differences but there were later differences. In each case, the later differences arose because the longest unemployed group (9 months or more) differed from each of the others. This group was more depressed, showed greater negative mood and was more external in locus of control than the other two groups (which did not differ). The means and standard deviations are shown in Table 5.6 (see Appendix).

There were statistically significant differences between the groups on all four scales introduced for the first time in 1984 (work involvement, anomie or social alienation, hopelessness and GHQ) with the exception of GHQ. In the other three cases, the 9 month group differed significantly from each of the others in displaying less work involvement, greater social alienation and greater hopelessness. Although the groups did not differ significantly with respect to GHQ, the 9 month group tended to score more highly than the other groups. The means and standard deviations are shown in Table 5.7 (see Appendix).

Different results according to age

The results from the second phase were quite clear-cut in showing that the longer term unemployed (9 months or more) were generally worse off than those unemployed for shorter periods. These results were inconsistent with the results from the first phase which had suggested that young people who had been unemployed for intermediate periods (3–6 and 6–12 months) were worse off than those unemployed for shorter or longer periods.

Although different time intervals were compared in the first and second phases, it seems unlikely that this would have accounted for the discrepant findings. A more likely explanation is that the effect of unemployment duration varies with age. During the first phase, the age range of our respondents was 16 to 20 years, whereas during the second phase it was 19 to 24 years. In other words, we were comparing a group of young people in their late teens, with another group in their early twenties. During the first phase of the study, the unemployment rate for young people in the 15–19-year age range was around 22–25 per cent. By comparison, the rate for young people aged from 20–24 years during the second phase was considerably lower, around 12–15 per cent. It is not unreasonable to assume therefore, that the fact that it is easier for young people in their early twenties to get jobs than it is for teenagers could be a factor resulting in greater social pressure being experienced by those in the older age group. This, in turn, could make it more difficult for the older group to adjust to their unemployment than was the case for the younger group.

A similar mechanism may operate in the case of middle-aged and older/elderly workers who have been made redundant. Because it is known that mature age is a factor that makes it difficult for unemployed people to obtain employment, the older unemployed person may be subject to fewer social pressures to find work than a younger person. This relative freedom from social pressure may enable the older person, like the teenager, to adjust to longer periods of unemployment, than is the case for those in the intermediate age range.

Economic factors may also contribute to such an age effect. Recent school leavers can usually continue to live in the family home and have their material needs met by their parents, and are not likely to have others who are dependent on them. Similarly, people in their fifties and sixties may well have fewer financial obligations and commitments than those in their twenties, thirties and forties. Their children are often grown up and independent and they may have paid off the mortgage on their home.

CONCLUSIONS

In considering factors that moderate the effects of unemployment, and which help people to cope with its potentially harmful effects, we have ignored the extensive literature on stress and coping. Much of this literature focuses on the efficacy of different cognitive coping strategies that people adopt in response to stressful (potentially harmful or threatening) environmental events. Lazarus and Folkman (1984) for example, have proposed a model of stress and coping according to which stress involves an interaction between the person and the environment where the critical mediating variable is the person's perception of a demand and their own ability to cope with it. Stress, according to this model, comprises three elements: environmental events that may be potentially stressful; primary appraisal – the individual's cognitive appraisal of the extent to which the events are potentially harmful or threatening; and secondary appraisal – the individual's cognitive appraisal of the adequacy of his or her ability to cope with the perceived threat or challenge. Secondary appraisal helps determine the type of coping response that will be used.

A variety of possible coping responses have been recognised both by Lazarus and Folkman (1984) and others (e.g. Moos, 1986). The two main categories of coping are problem-focused coping and emotion-focused coping, the former being assumed to be more appropriate (and therefore probably more effective) when the situation is controllable, and the latter being more appropriate when the situation is not controllable.

Although our data do not directly address the question of coping responses, future studies of unemployed young people might profitably do so. For example, in developing strategies for counselling young people, it would be useful to know what kinds of coping response are most effective in dealing with unemployment stress.

The main factors to have emerged from our study that seem to moderate the effects of unemployment are age, length of unemployment, financial security, social support and use of time. Of these, the individual would seem to have little or no control over the first four. However, clearly time use is often under the control of the individual. On the basis of our findings, it would appear that if young unemployed people can be counselled and persuaded to engage in purposeful activities and in activities involving other people, they will be able to cope better with the stress of unemployment than if they spend their time engaged in aimless activities, doing nothing in particular or in watching TV.

6 Theoretical implications

Several theories have been proposed to explain the psychological effects of unemployment which were described in Chapter 2. In this chapter we will review these theories in the light of evidence gleaned from our data, as well as that from other, related studies.

STAGE THEORY

Several writers have proposed that the psychological response to unemployment can be described in terms of several discrete stages. For example, Eisenberg and Lazarsfeld (1938), in reviewing the 1930s studies state:

> We find that all writers who have described the course of unemployment seem to agree on the following points: First there is shock, which is followed by an active hunt for a job, during which the individual is still optimistic and unresigned; he still maintains an unbroken attitude. Second, when all efforts fail, the individual becomes pessimistic, anxious, and suffers active distress; this is the most crucial state of all. And third, the individual becomes fatalistic and adapts himself to his new state but with narrower scope. He now has a broken attitude.
>
> (Eisenberg and Lazarsfeld, 1938: 378)

Similar versions of this stage theory have been proposed by Harrison (1976), Hayes and Nutman (1981) and others. Fryer (1985) provides a highly critical review of them, concluding that they are not well supported by the empirical evidence as well as being imprecise and inconsistent.

It should be recognised that stage theories are probably more applicable to the situation of the mature job loser than to that of the school leaver. It hardly seems appropriate, for example, to assume that the school leaver who fails to get a job will experience shock, given the current high unemployment rate amongst school leavers. On the other hand, a mature worker who has been in the same job for many years may well experience shock on being dismissed.

We found no evidence that young people who had lost jobs were any worse off than those who had never had a job (Winefield and Tiggemann, 1989a) and neither group was significantly worse off than they had been while at school. Moreover, we found that of those who had lost jobs, their psychological well-being was not related to the reason for job loss. Those who had been dismissed were no worse off than those who had left voluntarily (Winefield, Tiggemann and Winefield, 1992a).

Some longitudinal evidence that seems consistent with a stages account has been reported by Warr and Jackson (1987) in a study of male, blue-collar workers. They reported a curvilinear relation between unemployment duration and psychological distress, concluding that the men in their sample showed signs of adapting to the unemployed role after 25 months of continuous unemployment. On the other hand, Warr, Jackson and Banks (1982) reported no evidence of any correlation between distress and unemployment duration in their sample of recent school leavers and suggested that any association may be restricted to older samples and longer periods out of work.

We were able to examine the possible association between unemployment duration and affective well-being in our study. Interestingly, we found some evidence of a curvilinear relation in those unemployed from 1981–1983 (age range roughly 16–20 years). We found that those continuously unemployed for intermediate periods (3–6 months and 6–12 months) were worse off than those continuously unemployed for shorter (less than 3 months) or longer (more than 12 months) periods (Winefield and Tiggemann, 1989b).

By contrast, when we looked at those unemployed from 1984–1987 (age range roughly 19–24) we found no evidence of a curvilinear relation. Instead, we found no difference between those unemployed for less than 3 months and those unemployed from 4–8 months, but those unemployed for 9 months or more were significantly worse off than either (Winefield and Tiggemann, 1990b).

It may be that young people in their early twenties do eventually adapt to the unemployed role, but if so, it seems they need longer than do youngsters in their late teens. (Possible reasons for this were suggested in the discussion of age as a factor in coping with unemployment in Chapter 5.)

Overall, our results provide very little support for a stages account of unemployment.

DEPRIVATION THEORY

Jahoda's deprivation theory (Jahoda, 1981, 1982) was outlined in Chapter 2. It is based on a remark by Freud (1930) that work represents our strongest link with reality, and without it we are in danger of being overwhelmed by fantasy and emotion. The theory assumes that work, in addition to its manifest function (providing income) has five latent functions which are psychologically beneficial in that they keep us in touch with reality.

First, it imposes a time structure on the waking day; second, it provides regular social contacts with people outside the nuclear family; third, it imposes goals and purposes that transcend those of the individual; fourth, it defines status and identity; and finally, it enforces activity.

(Jahoda, 1981: 188)

In addition, Jahoda definitely implies that even bad jobs are preferable to unemployment, as the following quotations illustrate:

even unpleasant ties to reality are preferable to their absence. . . . Leisure activities . . . are fine in themselves as a complement to employment, but they are not functional alternatives to work

(Jahoda, 1981: 189)

That not all is well in the world of employment is beyond question. Though it provides the required categories of experience, their quality is on occasion so deplorable that many commentators regard unemployment (with adequate financial support) preferable to such employment. For reasons spelled out before, I cannot agree with this.

(Jahoda, 1982: 61)

First, if one assumes that school provides all of the assumed latent psychological benefits encompassed by Jahoda's five categories of experience, it would seem to follow that leaving school and becoming unemployed should lead to a deterioration in well-being. Our results provide no support for this expectation.

Second, we have shown in all our analyses conducted since 1984 (when we first measured job satisfaction), that those unemployed young people who regard their jobs as unsatisfactory (around 10 per cent of those employed) are no better off than the unemployed (Winefield, Tiggemann and Goldney, 1988; Winefield and Tiggemann, 1990a; Winefield, Winefield, Tiggemann and Goldney, 1991; Winefield, Tiggemann and Winefield, 1991b). This very consistent finding seems to be at variance with Jahoda's view that any job is better than no job.

A similar result has been reported recently by O'Brien and Feather (1990) who showed that skill utilisation seemed to be the main factor affecting job satisfaction. Kaufman (1982) in his study of unemployed professionals in New York similarly found that those who became re-employed in inferior jobs (the 'underemployed') were no better adjusted than the unemployed. All of this evidence calls into question Jahoda's assumption that even bad jobs are preferable to unemployment.

AGENCY THEORY — oppose Jahoda

Fryer (1986) has criticised Jahoda's deprivation theory, suggesting that the five supposed latent benefits of employment are all too often costs rather than benefits. He writes of: 'Arbitrary time structure without regard for human needs; autocratic supervision; activity for unclear or devalued purposes; a resented identity; the vacuous nature of imposed activities' (Fryer, 1986: 12–13). He proposes instead, what he calls an agency theory, which assumes that people are agents who strive to assert themselves, initiate and influence events and are intrinsically motivated. In short, agency theory assumes that people are fundamentally proactive and independent, whereas deprivation theory, by contrast, assumes them to be fundamentally reactive and dependent. He compares agency theory and deprivation theory in terms of the two dimensions proposed by Gergen and Gergen (1982) for evaluating theories of human behaviour. The first dimension concerns where the theory locates the source of action (person-centred or situation-centred); the second dimension concerns the degree of controlling force exerted (controlling or enabling). The two dimensions give rise to a 2×2 matrix so that theories can be classified within one of four cells. According to Fryer, deprivation theory would be classified as a 'controlling situation-centred' theory whereas his agency theory would be classified as an 'enabling person-centred' theory.

Gergen and Gergen (1982) acknowledge that it is often difficult to evaluate different types of theory in terms of their explanatory power, but suggest two other criteria: intellectual generativity and valuational implications. In terms of the former, they commend theories that challenge common scientific and cultural assumptions and shatter the orthodox consensus. Fryer sees agency theory as falling within this category. In terms of the latter, they suggest that situation-centred controlling forms of explanation support totalitarian systems of government whereas enabling person-centred explanations support radical libertarianism.

What Fryer finds disturbing about deprivation theory is that the supposed latent benefits of employment are imposed or enforced. He argues that this feature of the theory is inconsistent with much of what Jahoda has written which makes abundantly clear her opposition to authoritarianism and dehumanising social institutions. He also objects to the theory on the ground that it implies a view of human nature which is reactive and dependent. Politically he feels that deprivation theory 'can act, irrespective of the wishes of its supporters, as a tool of a reactionary world view'.

Fryer offers evidence in support of his agency theory from two studies. First, Fryer and Payne (1984) reported a study of a small group of eleven unemployed men who had adopted a proactive stance towards unemployment and coped very successfully despite material hardship. (Jahoda

(1988) has described the sample as highly atypical of unemployed people.) Second, Fryer describes a study with McKenna (Fryer and McKenna, 1987; McKenna and Fryer, 1984) in which they interviewed two groups of men from engineering factories. One group had been laid off for a period, negotiated as seven weeks, but the other group had been laid off indefinitely. Not surprisingly, they found that the second group was very much worse off than the first group, although according to deprivation theory, they argue, there should have been no difference. After interviewing the men, the investigators concluded that it was difference in orientation to the future that characterised the two groups. Whereas the temporarily laid off group planned carefully for their period off work, the indefinitely laid off group showed little sign of planning.

In summary, Fryer's agency theory suggests that the negative consequences of unemployment are that they inhibit the exercise of personal agency. The restrictions imposed by economic deprivation make it difficult or impossible for people to plan and organise personally satisfying life styles. Most people work for its manifest benefit and despite its so-called latent benefits. The regular income enables them to plan and organise personally satisfying leisure activities and to save for, and plan for, a satisfying retirement.

We have referred to two aspects of our findings that seem inconsistent with deprivation theory: first, the fact that school leavers who become unemployed show no deterioration in well-being; and second, the fact that those expressing dissatisfaction with their jobs were no better off than the unemployed. These findings suggest that it may be the quality of life, rather than the fact of being employed or unemployed, which is more important, thus they seem more compatible with agency theory.

Further evidence that seems to favour agency theory was obtained when we analysed how our young people spent their time. We looked at psychological well-being in relation to how much of their time our young people spent engaged in aimless activities (watching TV, doing nothing in particular), as opposed to purposeful activities (either alone or with other people). We found, for the unemployed and dissatisfied employed groups, that amount of time spent in aimless activities was negatively correlated with self-esteem and positively correlated with measures of psychological distress, whereas amount of time spent in purposeful activities was positively correlated with self-esteem and negatively correlated with measures of psychological distress. On the other hand, no such correlations were observed for the employed group (1981–1983) or the satisfied employed group (1984–1988) (Winefield, Tiggemann and Winefield, 1992a).

These results suggest a further deficiency in deprivation theory as compared with agency theory: as well as taking no account of the psychological significance of the quality of employment, it also takes no account of the psychological significance of the quality of unemployment.

Another limitation of deprivation theory is that it does not distinguish between work and employment. It implies, therefore, that those not in the workforce such as the idle rich and retired people should all suffer deprivation in that they are denied latent benefits provided by the five categories of experience described by Jahoda. It seems intuitively unlikely, however, that the idle rich suffer through not being employed, and studies of retired people suggest also that retirement is not an aversive experience for most people. Thus Talaga and Beehr (1989) in a recent review of the literature conclude:

> Virtually all previous reviews of the empirical literature, including Beehr's (1986), concluded that retirement is not stressful (i.e. does not have generally deleterious effects on mental or physical health), contrary to a lot of popular misconceptions. The recent research, reviewed here, again agrees with this conclusion.
>
> (Talaga and Beehr, 1989: 206)

Although our own results seem to support agency theory rather than deprivation theory, we do not subscribe to Fryer's global view of human nature. Indeed we believe that any global view of human nature must be mistaken. Some people, either for genetic or environmental reasons, are inclined to be reactive and dependent, others are inclined to be proactive and independent. Moreover, people who display reactance and dependence in one situation may display proactance and independence in another, and vice versa. We believe that the only realistic assumption to be made about human nature is its diversity.

VITAMIN MODEL

Warr's (1987) vitamin model is concerned with the effects of different environmental features on mental health. He proposes nine features of the environment (opportunity for control, opportunity for skill use, externally generated goals, variety, environmental clarity, availability of money, physical security, opportunity for interpersonal contact and valued social position) which, according to him affect mental health in an analogous manner to the way vitamins affect physical health.

Some environmental features, according to Warr, resemble vitamins A and D in that very high levels not merely cease to be beneficial, but are actually harmful (AD is a convenient abbreviation for 'additional decrement'). Others are assumed to resemble vitamins C and E in that very high levels, while ceasing to be beneficial, are not actually harmful (CE is a convenient abbreviation for 'constant effect'). He suggests that three of the environmental features, availability of money, physical security and valued social position, may reasonably be regarded as falling within the CE category, whereas the remaining six are regarded as falling within the AD category.

According to the vitamin model, there is no necessary distinction between work and non-work environments. The extent to which any environment is beneficial to mental health depends on the extent to which it provides the nine environmental features described above. Just as some work environments may be good and others bad, so may some non-work environments be good and others bad.

Mental health, according to the vitamin model, comprises the following five components: affective well-being, competence, autonomy, aspiration and integrative functioning. Moreover affective well-being is assumed to comprise three axes: discontented–contented, anxious–comfortable, and depressed–actively pleased.

Like agency theory, but unlike deprivation theory, the vitamin model draws no sharp distinction between employment and unemployment but rather sees the overall quality of the environment (assessed in terms of nine characteristics) as important for mental health. It goes beyond agency theory in specifying which features of the environment are important. On the other hand most of the features (for example, opportunity for control, opportunity for skill use, availability of money, physical security, opportunity for interpersonal contact and valued social position) would obviously facilitate the exercise of agency and are thus implied by agency theory.

In applying his vitamin model to the unemployment situation, Warr (1987) claims that the available evidence has shown significant effects for the three principal axes of affective well-being and limited support for competence, autonomy and aspiration.

Although, as pointed out in Chapter 2, Warr's vitamin model differs from Jahoda's deprivation theory in that it assumes no qualitative distinction between employment and unemployment, nonetheless Warr acknowledges the importance of Jahoda's theorising and its influence on his own thinking. For example, her second and fourth latent functions (contact with people outside the nuclear family, and personal status and identity) appear as environmental features eight and nine in the vitamin model (opportunity for interpersonal contact and valued social position) and her other three latent functions are incorporated within 'externally generated goals'. Jahoda (1986) has recently acknowledged that the omission of control was a weakness in her original analysis. Opportunity for control is the first of Warr's environmental features.

In applying the vitamin model to teenagers, Warr recognises that as a group they show significantly less impairment than do middle-aged people (Broomhall and Winefield, 1990; Rowley and Feather, 1987) and suggests that this is interpretable in terms of availability of money, physical security, opportunity for interpersonal contact and valued social position. This is because school leavers usually continue to live at home whether or not they are unemployed and consequently these features of their environment are unchanged.

In terms of the mental health of teenagers, Warr argues that the main areas of public concern relate to the possible effects of unemployment on autonomy, competence and aspiration. It is feared that unemployment during this crucial developmental period may have long lasting effects impairing the ability to adjust to later work roles. So far there seems to be no evidence to suggest that the desire to work (aspiration) for example, among teenagers is reduced by unemployment (e.g. Tiggemann and Winefield, 1980).

On the other hand, there is some evidence that both competence (or perceived competence) and autonomy, as measured by locus of control, may be affected by unemployment. Feather and O'Brien (1986b) for example, in a longitudinal study of Australian school leavers reported a reduction in perceived competence in those who became unemployed.

With respect to locus of control the longitudinal evidence suggests that, although teenagers become increasingly less external with age, those who become employed show greater decreases than those who become unemployed. Interestingly, we found no difference after one year (Tiggemann and Winefield, 1984) but differences in later years. For example, in each of the years 1984 (Winefield, Tiggemann and Goldney, 1988), 1987 (Winefield, Tiggemann and Winefield, 1991b) and 1988 (Winefield, Winefield, Tiggemann and Goldney, 1991) we reported significant differences in externality of control related to employment status. In general the satisfied employed were less external than the unemployed due to the satisfied employed (and in some years the dissatisfied employed too) showing significant reductions in externality and the unemployed showing no change. What is particularly impressive about these findings is that in each of the three years in question, the groups did not differ in locus of control while they were at school.

Similar results were reported by Feather and O'Brien (1986b). Their longitudinal data showed no difference in externality between employed and unemployed groups after one year but significantly greater externality in the unemployed after two years. Other results supporting the conclusion that unemployment leads to increased externality have been reported by O'Brien and Kabanoff (1979) and by Patton and Noller (1984).

Much more empirical evidence is required in which the nine

environmental features, as well as the different indices of mental health, are measured before the vitamin model can be evaluated. Also, the extent to which it makes predictions that are at variance with those from other theories needs to be articulated. It remains an extremely plausible conceptual framework for studying the psychological effects of different work and non-work environments.

The four theories considered thus far (stage theory, deprivation theory, agency theory and the vitamin model) are the four main theories that have been advanced specifically to account for the psychological effects of unemployment. The next four theories are more general, but have been applied to the unemployment situation. They comprise Erikson's life-span developmental theory, learned helplessness theory, Weiner's attributional theory and expectancy-value theory.

ERIKSON'S LIFE-SPAN DEVELOPMENTAL THEORY

Erikson's developmental theory (Erikson, 1959) is based on Freudian psychoanalytic concepts. It assumes eight developmental stages that encompass the life span as well as associated psychological conflicts which need to be satisfactorily resolved before the individual can proceed to the next stage. Healthy psycho-social development, according to Erikson, depends on the (successive) satisfactory resolution of the psychological conflicts associated with each developmental stage.

The eight developmental stages (with their associated psychological conflicts or challenges in parentheses) are as follows: (1) infancy (trust vs mistrust), (2) early childhood (autonomy vs shame, doubt), (3) play age (initiative vs guilt), (4) school age (industry vs inferiority), (5) adolescence (identity vs identity diffusion), (6) young adult (intimacy vs isolation), (7) adulthood (generativity vs self-absorption), (8) mature age (integrity vs disgust, despair).

The fifth stage, adolescence, involves acquiring a satisfactory identity, both occupational and sexual, according to Erikson. Unemployment has been seen by some commentators (e.g. Taylor and Gurney, 1984) as particularly significant for the adolescent in that it represents a threat, in terms of Erikson's theory, to healthy psycho-social development. Gurney (1980b) reported data from a longitudinal study of Australian school leavers which demonstrated some support for the Eriksonian view in that those who got jobs showed superior psycho-social adjustment than those who became unemployed.

Our own findings also provide some support in that, like Gurney, we found an improvement on the part of those who got satisfactory jobs as well as those who went on to tertiary studies (Tiggemann and Winefield, 1984;

Winefield and Tiggemann, 1985; Winefield, Tiggemann and Goldney, 1988; Winefield, Tiggemann and Winefield, 1991b; Winefield, Winefield, Tiggemann and Goldney, 1991; Winefield and Winefield, 1992).

Acquiring a satisfactory occupational identity, in Erikson's terms, does not seem to depend on getting a satisfactory job immediately after leaving school. Given that most professional careers require several years of tertiary training, it would seem to follow that embarking on a tertiary course leading to a professional qualification would fulfil a similar function. According to Erikson, the most obvious concomitants of an increasing sense of identity 'are a feeling of being at home in one's body, a sense of "knowing where one is going," and an inner assuredness of anticipated recognition from those who count' (Erikson, 1956: 72). Tertiary students would be expected to have a sense of knowing where they are going as well as an inner assuredness of anticipated recognition from those who count, consequently our findings that they show similar improvements in psychological well-being to those leaving school and getting satisfactory jobs (unlike those becoming unemployed or getting unsatisfactory jobs) seems consistent with the theory.

LEARNED HELPLESSNESS THEORY

Learned helplessness theory (Seligman, 1975), based on experiments with dogs, proposes that exposure to uncontrollable outcomes in one task will lead to impaired performance in a subsequent task where outcomes are controllable because of the following deficits: motivational deficits (reduced desire to control outcomes); cognitive deficits (belief that the outcomes are not controllable); and, if the outcomes are aversive, emotional deficits (anxiety and eventually depression).

The original theory was subsequently modified (Abramson, Seligman and Teasdale, 1978) in order to account for individual differences. The reformulated theory assumes that when people are unable to control outcomes they explain their inability in terms of three causal dimensions: internal–external, stable–unstable and global–specific. Whether the causal attribution is internal or external will determine whether the individual will experience self-blame (reduced self-esteem and increased depressive affect); whether the attribution is stable or unstable will determine whether or not the reaction will persist over time; and whether the attribution is global or specific will determine the extent to which the reaction will generalise to other situations.

The theory has attracted considerable interest, as well as criticism, as a theory of depression (Brewin, 1985; Costello, 1978 ; Coyne and Gotlib, 1983; Parry and Brewin, 1988), largely because it assumes that 'attributional style' is a stable personality characteristic that represents a vulnerability factor for depressive illness. For example, a depression-prone individual is one who is assumed to have a tendency to attribute negative outcomes to internal, stable, global causes and a tendency to attribute positive outcomes to external, unstable, specific causes. Attributional style is assessed using an open-ended Attributional Style Questionnaire (Peterson, Semmel, von Baeyer, Abramson, Metalsky and Seligman, 1982), although a much shorter version referred to as measuring pessimistic explanatory style has recently been published by Seligman (1991).

Criticisms of the theory have ranged from expressed doubts as to whether people spontaneously make causal attributions (Oakes and Curtis, 1982) to whether explanatory (or attributional) style is a stable characteristic.

The most recent revision by Abramson, Metalsky and Alloy (1989) proposes 'hopelessness depression' as a subtype of depressive illness. It differs from the earlier formulation in several respects. First, the assumed cognitive deficit is no longer included. Second, lowered self-esteem is assumed to depend not simply on whether an internal attribution is made:

> Lowered self-esteem will be a symptom of hopelessness depression when the event that triggered the episode was attributed to an internal, stable, global cause as opposed to any type of external cause or to an internal, unstable, specific cause. In contrast to the 1978 reformulation, then, the hopelessness theory postulates that attributing a negative life event to an internal cause does not, by itself, contribute to lowering self-esteem.
>
> (Abramson, Metalsky and Alloy, 1989: 363)

Our data permitted only limited testing of the helplessness theory because we only administered the full Attributional Style Questionnaire to a subsample in 1984: those classified as 'GHQ positive' and a matched control group. Too few of those tested were unemployed to permit comparisons between different occupational groups. Nevertheless, longitudinal comparisons from subsequent years permitted us to test the helplessness (hopelessness) theory of depression (Tiggemann, Winefield, Winefield and Goldney, 1991a; 1991b; Tiggemann, Winefield, Goldney and Winefield, 1992). Overall, these studies did not find strong support for the theory.

The questions included in the questionnaires relating to attributional style asked respondents when good things – and bad things – happened to them whether it was usually due to lack of ability (internal, stable attribution), lack of effort (internal, unstable), the situation (external, stable) or bad luck (external, unstable). In the case of those who were unemployed, a similar question was asked in relation to the main reason for their current unemployment. These questions, of course, only measure the internal–external and the stable–unstable dimension, not the global–specific dimension postulated by the theory.

In a paper by Winefield, Tiggemann and Smith (1987) we reported data from the third wave of our study (1983) in which we compared 813 employed with 138 unemployed. We found that in the employed, greater self-esteem was associated with internal attributions for good outcomes and lower depressive affect was associated with internal, stable attributions for good outcomes. Also, lower depressive affect was associated with external, unstable attributions for bad outcomes.

By contrast, in the unemployed neither self-esteem nor depressive affect were associated with attributions for good outcomes. However, both higher self-esteem and lower depressive affect were associated with unstable attributions for bad outcomes. Also, lower depressive affect was associated with external attributions for bad outcomes.

These ongoing associations were generally consistent with the attributional style hypothesis. However, causal attributions that were made three years earlier, when the respondents were still at school, were only weakly related to ongoing measures of self-esteem and depressive affect. Moreover, many of them changed their causal attributions over time, a finding that casts doubt on the validity of the theory.

WEINER'S ATTRIBUTIONAL THEORY

Weiner's theory (Weiner, 1985), like that of Abramson *et al.* (1978, 1989) is based on the earlier seminal work by Heider (1958) and by Kelley (1967). Weiner's attributional analysis of motivation and emotion can be applied to the unemployment situation. The theory assumes that the emotional consequences of causal attributions for negative outcomes (such as unemployment) will depend on their location within a dimensional space structured in relation to the three dimensions of locus (internal, external), stability (stable, unstable) and controllability (controllable, uncontrollable). The theory assumes that:

> success and failure perceived as due to internal causes such as personality, ability, or effort respectively raises or lowers self-esteem or self-worth, whereas external attributions for positive or negative outcomes do not influence feelings about the self.

(Weiner, 1985: 560)

The theory assumes further that because causal stability influences expectancies about future success and failure 'any emotion involving anticipations of goal attainment or nonattainment will be influenced by causal stability. One such affect has been labelled *hopelessness*' (Weiner, 1985: 563). Weiner's third attributional dimension, controllability or intentionality, is assumed to influence the emotions of anger, gratitude and pity.

Because we added a hopelessness scale to our questionnaire from 1984 (Beck, Weisman, Lester and Trexler, 1974), we were in a good position to test Weiner's predictions about the association between internality and self-esteem and between stability and hopelessness.

Using our 1984 unemployment data (Winefield, Tiggemann and Winefield, 1992a) we found the predicted association between internality of attribution (for unemployment) and self-esteem (those who gave internal attributions displayed lower self-esteem) as mentioned in the previous section. On the other hand, there was no evidence for any association between stability of attribution and hopelessness. Instead, we found an association between internality and hopelessness, such that those who gave internal attributions displayed greater hopelessness than those who gave external attributions. (We also found a high negative correlation of –0.67 between self-esteem and hopelessness.)

At first sight, the lack of association between stability of attribution and hopelessness seems surprising, but in relation to the specific negative outcome in question, current unemployment, it is perhaps explicable. Although in general stable attributions imply an unchanging situation, young people unemployed in the 18–20 age range are close to the boundary between the 15–19-year-olds and 20–24-year-olds and according to Australian statistics, there is a sharp decline in the unemployment rate between these two age groups. If unemployed people in this age range attribute their unemployment to stable causes (either lack of ability or the situation), the fact that they are on the brink of an age category for which the unemployment rate is substantially lower might well be expected to mitigate the hopelessness which they would otherwise feel. If this is so, then perhaps we were actually measuring an unstable, not a stable attribution. In other words, it is possible that our questions might have needed to be formulated rather differently in order to provide a fair test of Weiner's theory.

On the other hand, given the high negative correlation between self-esteem and hopelessness, it is not surprising that internality of attribution should have been associated with both of them. It is perhaps a shortcoming of the theory that it takes no account of the high correlation between these two measures of emotion.

EXPECTANCY-VALUE THEORY

This theory (or class of theories) attempts to relate behaviour to the expectation of success or failure, and to the perceived attractiveness or aversiveness of the possible outcomes. It has its origins in mathematical decision theory (Edwards, 1954), according to which rational decision making involves maximising the mathematical expectation of success based on the probabilities and values associated with success and failure (or winning and losing).

Unfortunately, the theory does not provide an accurate account of individual choice behaviour and it has been suggested that the main reason for this is that objective probabilities and values do not necessarily correspond to *subjective* probabilities (expectations) and *subjective* values (utilities or valences). For this reason, Edwards (1954) proposed an SEU (subjectively expected utility) model as a potentially more useful explanatory tool than the model based on objective probabilities and values.

Feather (1959, 1982) has been a leading proponent of expectancy-value theory and has recently applied it in the area of unemployment research (Feather and Barber, 1983; Feather and Davenport, 1981; Feather and O'Brien, 1987). For example, Feather and O'Brien (1987) showed that some aspects of job seeking behaviour can be explained in terms of the theory. Feather and Davenport (1981) showed that expectations of employment are related to an individual's past employment history and the affective response to unemployment is related to employment value. Feather and Barber (1983), however, failed to confirm the findings of Feather and Davenport. They found that depressive reactions to unemployment were not related to initial confidence about finding a job.

We have been able to use findings from our longitudinal study in order to test expectancy-value theory (Winefield and Tiggemann, 1992). Unlike the studies by Feather and Barber (1983) and by Feather and Davenport (1981) which both relied on cross-sectional data and retrospective report, we were able to use measures of work attitudes (perceived difficulty of getting a job and subjective importance of getting a job) taken while the respondents were at school in 1980 and use them to predict affective responses to employment or unemployment measured three years later (1983).

We predicted, in accordance with expectancy-value theory, that among the unemployed, those whose prior (at-school) expectations of finding work were high, would suffer more, in terms of both self-esteem and depressive affect, than those whose prior expectations of finding work were low. Those who had rated the importance of getting a job as (relatively) high (all rated it highly) were predicted to suffer more than those whose prior ratings had been (relatively) low.

In the case of the employed, we anticipated that those whose prior expectations of getting a job were low would show greater benefits through having got a job, than those whose prior expectations had been high. We also anticipated that those who had rated the importance of getting a job as (relatively) high would show greater benefits than those who had rated the importance of getting a job as (relatively) low.

In the event, the results provided limited support for the theory. As predicted, in the unemployed group, low prior expectation of getting a job led to a greater increase in self-esteem than high prior expectation of getting a job, although, contrary to prediction, depressive affect was unaffected by high or low prior expectation of getting a job. Also as predicted, in the unemployed group those who had rated the importance of getting a job more highly showed a greater increase in depressive affect than those who had rated it less highly. On the other hand, contrary to prediction, self-esteem was unaffected by prior rated importance of getting a job.

In the case of the employed, only one prediction was supported. As for the unemployed, low prior expectation of getting a job led to a greater increase in self-esteem than high prior expectation of getting a job. On the other hand, contrary to prediction, depressive affect was unaffected by high or low prior expectation of getting a job. Also, contrary to prediction neither self-esteem nor depressive affect were affected by rated importance of getting a job.

Although the results provide only partial support for the predictions based on expectancy-value theory, it is nonetheless impressive that prior measures of expectancy (of getting a job) and value (importance of getting a job) should have predicted changes in well-being three years later. Certainly our study represents a much more stringent test of the theory than that of Feather and Barber (1983), for example, who relied on retrospective measures of both expectancy and value.

It is perhaps not altogether surprising that prior rated importance of getting a job should have predicted later well-being less well than prior employment expectations. Because virtually all of our respondents rated job importance as either 'quite important' or 'very important' (ignoring the other three categories on the 5-point scale) we were forced to collapse the five categories into two. The lack of discrimination was no doubt an important factor in the poor predictability.

The other finding of interest was that self-esteem was sensitive to differences in prior expectations of getting a job (in both employed and unemployed groups) whereas depressive affect was sensitive to differences in rated importance of getting a job (but only in the unemployed). Although this finding is not accounted for by expectancy-value theory, intuitively it does not seem surprising that getting a job when you were not expecting to should boost self-esteem more than getting one when you were expecting to. Likewise, it does not seem surprising that failing to get a job when you were expecting to get one should diminish self-esteem more than failing to get a job when you were not expecting to. And finally, failing to achieve a highly valued goal might be expected to make you more depressed than failing to achieve a less highly valued goal.

SUMMARY

With respect to the four specific theories outlined above, our results provide little support for stage theory, challenge the implicit assumption of deprivation theory that even bad jobs are preferable to unemployment, but seem compatible with both agency theory and the vitamin model, without providing a real test of either.

With respect to the four general theories, our findings seem to be consistent with Erikson's life span developmental theory, but provide only limited support for learned helplessness theory, attributional theory, and expectancy-value theory.

7 Predictors of employment status and tertiary education

INTRODUCTION

Earlier chapters have documented that, relative to the employed, the young unemployed suffer a reduction in psychological well-being. People who continue as students into further education seem somewhere in between. The very act of leaving school and moving into whatever future, seems to carry considerable significance.

The major focus of this chapter is to see whether or not we are able to predict which students will subsequently become employed or unemployed (or continue onto further study), before this actually happens. Our prospective longitudinal research design enables us to test this, because we have information on the students while they are still at school. Moreover, this information is much more easily collected than it would be after students have left school.

Should we be able to predict future employment status, and particularly should we be able to identify individuals vulnerable to unemployment whilst they are still at school, then this 'at risk' group can perhaps be given special attention. The findings should be of practical value in providing feedback to school counsellors and guidance officers. Suggestions can be made as to what advice should be given to students and what sorts of preparation should be included in final year courses.

PREDICTORS OF UNEMPLOYMENT

We have already mentioned that current unemployment in Australia (and in most of the Western world) tends to be concentrated in the younger age groups, the people on whom this study focuses. A number of studies, however, have shown that there are other background and situational characteristics also associated with a disproportionately high unemployment rate. For example, young females, especially those who have left school early, are one of the more disadvantaged groups in the Australian labour market (Australian Industries Development Association, 1978). In fact, women, of whatever age, are more at risk of unemployment than men. In December 1980, the Australian Bureau of Statistics gave the unemployment rate for women as 8.2 per cent compared to 5.3 per cent for men. These figures, however, underestimate the discrepancy between the sexes, in that many women (particularly married women) are not counted as part of the labour force and form part of the 'hidden unemployed' (Smith, 1981).

The Department of Technical and Further Education of South Australia (Daley, 1983) lists certain groups among the young as more susceptible to unemployment than others. These include those in particular regional locations (primarily the outer, largely working-class, suburbs or rural areas), those of ethnic background, the disabled and Aborigines. There are virtually no reliable statistics available on Aboriginal unemployment rates, but estimates range as high as 60 per cent (Smith, 1981). The case is similar for minority or underprivileged groups in other countries. In the United States American Indians and urban blacks have much higher unemployment rates than do their white counterparts, as do those of West Indian descent in Britain.

While such differences in unemployment rate are very important for prediction, these demographic characteristics themselves are not amenable to change. Academic variables such as level of schooling attained are perhaps slightly more modifiable. Another group known to experience high levels of unemployment are early school leavers, i.e. those of low educational attainment who leave school prior to completion of secondary schooling (Daley, 1983). In Australia, the statutory legal school leaving age is 15, which normally occurs during Year 10, that is about half-way through secondary school.

The major interest for psychologists, however, lies in other sorts of variables, for example personality and attitudes. Here the evidence is more equivocal. While a number of cross-sectional studies have found personality differences between the employed and unemployed, only a longitudinal research design can distinguish between pre-existing differences and those consequent to the unemployment experience. Of the relatively few longitudinal studies published, most have found no predisposing factors. As Feather (1985) points out, these studies have generally been conducted on relatively restricted samples, for example, in terms of socio-economic status. Other more broadly based samples have reported some pre-existing differences in competence and depressive affect (Feather and O'Brien, 1986a, 1986b).

There has been very little investigation of attitudes as a predictor of unemployment. While attitudes to work have generally been found to be positive among young people (Feather, 1985), in our pilot study (Tiggemann and Winefield, 1980) we did find a few differences between those who subsequently became employed and those who became unemployed. For example, more of those who later became unemployed had said seven months earlier that they would claim unemployment benefits while looking for a job. Furnham and Stacey (1991) also note that there are a number of attitudinal differences between those who leave school early – a major predictor of unemployment – and those who stay on to complete secondary schooling. For example, compared to those who stay, early school leavers tend to see the school curriculum as irrelevant, and school as boring. Poole (1983) has also found early leavers to be characterised by low levels of achievement motivation and poor self-esteem.

PREDICTORS OF EMPLOYMENT STATUS UP TO THREE YEARS LATER

The major aim of the study reported here was to investigate how well a range of personality, attitudinal, background and demographic variables gathered from students could predict future occupational status, both in the near future (after one year), and in the longer term (three and five years). To this end, as described in Chapter 3, questionnaires were initially administered to more than 3000 students in normal (40-minute) lesson time, about three-quarters of the way through the school year in August 1980. Attempts were made to predict their employment status in 1981, 1983 and 1985, i.e. one, three and five years after initial testing. These results have been published by Tiggemann and Winefield (1989).

Data on four separate categories of variable, in increasing order of amenability to modification, were collected: background, academic, personality and attitudinal variables.

PREDICTION ON THE BASIS OF PERSONALITY

In order to assess prediction on the basis of personality, a series of discriminant function analyses was conducted, separately for each of the years 1981(Time 1), 1983 (Time 2) and 1985 (Time 3), for those respondents who had left school. Discriminant function analysis is a technique which statistically assesses the amount of separation or difference between groups. The predicted variable here was occupational status at the respective time, categorised as either employed, unemployed or tertiary student. Because of the increasing number of people who had left school over time, there were different numbers in each group at each time. The predictor variables were self-esteem, locus of control, depressive affect and achievement motivation. Table 7.1 provides the means for each variable as measured in 1980.

Table 7.1 Means of personality and attitudinal variables as measured in 1980 for subsequently employed (*E*), unemployed (*UE*) and tertiary students (*TS*)

Scale	T1 E	T1 UE	T1 TS	T2 E	T2 UE	T2 TS	T3 E	T3 UE	T3 TS
Personality									
Self-esteem	7.55	7.29	8.13	7.65	7.50	8.15	7.82	7.13	8.14
Locus of control	13.58	14.34	11.93	13.70	14.67	12.02	13.16	15.44	11.86
Depressive affect	1.41	1.56	1.30	1.39	1.56	1.29	1.33	1.41	1.25
Achievement motivation	5.80	5.56	6.25	5.82	5.58	6.24	5.87	5.93	6.31
Attitudes									
Job importance (self)	4.67	4.55	4.65	4.71	4.53	4.62	4.71	4.46	4.57
Job importance (parent)	4.36	4.27	4.33	4.43	4.23	4.21	4.37	4.32	4.14
Job control	3.29	3.11	3.27	3.33	3.27	3.34	3.35	3.16	3.28
Job time	2.52	2.65	2.48	2.60	2.84	2.60	2.58	2.81	2.66
Unemployment benefit	1.23	1.44	1.25	1.28	1.24	1.27	1.32	1.22	1.27

The group centroids (rather like grouped averages) of employed (−0.08), unemployed (−0.23) and tertiary students (0.33), show the primary discrimination to be between the unemployed and tertiary students, with the employed in between. Similar significant discriminant functions were replicated for both three and five years later.

As can be seen in Table 7.2, a similar pattern of correlations occurs each year. Using the accepted criterion of a loading of 0.45 or above (Tabachnik and Fidell, 1983), self-esteem, locus of control and achievement motivation emerge as the major predictors. Table 7.1 confirms that the unemployed displayed lower self-esteem, lower achievement motivation and more external locus of control in 1980, than the employed who, in turn, expressed lower well-being than the tertiary students. So we have confirmed and extended Feather and O'Brien's (1986a) finding of early differences in self-esteem. We are able to predict future occupational status from personality differences while students are still at school.

Table 7.2 Correlations of personality and attitudinal variables entered separately into the discriminant function analysis

Scale	T1	T2	T3
Personality			
Self-esteem	0.58 *	0.66 *	0.68 *
Locus of control	–0.82 *	–0.74 *	–0.81 *
Depressive affect	–0.27	–0.25	–0.22
Achievement			
motivation	0.65 *	0.67 *	0.51 *
Attitudes			
Job importance (self)	0.46	0.64 *	0.74 *
Job importance (parent)	0.25	0.80 *	0.55 *
Job control	0.61	0.13	0.40
Job time	–0.45	–0.44	–0.40
Unemployment benefit	0.59	0.17	0.39

* Loadings greater than 0.45 for significant functions

PREDICTION ON THE BASIS OF ATTITUDES

Similar analyses were conducted for the attitudinal variables. Here students were asked five specific questions about their attitudes and intentions for the future. They rated on 5–point scales how important obtaining a job was for themselves and for their parents, and how much control they felt over this. They also reported how long they expected it would take for them to obtain a job (1 = no time, 2 = less than 3 months, 3 = 3–6 months, 4 = more than 6 months), and whether or not they would claim unemployment benefits should they be unable to find a job (1 = yes, 2 = no).

The means in Table 7.1 show that in general attitudes to work were reasonably positive. Specifically, getting a job was rated as very important for both themselves and their parents, they felt a medium amount of control over the getting of jobs and most (85 per cent) expected to have a job within six months of finishing studying. Of the initial sample, a sizable minority (29 per cent) said that they would not go on the dole if unable to find a job.

In contrast to the personality variables, the attitudinal variables did not provide significant prediction for one year later. However, for both three and five years later significant discriminant functions emerge. The group centroids (T3: employed 0.08, unemployed –0.46, tertiary students –0.19) reveal that here the primary separation is between the employed and the unemployed. As can be seen in Table 7.2, it is the rated importance of a job which provides the major discrimination. The subsequently unemployed rated getting a job as less important for both themselves and for their parents than did the subsequently employed.

OVERALL PREDICTION

In order to assess the relative contribution of different kinds of variables, all the predictor variables were entered into a hierarchical discriminant function analysis in increasing order of amenability to modification. Background variables were entered first, followed by academic potential, then personality and finally attitudinal variables.

One year later, at August 1981 (T1), on the basis of all 15 predictor variables, two significant discriminant functions emerged. The first maximally separated tertiary students from those in the labour force. The second discriminated the unemployed from the other two groups. This same pattern emerged three years later. Five years later, however, while the first discriminant function was statistically significant, the second one no longer was. This means that, while we are able to predict who will be a full-time student in 1985 on the basis of data gathered five years earlier, one cannot offer a significant prediction as to who will be employed or unemployed at the latter time.

The loading matrix of correlations between the demographic and academic variables and the two discriminant functions is presented in Table 7.3. At each of the times, for the first discriminant function distinguishing tertiary students, the primary predictors are the academic variables of rated potential and the year level a student expected to complete before leaving school. Not surprisingly, more tertiary students (Time 1 56 per cent as opposed to 21 per cent and 17 per cent employed and unemployed, respectively) had been rated by their teachers as definitely capable of tertiary study, and intended to leave school at the end of year 12 (90 per cent vs 62 per cent and 65 per cent respectively).

Table 7.3 Correlations of demographic and academic predictor variables with discriminant functions 1 and 2

Scale	T1		T2		T3	
	1	*2*	*1*	*2*	*1*	*2*
Demographic						
Sex	0.09	–0.30	0.09	0.12	0.18	0.13
SES	0.24	–0.25	0.23	–0.51 *	0.26	–0.26
Ethnicity	0.06	0.65 *	0.12	0.48 *	0.26	0.04
Family						
unemployment	–0.26	0.49 *	–0.19	0.28	–0.08	0.28
Academic						
Potential	0.87 *	0.13	0.85 *	–0.13	0.76 *	–0.07
Year of leaving						
school	–0.49 *	–0.07	–0.57 *	–0.07	–0.55 *	0.02

* Loadings greater than 0.45 for significant functions

For the second function discriminating the unemployed, the primary predictors at Time 1 are ethnic background and family unemployment. Young unemployed people are more likely to come from a non-English-speaking household (27 per cent vs 12 per cent and 8 per cent). At Time 2 the unemployed are best discriminated from the other two groups again by ethnic origin, and also by socio-economic status, since 46 per cent of the unemployed came from low SES homes, compared with 28 per cent and 27 per cent of the employed and tertiary students. These form part of the set of background variables over which people have little control. As already mentioned, at Time 3 there was no significant prediction of the unemployed.

Looking at all the variables together, at each time background and academic variables offered significant prediction, but personality and attitudinal variables offered no unique prediction over and above that. That is, when investigated on their own, there are personality characteristics and attitudes which can predict subsequent unemployment, but these are in fact a function of the background characteristics. Yet there is little individuals can do to change their background. Attitudes are much more modifiable, but we have no guarantee that adopting different attitudes will make students more employable. For example, perhaps people who in reality have little hope of getting a job are wise to rate it as less important than those with a better chance (even though the overall rating is still 'very important'). It is likely that these attitudes represent a realistic appraisal of their future prospects.

In conclusion, we have been able to identify individuals vulnerable to unemployment one and three years after the gathering of the initial information. Perhaps it is reassuring that this prediction appears to become weaker with time, and is no longer significant after five years. If we are to identify an 'at risk' group while still at school from our findings, we would choose those of ethnic origin, of low socio-economic status and with an unemployed member of the immediate family. Such students are likely also to view the getting of a job as less important for themselves and for their parents than their peers, and to have lower self-esteem, a more external locus of control and lower achievement motivation. What use is made of this information, however, is largely in the political arena. Attempts to make 'at risk' people more similar to people who obtain jobs, simply may not work.

PREDICTION OF ENTRY INTO TERTIARY EDUCATION

In the study outlined above which was concerned with predicting unemployment, perhaps somewhat surprisingly, the greater discrimination was always between full-time students and those in the labour force, rather than between the employed and unemployed. It is those who continue with further study who are the most different, rather than those who subsequently become unemployed. Encouragingly, the best predictors of further education are students' rated academic potential and the level of schooling they intend to complete, rather than some background characteristic such as socio-economic status or sex. The fact that the same pattern was replicated across the three time spans allows confidence in the result. It also provides evidence for the validity of teacher judgements. Even five years after initial testing, we obtained very strong predictions of further education.

The decision to continue formal education is a major one, and for most people not subsequently reversed. For those young people who are intellectually able, entry into tertiary education rather than into the workforce raises the probability of attaining long-term goals relating to material security, job satisfaction and quality of life. In the short term, entry into tertiary education offers able school leavers social and intellectual stimulation and encouragement to spend several years in exploration of their talents and interests and in psychological maturation before they assume workforce responsibilities. Of course, there are also economic costs associated with this course of action.

We have seen above that academic ability is, appropriately, the major determinant of whether young people continue on to further education. However, it is quite clear that not all academically able young people adopt this course of action, so academic potential is not the only determinant. A number of studies present stable associations between social class, cultural background and sex and entry into higher education. These associations arise mainly because sex and social background influence young people's expectations, aspirations and self-confidence (Gallatin, 1975). So we thought that the decision to continue further education warranted closer investigation.

To this end, as reported in Winefield, Winefield, Tiggemann and Goldney (1988), the tertiary students were compared in more detail to the other occupational groups. This comparison was undertaken four years after initial testing, that is when all of the respondents would normally have left school, but only a few would have finished any tertiary study they had undertaken. At the time, there were 128 men and 100 women (23 per cent of the total group) with an average age of 19.6 years, involved in tertiary study.

In addition to academic potential, a number of other variables differentiated those involved in further education from their employed or unemployed peers. First, tertiary study was being undertaken by more of the males than the females (27.4 per cent vs 20.0 per cent). This difference was more striking amongst those adolescents rated as definitely capable of tertiary study, with 43.4 per cent of the males and 32.9 per cent of the females proceeding into tertiary education. More of the male than female students

(78.9 per cent vs 64.0 per cent) were enrolled at universities rather than at the less prestigious colleges of advanced or further education. This is consistent with notions that young men are expected to prepare themselves for the world of work, but young women tend to have less clearly defined ambitions. Coleman (1980) reviewed arguments that identity development and vocational choice are correspondingly more complicated for young women. A 'feminine' gender identity certainly does not depend on high academic achievement, in fact achievement may even conflict with such an identity. So the determinants for young men and young women may well be different.

An alternative explanation for the sex difference is the marked segregation within the Australian labour market and the fact that it is colleges of advanced education, rather than universities, which offer courses in vocational subjects like nursing, social work and primary school teaching which (in the past) have tended to attract women rather than men.

While cultural background *per se* did not predict tertiary study, young women from non-English-speaking homes were significantly more likely than others to be students (38.1 per cent compared with 16.5 per cent of English only). This was not the case for males. In fact, young men from non-English-speaking homes were the most likely to be unemployed. We further found that young women who subsequently entered tertiary education had had higher self-esteem and a more internal control orientation while still at school, than the other occupational groups. In contrast, young men who entered tertiary education had not differed in earlier personality.

As mentioned in Chapter 3, a subsample of the students was selected for further testing at the four-year follow-up stage. These respondents completed the EMBU, which is a self-report measure describing parental rearing patterns during childhood (Winefield, Goldney, Tiggemann and Winefield, 1989, 1990). Scores were obtained on three scales for each parent: mother/father, affectionate, performance-oriented and stimulating. Previous work notes consistent reports by high achieving women of encouragement from their fathers (Barnett and Baruch, 1978). A contrary hypothesis derived from the work of Kelly and Worell (1976) was that achievement encouragement from the mother might distinguish young women who entered tertiary education. Our results showed that female tertiary students reported *fathers* who were more performance-oriented (sample items: 'Did your parents try to spur you on to become the best?' 'Did your parents usually show they were interested in your getting good marks?'), and who were more stimulating ('If you had a difficult task in front of you, did you then feel support from your parents?'). The corresponding results for male students showed no significant effects. Neither sex reported significantly different patterns of maternal behaviours.

So which young people enter tertiary education? The males are not very different from their non-student peers, except in being more academically capable, and having a tendency to come from higher socio-economic status homes. The females are also more academically capable, but that is not sufficient. Young women who enter tertiary education are additionally distinguished by high self-esteem and internal locus of control during school days, a non-English-speaking cultural background and fathers who encouraged them to achieve success in the world. It seems that tertiary education is a 'normal' activity for young men to engage in, whereas for young women it still requires special characteristics and circumstances.

A NINE-YEAR FOLLOW-UP OF ACADEMICALLY CAPABLE SCHOOL LEAVERS

If one accepts that tertiary study is the developmentally optimal vocational choice for intellectually capable young people, then the choices made by the specifically academically able group of students warrant particular examination. At the end of our study, that is nine years after initial ratings of academic potential by teachers, we were able to see what those capable individuals remaining in our sample had achieved (Winefield, Tiggemann, Goldney and Winefield, 1992). In 1989, there were 169 individuals remaining in our sample who had been rated in 1980 as definitely capable of tertiary study. Of those, 24 were current tertiary students, 95 had undertaken tertiary studies in the past of at least two years duration (97.8 per cent had gained at least one degree or other formal tertiary qualification), and 50 had never been tertiary students. Their average age was 24.6 years.

By investigating only academically capable individuals, we have removed the effect of academic ability, so influential above. The first question was whether we could predict tertiary study in this select group. Discriminant function analysis showed that those who had never entered tertiary study did not differ in 1980 from those who had, in age, sex, ethnicity, self-esteem or depressive affect. They did at school have a more external locus of control, and came from lower socio-economic status homes. Only 30.4 per cent of the never students' fathers had high occupational status, compared to 54.9 per cent of the past and 60.9 per cent of the current students'. Of course, there are other variables not included in the present study which might affect the probability of tertiary entry by the academically capable. One which seems likely to be relevant is the presence for the school leavers of highly educated role models. The correlation with father's occupation is consistent with this possibility, although we have no direct information on how many or which members of our subjects' families may themselves have undertaken tertiary study.

A second question which arises is what were the consequences, both in social status and psychologically, of undertaking tertiary study? Does tertiary study offer benefits to students which are not available to their equally academically capable peers? With respect to financial status, past students did earn significantly more per week ($400–$500 on average) than did the never students ($300–$400), whose incomes in turn were higher than the current students ($200). Correspondingly, past students had higher occupational status than the never students.

With respect to psychological well-being, somewhat surprisingly, the current students had higher scores for depressive affect and GHQ, a measure of psychological distress, than the other two groups which did not differ. Analyses showed that these differences were not completely attributable to the relative poverty of the current students.

Perhaps, studenthood at this (late) age, which is often accompanied by part-time or casual work, might be particularly stressful. This does not deny that psychological benefits might accrue much later, when these people are in their thirties and forties, when job satisfaction might well depend on having obtained the appropriate academic qualifications. Nevertheless, tertiary study, contrary to what many educators believe, does not confer general psychological benefits on individuals while they are pursuing it. Rather it is being in the workforce and out of the education system which results in improved psychological well-being. This conclusion is supported by the longitudinal and cross-sectional findings reported in Chapter 4. In general, although the tertiary students were better off than the unemployed and the dissatisfied employed on all our measures of well-being, they were less well off than the satisfied employed on four of them: depressive affect, negative mood, GHQ and hopelessness. They did not differ from the satisfied employed on self-esteem, locus of control or anomie (see Tables 4.1 to 4.12 in the Appendix).

OVERALL SUMMARY

In this chapter we have attempted to answer three questions concerning the predictors of occupational status. First, can we predict who will become unemployed from information collected while people are still students at school? The answer is yes, we can, up to three years later. Those most vulnerable to unemployment are students of ethnic origin, of low socio-economic status and with an unemployed member of the immediate family. Such students also view the getting of jobs as less important for themselves and their parents, and have lower self-esteem, a more external locus of control and lower achievement motivation.

The second question was: Can we predict who will go on to further tertiary education? The answer is again yes, up to five years later. For men, it is the academically most able. For women, however, other factors contribute. Women who go on to further study also have higher self-esteem, a more internal control orientation, a non-English-speaking cultural background and fathers who encouraged them to achieve success in the world.

The third question represents a refinement of the second. Targeting specifically the academically capable, over the entire nine years of the study, who did or did not undertake tertiary study? Among the academically capable, those students who had never undertaken any tertiary study, had a more external locus of control and came from lower socio-economic status homes.

8 The prevalence of psychological ill health and suicidal ideation

INTRODUCTION

Whereas previous chapters have addressed the relationship of a number of psychometric variables to unemployment, this chapter looks at the possible association between clinically significant psychological illness, suicidal ideation and unemployment.

There is a general feeling in most communities that unemployment *per se* must be bad, and it is easy to attribute one's problems to unemployment rather than examining more painful interpersonal issues. However, it is a complex problem, made more difficult both by the increasing rates of unemployment in most countries and by the fact that psychological illness itself is quite prevalent. Indeed, it is important to reflect that there have been a number of epidemiological surveys in England, North America and Australia which have produced remarkably similar results, with 15–20 per cent of the populations studied having a diagnosable psychological illness. This has been confirmed in the recent authoritative Epidemiologic Catchment Area study in the USA (Robins and Regier, 1991), the most comprehensive study of its type. Furthermore, young adults, the segment of the population most commonly referred to in media publicity about unemployment, are not spared from such psychological illness. It is fair to note that this 15–20 per cent prevalence of psychological illness is predominantly comprised of less serious conditions, but nevertheless such a prevalence must make researchers cautious in attributing any such illness to any specific factors.

EARLY STUDIES

There is a long tradition of research elucidating the association between psychological illness and unemployment. Two of the earliest contributions were those of Lewis in England in 1935 and Eisenberg and Lazarsfeld in the USA in 1938, studies which arose out of the effects of the Great Depression.

Lewis was somewhat cautious in his conclusions, which were drawn from a clinical assessment of 52 male subjects between the ages of 20 and 67 years. He noted that symptoms of 'anxiety, irritability, hypochondria, depression, querulousness or resentment, and (hysterical) conversion symptoms were found' (Lewis, 1935: 293), and added that

> outstanding features were a preoccupation with discomforts, whether expressed in physical, mental, or social terms, a feeling of dissatisfaction or resentment in regard to them, and various expressions of anxiety; trembling was frequent. The complaints were commonly vague, but expressed with great earnestness, often also with rich prolixity and as though learnt off by heart.
>
> (Lewis, 1935: 293)

He indicated that the symptom complex bore 'a close likeness to the syndrome of the chronic "compensation or pension-neurosis" ' (Lewis, 1935: 293).

Lewis acknowledged the difficulty of determining the aetiology of these symptoms, and although he noted that his subjects' previous history yielded evidence of inherent deficiencies of adaptation, he concluded that, 'regular occupation with trained supervisors seems the most important requirement for their recovery' (Lewis, 1935: 297), a clear acceptance of the significance of unemployment in their emotional distress.

Eisenberg and Lazarsfeld reviewed over 100 studies of the psychological effects of unemployment, and it is fascinating that they introduced their paper by stating, 'when we try to formulate more exactly the psychological effects of unemployment, we lose the full, poignant, emotional feeling that this word brings to people' (Eisenberg and Lazarsfeld, 1938: 358). There is no doubt that is the case.

They noted depression, hopelessness, boredom, criminal behaviour and prolonged dependence upon parents as being associated with unemployment, but few conclusions were drawn. They pointed out the different effects on different age groups, and even the potential different effects that unemployment would have in youths with either employed or unemployed parents. Indeed, it is sobering to note that although these methodological issues were canvassed over fifty years ago, much research still ignores these pitfalls, and sweeping assertions are sometimes presented as scientifically proven facts applicable to all unemployed.

RECENT STUDIES

In the last fifty years there have been numerous studies addressing the impact of unemployment upon health. Perhaps the overriding theme has been summed up rather pithily in an Editorial in the *Lancet* (1984) where it was stated that:

most people already 'know' or believe that unemployment makes people unhappy, leads to relative poverty, and causes a sense of futility. It would be surprising if these effects did not sometimes cause stress and psychological ill-health.

(*Lancet*, 1984: 1019)

Not all have agreed. In a provocative paper entitled 'Unemployment causes ill health: the wrong track', Kagan (1987) states quite bluntly that

It is not unemployment *per se* that causes ill health. It can be a very desirable state. There are no diseases specific to unemployment. Contrast this with employment. Unemployment shares with all other socio-environmental situations risk of exposure to common physical, social and psychological stressors that predispose to disease.

(Kagan, 1987: 217)

Kagan coined the term 'cratogenic' disease, a term meaning disease caused by authorities, and proposed that, 'As an immediate first step, that will reduce "cratogenic" disease, people in authority should stop misleading the public into believing that unemployment is the cause of ill health' (Kagan, 1987: 217).

This devil's advocate view is not without merit, and reminds one of the Greek philosopher Epictetus who stated that 'People are disturbed not by things, but by the view which they take of them.' It is also consistent with recent research into the aetiology of neurotic illness in which it is the perceived adequacy of support or rejection, rather than the reality of the situation, which is important (Henderson, Byrne and Duncan-Jones, 1981). This leads back to observations such as those of Lewis (1935) who attributed his unemployed subjects' emotional distress as much to their 'inherent deficiencies' of adaptation to their environment, as to the unemployment *per se*, and the cynic could be forgiven for opining that little has been gained in over fifty years of research.

Such a view is unduly pessimistic. Significant advances have been made in our understanding of the effects of unemployment. At a national level, Brenner (1979b) has correlated economic data with a number of measures of health, both in the UK and USA, and found associations between national economic performance and admissions to psychiatric hospitals, homicide, suicide, cirrhosis (an index of alcohol consumption) and general mortality (see Chapter 3). In fact, he asserted that unemployment rates were the most important economic factor in influencing health. His more recent work has suggested that there are two peaks of health change following economic recession. In the first two years he demonstrated an increase in parameters of aggression and also premature death in vulnerable populations, such as infants and the chronically ill; and the second peak, two or three years after a recession, appears to be comprised of a general deterioration of health with an increased mortality from cardiovascular disease (Brenner, 1987).

At the individual level, clinicians such as Fagin (1983) have very clearly described the psychological phases which occur following unemployment. These include the phases of disbelief, denial and anxiety and then there is the assumption of the 'unemployed identity'. Such work emphasises the salience of the earlier comments of Eisenberg and Lazarsfeld (1938) about the poignancy of the individual's emotional reaction to unemployment.

Between these two broad types of study there have been numerous research projects designed to tease out the health consequences of unemployment in specific groups. Although there have been studies addressing specific occupational groups, such as shipyard workers (Iversen, Sabroe and Damsgaard, 1989) and factory workers (Beale and Nethercott, 1985) following closure of the worksite, and of specific age groups such as British men aged 40–59 years (Cook, Bartley, Cummins and Shaper, 1982) and Finnish men aged 30–54 years (Martikainen, 1990), the majority of studies of the unemployed have focused on the young (e.g. Banks and Jackson, 1982; Cullen, Ryan, Cullen, Ronayne and Wynne, 1987; Donovan, Oddy, Pardoe and Ades, 1986; Feather and O'Brien, 1986a, 1986b; Winefield, Tiggemann and Goldney, 1988; Winefield, Tiggemann, Winefield and Goldney, 1991).

The focusing of attention upon more discrete groups of unemployed is important, and consistent with the view of Smith (1987a) who warned of the dangers of talking about the unemployed as if they were a homogeneous group.

PSYCHOLOGICAL ILL HEALTH IN YOUNG ADULTS

A number of parameters of psychological ill health have been addressed elsewhere. Measures of self-esteem, depressive affect, locus of control, anomie, hopelessness and negative mood all give results which indicate that the unemployed are disadvantaged. However, in our study they are not always more disadvantaged than those who are dissatisfied with their employment. Furthermore, the disadvantage appears to be related to a lack of change in those parameters over time, rather than a definite deterioration in the unemployed.

It could be argued, quite correctly, that the above measures do not delineate clinical psychiatric illness. In fact, there are remarkably few studies which have concurrent measures of psychiatric morbidity as assessed by rating scales and that assessed by experienced clinicians.

The most commonly used instrument in these studies is the General Health Questionnaire (GHQ) (Goldberg, 1972). The use of such instruments has been questioned, as even if there is, for example, a correlation of 0.8 between the GHQ and a more comprehensive clinical assessment instrument such as the Present State Examination (Wing, 1980), either assessment can only account for 64 per cent of the variation in the other (*Lancet*, 1984). Nevertheless, the utility of the GHQ in such research has been defended (Banks, Clegg, Jackson, Kemp, Stafford and Wall, 1980), and it has been used in a number of subsequent studies.

There are a number of different versions of the GHQ, with those most commonly employed being the 12, 28 and 30-item instruments. There are also two scoring methods, with either a binary or Likert system being used to give a differing range of scores.

Using three different versions of the GHQ, in the 1984 sample the unemployed consistently scored higher, indicating a greater likelihood of psychological illness, than the satisfied employed. However, it was striking that the dissatisfied employed scored in a similar manner to the unemployed, as has been discussed in some detail in Chapter 4. In fact the scores translate into there being 39.7 per cent of the unemployed, 21.4 per cent of the satisfied employed and 39.2 per cent of the dissatisfied employed, respectively, who could be considered as probable psychiatric cases. These figures are of the same order as other studies presented in Table 8.1 in the Appendix.

The question arises of how closely do these 'probable cases of psychiatric disorder' approximate clinical conditions assessed and treated by experienced psychiatrists. In order to examine this issue further, in 1984 we selected all those subjects who rated greater than 4 on the binary scored 28-item GHQ. Of the 1013 young people, mean age 19.6 years, there were 291 GHQ-positive and 188 were interviewed by experienced psychiatric clinicians on the basis of their availability. These psychiatrists judged only 31.4 per cent of the GHQ-positive subjects to show evidence of a probable or definite psychiatric disorder as delineated by the criteria of the DSM-III (American Psychiatric Association, 1980). This is a not-unexpected finding, as it is recognised that instruments such as the GHQ tend to give a high misclassification rate of 'cases' (Rabkin and Klein, 1987; Winefield, Goldney, Winefield and Tiggemann, 1989).

A control group of GHQ-negative subjects was also examined, and 10.2 per cent of these warranted a clinical psychiatric diagnosis. Notwithstanding the difference in psychiatric diagnosis by the psychiatrists, a standardised Global Assessment Scale measurement of general coping (Endicott, Spitzer, Fleiss and Cohen, 1976) showed scores of 76 and 84 for the GHQ-positive and GHQ-negative subjects respectively, a difference which, although statistically significant, is of marginal clinical importance.

In 1988 the GHQ-12 was administered again and the unemployed (12.32) scored higher than the satisfied employed (9.73), but in fact the dissatisfied employed (13.77) scored even higher, emphasising the importance of examining attitudes to work as well as employment *per se*. No clinical interviews were undertaken at that time, and we cannot speculate on the clinical significance of these figures.

What can be concluded from these data? The GHQ figures for both 1984 and 1988 are similar, and when clinical psychiatric interviews were undertaken in 1984 only 12.6 per cent (31.7 per cent of 39.7 per cent GHQ-positive) of the unemployed had a clinically significant psychological illness. It is sobering to note that such a figure is not dissimilar to a number of community psychiatric prevalence studies, as noted before, where an appreciable degree of psychological illness has been reported in communities in England, North America and Australia. This, and the relatively benign nature of the overall morbidity as judged by the Global Assessment Scale, indicate that caution should be exercised before placing great emphasis on the clinical significance of the effect of unemployment.

Such a cautionary conclusion is congruent with our findings that the self-perception of general health did not reliably distinguish the employment groups (see Chapter 9). It is also consistent with the longitudinal analyses of the data which showed that when there were differences between the unemployed and the other groups, those differences were attributable to improvements shown by some groups rather than to a deterioration in any group. Typically, the psychological health of the satisfied employed improved and the well-being of the dissatisfied employed and unemployed did not significantly change (see Chapter 4).

SUICIDAL IDEATION AND BEHAVIOUR

It has long been presumed that there is an association between unemployment and suicidal ideation and behaviour. In a comprehensive review of the literature in 1984, Platt noted that Falret in 1822 asserted that suicide increased in times of economic depression, and Durkheim in the late nineteenth century appears to have confidently accepted that assertion.

Broad population studies demonstrated an increase in suicide rates in the economic depression of the 1930s (Sainsbury, 1986), and other studies of European countries (Boor, 1980) and India (Rao, 1975) have come to similar conclusions. However, a recent report of Dooley, Catalano, Rook and Serxner (1989), using more sophisticated aggregate time-series statistical methods, has cast some doubt on these earlier studies. They concluded that

> aggregate-level analyses do not support the contention that economic contraction has a strong or widespread effect on suicide in the general

population. The results suggest, rather, that any effect a regional economy has on suicide is complex and depends on individual-level factors.

(Dooley, Catalano, Rook and Serxner, 1989: 334)

With regard to attempted suicide a similar conflicting picture emerges. Platt (1986a) reported that at least twenty studies demonstrated an association with unemployment, and the proportion of suicide attempts in the unemployed compared to the employed has been as high as 15.4:1 (Hawton and Rose, 1986). In a number of studies from Edinburgh, Platt and his colleagues have reported that the ratio has been approximately 10:1 over a period of twenty years (Platt and Kreitman, 1984, 1990; Platt, 1986a, 1986b). These figures are somewhat greater than those of Bland, Stebelsky, Orn and Newman (1988) who in a community sample in Edmonton, Canada, reported a lifetime prevalence rate of attempted suicide for the unemployed as 9.4 per cent, compared to 2.5 per cent for those who were employed. There are also data which indicate that the longer the duration of unemployment, the greater the risk of suicidal behaviour (Hawton, Fagg and Simkin, 1988; Platt and Kreitman, 1984).

Although there appears to be a firm association, there have been intriguing variations when the data have been more closely examined. Thus, for men in Edinburgh between 1968 and 1975 there was a highly significant positive correlation between unemployment and attempted suicide, but a negative association was evident between 1976 and 1983 (Platt and Kreitman, 1990). Similar findings were reported from Oxford (Hawton, Fagg and Simkin, 1988).

Platt and Kreitman suggested that the more widespread unemployment was in a community, then the lower was the risk of attempted suicide among the unemployed. This observation was consistent with the fact that in Hartlepool in England between 1974 and 1983 unemployment increased four-fold, but attempted suicide remained relatively constant (Furness, Khan and Pickens, 1985).

This phenomenon could be related to a progressive dilution of the number of the more vulnerable unemployed who may have attempted suicide, or it could be related to a reduction in the stigma associated with unemployment. Thus as unemployment became the norm for certain communities, there would be less alienation and societal denigration of these persons. In fact, Platt and Kreitman (1985) have demonstrated that communities where unemployment has always been endemic have fewer behaviour problems in the unemployed than those in areas with historically low unemployment rates.

The question must be posed as to why there is an association between unemployment and suicidal behaviour. In broad terms there are two theories. The first is the selection or vulnerability theory that those who are predisposed to, or already suffer from, emotional difficulties which could lead to suicidal behaviour will be those who become unemployed. The second is the causal theory that unemployment *per se* leads to emotional distress and suicidal behaviour.

Platt and Kreitman (1984) presented data which they interpreted as being 'consistent with the view that unemployment, especially if long term, increases the incidence of parasuicide' (Platt and Kreitman, 1984: 1029). However, colleagues from their own university department disputed their conclusions, noting that no causal connection should be made from such observations (Shapiro and Parry, 1984). Subsequently, Platt and Kreitman (1985) reaffirmed their stand, and Platt (1986a) more specifically stated that 'the attributable risk analysis shows that over 50% of the overall parasuicide rate may be attributable to unemployment in recent years' (Platt, 1986a: 403).

On the other hand, to temper those conclusions Platt and Duffy (1986) later reported an association between unemployment and early separation from mother. This factor is well recognised as being associated with suicidal behaviour (Goldney, 1981), but replication of its rather unexpected association with unemployment remains to be demonstrated before concluding that unemployment and suicidal behaviour are only associated because of their common relationship to early parental separation.

Caution about such conclusions has also been expressed by other workers. In their study of female unemployment and attempted suicide in Oxford, Hawton, Fagg and Simkin (1988) stated that their results added 'some weight to the argument that it is prior predisposition rather than unemployment itself which increases the risk of attempted suicide in the unemployed' (Hawton, Fagg and Simkin, 1988: 636).

Crombie (1989) examined suicide and unemployment in men in Scotland and concluded 'these data do not support the hypothesis that the rise in unemployment is a direct cause of the rise in suicide rates among men' (Crombie, 1989: 782).

Finally, Jones, Forster and Hassanyeh, (1991) compared 64 subjects with 'deliberate non-fatal self-poisoning' with community control subjects and concluded that there was

> no firm evidence to support the hypotheses that unemployment was causally related to self-poisoning in an indirect manner or that it increased the vulnerability of individuals who self-poison to other stressful life events and difficulties.
>
> (Jones, Forster and Hassanyeh, 1991: 169)

The association is obviously by no means simple. Platt (1986a) has indicated that when statistical analysis of his data controlled for the level of poverty, the correlation between unemployment and attempted suicide was no longer significant, leading him to conclude that 'unemployment appears to be associated with parasuicide only in so far as it relates to poverty or to some other variable closely connected with poverty' (Platt, 1986a: 402).

Another indication of the difficulty in establishing causal links has been provided by Kreitman (1988) who observed that:

> It can be shown for example that there is a substantial correlation between male unemployment and female suicide. This could be because male and female unemployment are themselves correlated, but equally plausibly one could be seeing here the effects of male unemployment on family stability and the stresses falling on the wife and mother. None of this implies that unemployment is not important in a causal sense, but it does indicate that the causal chain may be highly complex.
>
> (Kreitman, 1988: 370)

Of this there can be no doubt.

In order to tease out these factors in more detail the ideal study would have a prospective design. However, one of the inherent problems in research into suicidal behaviour is that although it is a dramatic event, and although there may have been increases in such behaviour, the reality of the situation is that it is still an infrequent event in an overall population context; that is, it has a low base rate. This problem has been referred to in attempts to provide instruments which could predict suicide (Goldney and Spence, 1987; Pokorny, 1983). Similarly, in regard to the further elucidation of unemployment and subsequent suicidal behaviour, Platt (1986b) has commented that 'a longitudinal study of such a relatively unusual behaviour would be a most wasteful misuse of scarce resources' (Platt, 1986b: 30).

Whilst one can agree with Platt's comment in general terms, we believe that our longitudinal study of a cohort of young subjects provides an opportunity to examine this issue. However, the expectation that this could be performed by examining those who actually attempted suicide must be put to rest. Thus of the original 3130 students examined in 1980, only twelve who were still in the cohort in 1988 acknowledged ever having attempted suicide. We accept that this is almost certainly an under-estimate, as no fewer than 40 per cent of those who recorded suicidal ideation in 1984 denied ever having had suicidal ideation during their lives when re-examined in 1988 (Goldney, Smith, Winefield, Tiggemann and Winefield, 1991).

With the small number of twelve who had attempted suicide, only one of whom was unemployed, it is quite evident that despite the initial size of our cohort, any conclusions based on so few cases would be of doubtful validity.

In order to expand the numbers, we believed it was reasonable to include subjects with suicidal ideation in addressing this issue. It is acknowledged that those who simply have suicidal ideation may be different from those who actually attempt or go on to commit suicide, but nevertheless it cannot be denied that there are certain similarities. At the very least it can be asserted that we have demonstrated a highly significant association between suicidal ideation and a number of measures of psychological distress, including depressive affect, low self-esteem, hopelessness, anomie and scores on the GHQ. This is so not only for cross-sectional analyses (Goldney, Winefield, Tiggemann, Winefield and Smith, 1989), but also for the longitudinal data, indicating that suicidal ideation appears to be associated with appreciable morbidity over a number of years (Goldney, Smith, Winefield, Tiggemann and Winefield, 1991).

When confining the analysis to those who had had suicidal ideation in the six months prior to their assessment in 1988, only 22 of 432 acknowledged such thoughts. Furthermore, only one of the 21 who were unemployed reported being suicidal in the last six months. Such a figure would appear to vindicate Platt's comment!

However, by expanding the suicidal ideation criterion to those who had ever had suicidal ideation, a sample size of 105 young adults with a mean age of 23.6 years (SD: 1.1 years) was obtained. Those 105 subjects who acknowledged having had thoughts of killing themselves at sometime in their lives comprised 69 (20 per cent of 345) satisfied employed, 15 (48 per cent of 31) dissatisfied employed, 8 (38 per cent of 21) unemployed and 13 (37 per cent of 35) tertiary students. Young men and women were evenly represented, with 34 men and 35 women; 8 men and 7 women; 4 men and 4 women; and 6 men and 7 women being in the respective groups. There was a significant difference between the groups, with the satisfied employed being under-represented, and the other three groups all being over-represented in those who acknowledged lifetime suicidal ideation.

When the psychometric variables for the different groups who acknowledged suicidal ideation were compared, only scores on the measure of depressive affect and the GHQ were significantly different, and in both cases it was the satisfied employed who scored in the least disturbed manner, with the dissatisfied employed reporting more emotional distress, rather than the unemployed (see Table 8.2, Appendix).

These results certainly do not lend strong support to an association between unemployment and suicidal ideation. However, it could reasonably be argued that the number of unemployed with suicidal ideation, only eight, is insufficient to demonstrate differences, and that Platt's cautionary advice has again been vindicated; that the presence of students, not usually included in research into the effects of unemployment, could be confounding the results; and that the definition of unemployment as simply indicating that state at the time of assessment could preclude subjects who may have been unemployed for a prolonged period of time shortly before gaining work. Further data analysis appeared warranted.

In the first instance, students were excluded, and then the definition of unemployment was addressed. At the 1988 assessment, subjects were asked to state how many weeks of paid employment they had had in the preceding year. Three hundred had had 52 weeks of employment, and 40 had had 26 weeks or less of employment. There were 54 subjects who reported having had between 28 and 51 weeks of employment, and it was decided to exclude those from the analysis in order to optimise any differences between those who had had full-time employment and those who had had at least six months' unemployment in the year prior to assessment. We believe that a period of six months' unemployment can reasonably be considered sufficient to provide a valid cohort of subjects for comparison with those who had had full-time employment. Furthermore, our data presented in Chapter 5 indicate that the maximum psychological impact of unemployment does not occur before about six months.

Of the 340 subjects selected in this manner, 13 (32.5 per cent) of those 40 who had had at least six months unemployment and 66 (22.0 per cent) of the 300 who had had full-time employment reported having had suicidal ideation at some time in their lives. There was a trend for more of the long-term unemployed to have reported suicidal ideation than the full-time employed, but this was not statistically significant. Again it appears that the dissatisfied full-time employed are more disadvantaged in terms of suicidal ideation than the unemployed. This is also demonstrated when scores of the psychometric variables examined in 1988 are compared for these three groups, with the only significant difference being between scores on depressive affect, with the dissatisfied employed being higher than the virtually identical scores of the satisfied employed and unemployed (see Table 8.3, Appendix).

Overall, our data do not provide much support for an association between unemployment and suicidal ideation (Goldney, Winefield, Tiggemann and Winefield, 1992). Indeed, there appears to be a stronger link between suicidal ideation and unsatisfactory employment, a finding consistent with our other results. Perhaps what can more firmly be stated is that satisfactory employment is related to less suicidal ideation, but the direction of causality can not be assumed. However, on the basis of our finding that suicidal ideation is not strongly associated with unemployment, whereas psychometric measures of suicidal subjects versus non-suicidal subjects taken in 1988 show significant differences not only then, but also in 1984 and 1980 for those same subjects (Goldney, Smith, Winefield, Tiggemann and Winefield, 1991), it is likely that suicidal ideation is essentially independent of employment status and related to more enduring personality or health related traits.

CONCLUSIONS

Although the results of this study indicate that the effects of unemployment on psychological health and suicidal ideation are relatively modest, one can still agree with the earlier comment of Eisenberg and Lazarsfeld (1938) that the poignancy of the individual's emotional experience is lost when overall psychological effects are quantified. This was evident in the clinical interviews performed in 1984, where a number of subjects reported having felt depressed and frustrated when they had been unable to find work, or had been retrenched.

The complexity of the personal experience of unemployment is illustrated by reference to just two individuals. A young man reported a considerable degree of depression, and it emerged that he had given up his work in another city in order to return to his dying grandmother who had raised him after his parents' separation. Another subject, a young woman, was depressed, angry and frustrated that she had been sacked in order that her boss's new girl friend, without any training or qualifications, could take the position in which she had worked effectively for two years. Whilst both these subjects were unemployed, neither blamed the unemployment *per se* for their emotional distress. Nevertheless, it could be argued that if there had been readily available alternative work, then it would have been to their advantage.

There were also some subjects, both employed and unemployed, who had definite evidence of psychological illness. This was usually depression, but symptoms of schizophrenia were also present in several, and it was quite evident that such subjects would have had problems in impressing a potential employer in a tight labour market. It is of interest that almost invariably the clinicians elicited information suggesting that the symptoms ante-dated leaving school, a finding that is consistent with the recent American Epidemiologic Catchment Area study which found that most psychological illness had its onset early in life, at a median age of 16 years (Robins and Regier, 1991).

Finally, there were those who reported that they had used a period of unemployment in order to travel and think through their life's ambitions, much in the manner of the more socially condoned 'year off' that many young Australians take before pursuing further studies or a career. It is fair to note that such comments sometimes lacked conviction, and were probably rationalisations or examples of dissonance reduction (Festinger, 1957) to make unemployment more acceptable. Nevertheless, such an approach is certainly adaptive.

There is no doubt that unemployment can affect an individual's psychological well-being, and this is a uniquely personal experience.

However, notwithstanding the intensity of emotional arousal which may be seen in susceptible individuals, when one attempts to quantify the broader impact of unemployment as a cause of clinically significant psychological ill health and suicidal ideation, the overall effects are at most quite modest.

9 Drug use, health and finances according to employment status

In this chapter we review our longitudinal findings concerning how both drug use and physical health relate to employment status. We asked our subjects about their consumption of alcohol, cigarettes, prescription drugs, non-prescription (or over-the-counter) drugs, and 'other' drugs, deliberately including the possibility of illegal substances such as marijuana, heroin and cocaine, etc. The measures of drug use were simple reports of frequency and, in some cases, especially where subjects were asked to report illegal usage, can be expected to under-estimate what they actually consumed. Similarly with health, exact measurement is extremely problematic, as will be discussed further below. A rating of financial state which subjects provided each year adds another valuable dimension to the total picture of unemployment effects, as poverty and ill health are traditionally linked although the direction of causal influence is unlikely to be simply one-way.

Thus in this chapter, in giving the results of questions about drug use, health and financial state, we are not able to describe standardised assessment techniques as we were able to do for the psychological aspects of our subjects' adjustment. Nonetheless, it is important in any overview of the consequences of unemployment to take what account is possible of the physical aspects of the life of subjects in addition to the psycho-social.

DRUG USE

There are several reasons for interest in the drugs consumed by young people. First, in the public mind at least, is the expectation that unemployed youth become prone to drug addiction and consequent lawlessness. The rising crime rate observed in Western societies during the period of high youth unemployment causes anxieties related to 'law and order' issues, and 'drugs' have frequently been referred to in this context as a factor which stimulates crime due to the expenses involved in their acquisition, or the reduced commitment to social conformity which unemployment might bring about.

Public health professionals are also concerned about the use of hard drugs by young people, but they are more concerned about the commercially available legal drugs of alcohol and tobacco, which are consumed by very large numbers, than about the illicit substances consumed by a small but highly publicised minority of young people. Tobacco smoking, which usually begins in early adolescence, is one of the largest single causes of preventable illness and mortality in our society, while alcohol is of concern not only because of its association with the health and social impairment caused by alcoholism, but also because of the high rates of injury and death caused to young people by drink-driving.

Finally, from the viewpoint of developmental psychology, drug use is of interest in that consumption of socially acceptable drugs such as alcohol and tobacco acts somewhat as a marker of entry to independent adulthood, or is often perceived to do so. The task of learning to use the drugs accepted in ordinary society in a responsible manner can almost be seen as a test of psychological maturity.

In our longitudinal study we included questions about the use of alcohol, tobacco and other drugs for the first time in 1984, when the subjects had an average age of 19.6 years. Thereafter these questions were repeated annually until 1988, giving us a five-year history of drug use patterns in the stay-in subjects. Drug use can therefore be related to demographic factors, including employment status, and psychological factors, both concurrently and predictively.

Unfortunately drug use was associated systematically with drop-out from the study. Heavier users of both alcohol and tobacco in 1984 were more likely to have ceased participation in the study by 1988 (Winefield, Winefield and Tiggemann, 1990), and thus our data under-represent the amount of drug use in Australian young people overall. A further consequence is that we have been unable to report fully on perhaps the most interesting group from a health point of view, that is the heavy users.

A question which immediately occurs when contemplating the current results concerns the degree of accuracy which we could expect in replies to a postal survey, particularly with regard to behaviours which, like drug use, may be illegal or at least socially stigmatised. Naturally this question is difficult to answer without being able to make comparisons between self-reported and actual levels of drug use, the latter being measured by some objective criterion. The fact is that there are few objective and reliable measures of drug use. Physiological methods involve taking blood or urine samples (or salivary swabs in the case of one method to check for smoking), and all such methods are expensive and intrusive to various degrees. Thus their use is constrained by both financial and ethical considerations. In addition, because the subject's informed consent is required, the results can be manipulated, for example by the user giving up the drug for the period immediately before the test. Results can also be distorted by the consumption of other substances than the ones of interest: for example, certain foods and air pollution bias the indicators of cigarette use.

While one might suspect that the usual direction of any distortion in self-report would be to understate the drug use, this should not automatically be assumed to be true. Especially in the case of socially acceptable or 'mainstream' drugs such as alcohol and tobacco, use may be over-reported by those wishing to impress as grown up, for the reason referred to above.

In the final analysis self-report is a necessary component of gaining information about drug use, as about psychological state and many of the other variables of interest in this study. The validity of self-report in relation to drug use has been shown to be reasonable in young people (Kline, Canter and Robin, 1987). It also seems fair to assume that subjects who continued participation in our longitudinal study, where they knew that their results were seen by the research team only, had accepted responsibility for contributing to scientific knowledge and were motivated to answer honestly.

ALCOHOL

Alcohol use has a complex but important role in Australian society. As noted by the National Health and Medical Research Council (NHMRC, 1987: 20 ff.), alcohol use is seen as 'integral to being an acceptable, healthy, sociable person; a "real Australian" '. Being able to enjoy a drink, especially in celebration and with friends, is almost a definition of culturally acceptable behaviour (Wilks and Callan, 1988). At the same time, excessive drinking, particularly alone or to seek psychological oblivion, is regarded with contempt – with the exception that getting completely drunk with friends has been tolerated and even expected as a rite of passage into adulthood for young men. Hill, White, Pain and Gardner (1990) found that by the age of 17, 50 per cent of Australian boys and 40 per cent of girls were buying alcohol for themselves, despite the illegality of alcohol sales to minors.

Alcohol abuse which becomes continuous is associated with a range of serious health problems such as liver disease and brain damage, and deterioration in social adjustment goes along with the alcoholic's greater risk of becoming unemployable, violent and socially isolated (NHMRC, 1987). However, in young adulthood such problems associated with chronic alcohol abuse are not common. The greatest anxiety is the involvement of young drinkers, especially males, in road accidents which can kill or permanently disable them or their passengers and other road-users. Figures provided by the Road Accident Research Unit in Adelaide in 1991 showed that while the majority of injuries occur to drivers who have consumed no or very little alcohol, having a high Blood Alcohol Concentration clearly raises the risks of becoming a casualty. For example, of all male casualties aged in their twenties in 1988, 17 per cent had a BAC of three times the legal limit (0.15). Ferrara (1987) reviewed numerous international studies and concluded that the risk of traffic accidents is forty times higher with this concentration of alcohol in the blood than at the legal limit (0.05).

Drinking by young women has, until recently, been less socially acceptable than for young men, but attitudes are changing. Corti and Ibrahim (1990) found an overall increase in consumption by women since 1977, particularly by women aged 18–24 years. Financial independence and increased social acceptability were two factors the authors identified as likely causes. With about 16 per cent of women drinking at hazardous levels by 1985 (i.e. 2–4 drinks per day), they predicted a future increase in alcohol-related health problems for women, and advocated education and improved labelling to minimise such risks.

To see if increased exposure to the workplace would result in greater risks of alcohol abuse for women, Shore and Batt (1991) recruited a large sample of middle-aged Kansas women lawyers, accountants and business owners, then asked about their drinking and any negative consequences such as forgetting to do things, having family or work disputes, being charged with drink-driving or becoming less particular about choice of sexual partner after drinking. Few of these subjects drank at hazardous levels, and the more organisations they belonged to, the less alcohol they consumed. The authors concluded that employment and multiple roles may in fact protect women from alcohol abuse, by boosting their self-esteem and decreasing their opportunities for secret drinking.

In the present research, alcohol consumption was reported in terms of number of glasses of beer, wine, spirits and fortified wine taken during the preceding week (assuming as is commonly done, that a standard-sized drink of each sort of beverage contains roughly the same amount of alcohol: 10 gr.). The definitions of 'moderate' and 'excessive' levels of consumption which we have used are those recommended by the National Health and Medical Research Council of Australia in 1987: moderate drinking is up to 2 glasses per day for women and 4 for men. It is relevant to note in passing that specific and easily-understood information of this kind has only quite recently been readily available to the public, as health authorities and the alcohol industry begin to make serious efforts to make educative use of television and the print media.

In 1984 when a question about alcohol was first included, our subjects (at an average age of 19.6 years) reported that about three-quarters of the men (74 per cent) and two-thirds of the women (65 per cent) had drunk some alcohol in the past week (Winefield, Winefield, Tiggemann and Goldney,

1989). Over the next four years the proportion of moderate drinkers remained similar in both sexes (62–68 per cent for men; 56–59 per cent for women). The proportion of heavy drinkers also remained stable over time, at 6–10 per cent for men and 6–7 per cent for women, showing no particular trend over time.

A feature of youthful drinking which causes concern is the habit of binge drinking, i.e. consuming what would be a safe amount of alcohol if taken evenly over a week, in one or two drinking sessions, usually on Friday and Saturday nights. The proportion of binge drinkers is therefore probably higher than the proportion of 'heavy' drinkers based on the amount consumed per week. For example, in a student sample of similar age to the 1988 subjects, Winefield, Goldney, Winefield and Tiggemann (1992) found binge drinking in 27 per cent of male drinkers and 14 per cent of female drinkers – in a sample where only 9 per cent of men and 4 per cent of women were 'heavy' drinkers – when binging was defined as consumption of more than twice the 'moderate' amount on the heaviest drinking day last week. The risk of driving after a bout of alcohol consumption over a short period of time is obvious; unfortunately in the longitudinal study we did not ask a question which would have provided information about binge drinking.

Alcohol and employment

Dividing subjects into the abstinent (non-drinkers), the moderate and the heavy drinkers according to the NHMRC guidelines for each sex, we searched for relationships between drinking category and employment status, but found very few which reached statistical significance. The exception was that in 1984 (at 19.6 years) the unemployed males, and unemployed and dissatisfied employed females, were more likely to be heavy drinkers than were the other occupational groups. As will become apparent, this lack of association between drug use and employment is characteristic of all the drugs studied in our sample.

Predictors of alcohol abuse

In order to check the predictability of becoming a heavy drinker, we looked back at the demographic and psychological characteristics of the 1988 drinker groups (abstinent, moderate, heavy). Father's occupation, ethnicity, negative mood, self-esteem, locus of control, depressive affect, need for achievement, social alienation and hopelessness were all variables for which comparisons could be made. The males who were drinking heavily in 1988 turned out to have had, four years previously in 1984, lower self-esteem, higher depressive affect, more social alienation and more hopelessness.

Patterns of drinking showed considerable stability over this age range (19.6 to 23.6 years), but taking psychological variables into account increased the accuracy of predictions based on how much the man drank last year. As drinking habits were not studied before 19.6 years of age but may well have been quite well-established by then, the results are not conclusive in determining which comes first for young men: heavy drinking or psychological distress. The association is potentially an important one to note, however, as one implication might be that educational campaigns or treatment approaches need to suggest other methods than alcohol use for men to cope with negative feelings.

There was no association between heavy drinking for young women and demographic or psychological characteristics. There was another interesting sex difference in the form of alcohol consumed: beer was the preferred beverage for men and wine for women (Winefield, Goldney, Winefield and Tiggemann, 1992).

CIGARETTE SMOKING

The factors which influence people to start smoking, often during early adolescence, are well understood. Peer pressure is a primary influence, and children whose parents smoke are also more likely to smoke themselves (Ary and Biglan 1988; Charlton and Blair 1989). Accordingly, a major component of anti-smoking educational efforts in schools has been to help children resist social pressures to smoke, and to develop skills in declining offered cigarettes without feeling anxious or uncomfortable. For adults, educational messages stress the health damage which smoking can cause, which includes respiratory and circulatory problems in addition to the increased risk of lung cancer. Health warnings have been displayed on cigarette packets for several years now, and tobacco consumption has been decreasing in Australia according to large-scale surveys (Hill, White and Gray, 1988).

Very recently, evidence of the negative effects on bystanders of 'passive smoking', that is of inhaling other people's smoke as air pollution, has led to court decisions upholding the right to a smoke-free environment, with corresponding pressure on employers to ban smoking in workplaces or risk having to make compensation payouts. However, at the time our data were gathered, this development had not occurred, and health educators were concerned by the susceptibility, especially of young women, to advertisements suggesting that cigarettes conveyed sophistication and independence.

At 19, 27 per cent of our men and and 29 per cent of our women subjects smoked; each year there was a similar small preponderance of women smokers compared to men. Smoking in both sexes showed a slight downward trend over time so that in the 1988 sample, 18 per cent of men and 24 per cent of women reported smoking. An analysis of individual paths reveals considerable changing over from being a smoker to being a non-smoker, in successive years (Winefield, Winefield and Tiggemann, 1992b). About half the 1988 smokers had reported smoking in each of the preceding four years, but the other half had had at least one year of not smoking, perhaps related to efforts to quit.

Smoking and employment

In 1984 both male and female students were less likely to smoke than the other occupational groups, but on the whole there were few relationships between smoking and employment status. Unemployed men in 1987 and unemployed women in 1988 were more likely to be smokers, and satisfied employed men in 1987 were less likely to smoke. Lee, Crombie, Smith and Tunstall-Pedoe (1991) found that more unemployed than employed Scottish people smoked, in middle age, although their knowledge about health damage from smoking was the same. However, there was an interesting sex difference: unemployed male smokers consumed fewer cigarettes than did employed male smokers, while unemployed women smokers consumed more cigarettes than employed women smokers. Perhaps as Graham (1987) found for socio-economically deprived women, smoking represents an affordable luxury and symbol of adulthood to those who have few other opportunities for self-indulgence.

Prediction of smoking

Those who smoked in 1988 had scored higher than non-smokers in hopelessness in 1984, although the difference was not dramatic enough to allow clear predictions. In fact by 1984 when the first questions were asked, smokers had probably been engaging in the practice for several years. Extraversion and parental example are probably the best predictors, but our study gathered no information on these.

ILLICIT DRUGS

In South Australia during the data-gathering period, it was illegal to use marijuana, heroin, cocaine and their derivatives, but there was considerable community acceptance at least amongst those aged under 40, for legalisation of personal use of marijuana (McAllister, Moore and Makkai, 1991). From 1984 to 1987 the relevant question in our survey, after those referring to alcohol, cigarettes and medications, was 'Are you regularly using any other drugs (e.g. marijuana)?' At 19.6 years in 1984, 11 per cent of men and 5 per cent of women replied affirmatively. These proportions remained steady during the next five years of the survey, at 9–11 per cent users for men and 3–5 per cent for women, with no particular pattern over time. In the last year the wording of the question was slightly changed, to 'Are you regularly using any illegal drugs?' with options for answers: 4.6 per cent marked yes, marijuana, 0.8 per cent marked yes, hard drugs, 0.2 per cent were taking both; 1.0 per cent marked 'I prefer not to answer', and 93.3 per cent marked no.

Clearly these frequencies are too low to do anything other than aggregate all those concerned even though this may well blur important distinctions between the marihuana users and those taking less socially acceptable drugs. It does appear that marijuana was much the most commonly used of the illicit drugs (Winefield, Winefield, Tiggemann and Smith, 1988).

Illegal drugs and employment

During the first three years (1984–1986 inclusive) there was a significant association for men between taking illegal drugs and being unemployed.

Predictors of drug use

In the 1980 and 1984 demographic and psychological variables described above, there were no significant differences between users of illegal drugs and non-users.

MEDICATIONS

One of the largest sex differences anywhere in the data from this survey comes in the area of the use of prescription drugs. A fairly constant 6–9 per cent of men, and 30–58 per cent of women, reported regular use of these. The very large proportion of women reporting use (58 per cent) came in 1988 when their average age was 23.6; before then the average ranged from 30–35 per cent. In this last year subjects were asked also, to indicate for what conditions these drugs had been prescribed: 52 per cent of women were taking oral contraceptives, 1 per cent suffered from each of headaches and diabetes, 4 per cent from asthma or other allergies and 4 per cent for a heterogeneous mixture of other conditions. Men reported taking medications for asthma (3 per cent) or 'other' conditions (5 per cent).

A constant 1–3 per cent of men and 4–6 per cent of women reported regularly taking non-prescription or over-the-counter drugs 'e.g. aspirin'. This practice was even more closely linked to poor health than was the taking of prescription drugs, which is reasonable in the context that many of the prescription drugs may have had preventive purposes so that people could take them without necessarily defining themselves as sick in consequence.

There were no associations between prescription drug use and employment status with the exception that full-time students were the least likely women to take them in 1988.

HEALTH

How to measure health quantitatively is always a problem for behavioural scientists, as indeed for medical researchers. For some purposes, the outcome 'alive or dead' might be enough information to make useful decisions, but usually we are interested in much subtler distinctions between levels of health and ill health.

Once we reject mortality as a useful index, there are difficulties in describing health numerically. A person with many physical symptoms, for example, may actually be better able to enjoy life and to function independently, than a person with a disabling cognitive dysfunction or even one with severe social anxiety. The World Health Organisation's (1948) definition of health as 'physical, mental and social well-being, not merely the absence of disease and infirmity' reflects the desire of many researchers to capture the quality of life in health measures.

In young people deaths are few and are most commonly caused by accidents and violence (including suicide), rather than by diseases. Checklists of illness symptoms including pain and mobility problems, which might apply to older populations, are therefore not useful. Problems such as headaches, appetite and sleep disorders are often related in youth to psychological stress rather than to disease processes. Thus we are forced to rely on global self-ratings of health, judgements about relative energy levels, and rather insensitive correlates of illness such as doctor visits or medication use. Both of the latter can and do occur in healthy people, of course (e.g. for check-ups and preventive measures, sporting injuries and contraception).

From 1984 to 1988 we asked our subjects to rate their health on a 5-point scale from 'very healthy most of the time' to 'always ill'. Throughout this period there was a marked skew in the answers, with fewer than 10 per cent using any of the three ratings denoting poorer health. Men and women were equally likely to describe themselves as very healthy, even though many more women took prescription drugs than did the men, and each year rather more women than men used non-prescription drugs.

Health and employment

The results of our study provide little evidence for poor health being a reason or a consequence of unemployment in these young people. In 1986 and 1987 the unemployed men had poorer health, and in 1987 the dissatisfied employed men also reported poorer health, but in the other years and for all the women, health and employment were not closely associated. It must be remembered that, as the main focus of the research was upon the psychological aspects of unemployment, the assessment of physical health was not particularly searching.

The relationship between physical health and psychological well-being, however, was shown to be a consistent one. Self-esteem was significantly higher for men and women in good health in three of the five years, depressive affect was lower for women in good health in all five years and for men in four, and the GHQ showed less psychological disturbance in women with good health in four of the years and in men for three. Thus the association of physical health and psychological well-being holds for both sexes, and if anything for women even more reliably than for men.

Health and drugs

Men who drank heavily reported poorer health in 1984 and 1987, and smokers of both sexes reported poorer health in 1984, while women smokers reported poorer health in 1985. Men taking illicit drugs reported poorer health in 1984 and 1987, and women in 1985. Thus the relationship between drug abuse and poorer health, although in the predicted direction, often failed to reach statistical significance and must be concluded to be fairly weak.

As might be expected, poor health was associated with the taking of medication. Both women and men who regularly used prescription drugs reported worse health in two of the five years; an even clearer connection was that between poor health and regular use of non-prescription drugs. This association reached significance in all five years for the women subjects and in two years for the men. It appears therefore that over-the-counter medications cater to those who perceive themselves as unhealthy, while the drugs prescribed by doctors do not necessarily have this meaning, for example for those young women taking the contraceptive pill, which is only available on prescription.

POVERTY

Financial state might be expected to moderate the health effects as well as the psychological effects of unemployment (see Chapters 2 and 5). For example, a person with no paid work but a large inherited income might be thought to be in a psychologically desirable situation, if he or she could obtain Jahoda's 'latent benefits of work' such as sense of purpose and social value, stimulation and social contact, through whatever pursuits filled his or her time. At the same time a person with a steady and even satisfying job might still be severely stressed if the salary earned was not sufficient to meet financial responsibilities.

For these reasons we included self-ratings of financial state in the questionnaire and in this section describe the results in relation to occupational status, drug use and health. Subjects provided a rating of their financial state from 'very comfortable' to 'desperately hard up', and from 7 to 15 per cent of subjects described themselves as hard up or desperately hard up, each year. In the earlier years (1984–1986) the men were slightly more likely to refer to themselves this way than the women, but in the last two years the women tended to express more financial strain than the men. Perhaps this change has something to do with the ages of greatest financial commitments for the two sexes.

Poverty and employment

There was a strong link between being unemployed and describing one's financial state as hard up or desperately hard up. This association was significant for both sexes every year, although the proportion of the unemployed who were experiencing poverty never quite reached half. It is possible of course that some of the unemployed had other sources of income such as an inheritance or work of a casual sort for which they might be paid in cash and which they might not declare for taxation purposes.

Another possibility is that adaptation to unemployment can mean, especially in the young, the development of a frugal life style, perhaps with sharing of resources amongst peers, where well-managed income from welfare payments is indeed adequate for needs. In Australia references to young people who pool their unemployment benefits and live in idle luxury, refusing to search for work, surface whenever there are calls to increase the amount of unemployment benefits. However, the data from this study suggest that for many of the unemployed, there is financial hardship. Whether these young people really have opportunities to find paid work in our declining economy, and whether or not people necessarily regard poverty as undesirable, are wider issues than we can discuss here in any detail. The role of parents in financial support of the young unemployed has not been investigated here.

Perhaps a more surprising finding from our study was the equally clear association between poverty and the condition of being a full-time student.

Again, this association was significant for both sexes every year; in fact the proportion of hard up students was often close to the proportion of hard up unemployed. The government financial support offered to students in Australia is lower than that provided to the unemployed, so it is not surprising that full-time students should report hardship (especially considering the expensive textbooks which many need to buy and the lack of spare time to find casual jobs). These financial stresses contribute to the greater psychological disturbance which Winefield, Tiggemann, Goldney and Winefield (1992) found in academically capable subjects who were still studying at 24.6 years of age, compared to those who had completed their studies and those who had not undertaken higher education. Part-time students, who usually gain income from employment at the same time that they study, suffer other difficulties of role strain and lack of leisure time (Winefield, 1992).

Poverty and drugs

There were no significant associations between being hard up and level of alcohol intake or smoking with the exception that male smokers in the last two years (1987 and 1988) were likely to report being hard up. Consumers of illicit drugs reported being hard up for the females in 1984 and the males in 1987. The only association between poverty and medications was for males taking prescription drugs in 1986.

Poverty and health

The relation between poverty and ill health was always in the same direction, but only reached statistical significance in two of the ten tests over the five-year period. However, especially for the younger men, there was a clear relationship between poverty and psychological distress, with men who reported being hard up scoring lower in self-esteem (1984–1986 inclusive) and higher in depressive affect (1984–1986 inclusive) and psychological disturbance (GHQ: 1984–1985). This finding contrasts with the results for women, which showed a closer connection between poor health and psychological distress.

SUMMARY

This chapter has surveyed a collection of issues which were peripheral to the main hypotheses and goals of the study as it was originally conceived, but which nonetheless have relevance for understanding the process of growing up psychologically during a decade of high unemployment. As the phenomenon of high youth unemployment has not vanished but rather appears to be more and more prevalent, the most comprehensive understanding is needed and some of these results may inspire further investigations. It was unfortunately the case that those who ceased participating in our study tended to be the heavier users of drugs, which reduces the generalisability of our findings to all Australian youth. Yet because of the size and randomness of the original sample, our data are less affected by bias than those in many available reports referring for example to tertiary students only. The material covered in this chapter is based on survey questions answered by the subjects during the five years when their average ages increased from 19.6 to 23.6 years.

As has been concluded by other large-scale surveys, moderate drinking is now modal for well-adjusted young people of both sexes in Australia. The implication which follows is that abstinence is not a realistic goal for health-promotional efforts to adopt: rather educators need to give usable information about what level and pattern of drinking could be regarded as responsible, and how individuals can reach decisions and learn the social skills to implement the habits of alcohol consumption which suit them. With the dangers of binge drinking acknowledged, there is scientific evidence that moderate consumption of alcohol is not necessarily injurious for humans, which contrasts sharply with the current state of our knowledge about cigarettes. Heavy drinking is associated with health and psychological damage for young men in particular.

The proportion of young people who smoke seems to be declining slowly, and the habit is weakly associated with health problems and unemployment. For men aged 19–22, there seemed to be greater consumption of illegal drugs amongst the unemployed. Our results show a high rate of usage of medications, and indicate that regular use of non-prescription drugs especially, is closely related to perceptions of poor health. For women subjects in particular, good physical health and psychological well-being are strongly related.

Financial hardship was a common correlate of being unemployed, and full-time students were equally likely to report living in poverty: a state clearly related to psychological distress for men in the 19–22 age range. The basis for government policies requires fuller information than was gathered here, but it does seem anomalous to encourage young people to undertake higher education without providing them with adequate financial support.

In this chapter as in others, the age of our subjects is a key issue and it seems likely that the relationships between variables would be quite different in older samples. There has been little detailed psychological study of the process of 'growing up' in large and representative Australian samples followed for long periods of time, such as ours. Although the measures described in this chapter were relatively simple ones we believe that the results have value for developmental psychology.

10 Overview

This final chapter will present a discussion of the study and its findings, and then attempt to draw some conclusions. Finally, we will discuss the implications of these, both for further research and for practical strategies in dealing with unemployment in an uncertain future.

DISCUSSION AND IMPLICATIONS

The first general conclusion to emerge is that psychologically, unemployment is a very complex phenomenon. It certainly has some negative consequences, but they are by no means uniform and answers to any of the questions that we have raised are not clear cut.

If the findings themselves are not straightforward, then any recommendations for education or policy are likely to be even less so. Armed with all the information we have gathered, what suggestions can we make? The best we can do is to indicate possible courses of action rather than make firm recommendations.

Work attitudes

Our respondents expressed very positive attitudes to work throughout the study (Chapter 3) and, as mentioned earlier, roughly 90 per cent of those in jobs expressed overall satisfaction with their jobs.

We did not find, as others have done, that employment commitment is a moderating factor in coping with unemployment (Jackson, Stafford, Banks and Warr, 1983). This was a somewhat surprising finding because intuitively it seems likely that a person who is strongly committed to work should find it harder to cope with being unemployed than someone who is not so strongly committed. This result might have been due to the fact that employment commitment was not measured until after our respondents had left school (from 1984). Consequently it is possible that the employment commitment expressed by our unemployed respondents might have been affected by the fact of their being unemployed. Perhaps it is a form of adaptation to redefine one's attitude to the importance of work if one is unemployed. Warr and Jackson (1987), in their study of unemployed men, identified two forms of adaptation: resigned and constructive adaptation. Stokes (1983) similarly, in his study of unemployed young people, found that as a result of redefining their attitudes towards the value of work, the youngsters no longer experienced unemployment as a significant personal crisis. Nevertheless, they had also become 'lethargic, apathetic, disinclined to participate in constructive leisure activities and had little commitment to a society that seemed to be offering no worthwhile future' (Stokes, 1983: 271).

Interestingly, there were some historical changes that we noted, comparing work attitudes expressed in 1986 with those expressed in 1980 from some of the same schools. Not only were the students more optimistic about their chances of employment (which statistically had not improved), but the attitudes of the children of lower socio-economic status in relation to the need for qualifications and the importance of study, had become more similar to those of the children from higher socio-economic status backgrounds.

These findings certainly run counter to the suggestion of some writers, such as Kelvin (1980), that we are witnessing a decline in the work ethic. Kelvin suggests that in a society where full employment is no longer a realistic goal, the value or significance of work will inevitably undergo a gradual decline, so that by the end of the century the work ethic will have been largely eroded. He concedes that such a change in values may be a slow process lagging behind structural changes in society. Even so, our finding provides no evidence to support such a proposition. On the contrary, the young people surveyed, if anything, displayed a heightened level of aspiration. This could have been due to an increase in formal education or, as Jahoda (1982) suggests, to the impact of television presenting a view of life replete with material benefits. On the other hand, it might reflect the importance of latent functions of work, such as social contact and a sense of personal identity, that are additional to its manifest function of earning a living.

While this finding may be reassuring for society as a whole, the attitudes expressed by the students were unrealistic. They expected to find quite high level jobs relatively easily, yet many experienced a very different outcome. In psychodynamic terms, it seems that some defence mechanism, denial perhaps, is in operation whereby young people, although aware of the high unemployment rate, nevertheless do not think it will affect them personally. In this way they are likely to be unprepared for the experience of unemployment.

To the extent that an individual has high unrealistic expectations, the normal negative consequences associated with failure or frustration are likely to be exacerbated. The assumption that jobs are available to all those who try sufficiently hard may serve to maintain motivation. It also, however, implies that an individual who has been unable to obtain a job should feel personally responsible, a view often reinforced by the media and others. This kind of internal causal attribution is what we found led to lowered self-esteem and increased hopelessness (Winefield, Tiggemann and Winefield, 1992b).

So long as attitudes of this kind prevail, society need not fear social disruption from the unemployed. People who believe that they personally will get jobs are unlikely to question why there are so few jobs or to direct their anger and frustration externally towards the system. Instead, they are likely to direct them internally and become apathetic and depressed, like the unemployed workers in Marienthal (Jahoda, Lazarsfeld and Zeisel, 1933). They will perceive themselves as failed members of a reasonable society rather than victims of an unjust social system.

The question arises as to whether this can be avoided. A devaluation of work may indeed be the most psychologically adaptive response for the unemployed young person, although it may not be desirable for society as a whole. Perhaps there are other strategies that may assist the individual in coping with unemployment that do not share this socially undesirable characteristic.

Psychological well-being

One very clear conclusion from this study is that employment status does have significant psychological consequences for the young person. It has confirmed the observations from other studies, both anecdotal and systematic, that the young unemployed are generally less well adjusted than their employed counterparts. The picture presented by the media of unemployed youngsters as bored, lonely, depressed and watching a lot of daytime TV is not inaccurate, for many.

Our interest, however, extended beyond merely documenting differences to understanding how they arose. The overall finding was that the negative consequences of unemployment were, in most cases, lost benefits rather than absolute losses. That is, in general, getting a job results in an improvement in psychological well-being rather than unemployment resulting in a decline. Closer analysis of those in jobs, however, revealed that the psychological benefits were restricted to those (admittedly the large majority) who were satisfied with their jobs. The rest were generally no better off than the unemployed. This should not be seen as an excuse for complacency, however. It suggests that satisfying paid work is an important factor leading to healthy psycho-social development in the young person. Without it, there may well be a real danger that they will not develop a satisfactory self-concept or sense of identity, as Erikson (1959, 1971) has suggested. That the psychological damage due to unsatisfactory employment was comparable to that due to unemployment, was an unexpected finding with implications that we cannot fully explore here. We do not know why some respondents felt dissatisfied with their work. Perhaps some felt underemployed, some disliked the nature of the work, or the pay, or the supervisors or workmates, and some may have experienced disappointment at not gaining some different, preferred form of employment. The fact is that in our sample those who expressed overall satisfaction with their jobs tended to express satisfaction with all aspects of their jobs. Similarly, those who expressed dissatisfaction tended to express dissatisfaction with all aspects of their jobs. It seems that the young are somewhat undiscriminating about their conditions of employment.

Without more information we would not feel justified in advising young dissatisfied workers to change to a more satisfactory job for the sake of their psychological well-being. Whether resigning oneself to the job one has, or agitating to improve the unsatisfactory aspects, would be helpful strategies must be a question for future research.

Leaving school

It seems clear that school leavers are a special group and findings from observations on older workers may not generalise to them. The school leaver who fails to obtain a job is often in much the same position of dependence as when he or she was still at school. It is the school leaver who obtains a full-time job who experiences a significant change in status. Also, of course the older unemployed worker who is made redundant is almost certain to experience a reduced standard of living, as will his (or her) dependents, and may well have little or no prospect of re-employment at a similar level.

While our study was concerned primarily with the effects of employment status, we also learned a lot about the effects of leaving school. Although we were not surprised to observe that youngsters who left school and became employed displayed improvements in self-esteem and depressive affect, we were surprised to observe similar, albeit less marked, improvements in those who became unemployed.

Contrary to expectation, in many ways it seems as if leaving school, rather than getting a job, is the more psychologically significant transitional event in the young person's life. In the past, with more or less full employment, the two events have been almost perfectly correlated, unlike the situation today.

While getting a job may be seen as a sign of adulthood, perhaps leaving school is seen as the end of childhood. It usually entails leaving an authoritarian environment, becoming responsible for oneself and receiving an independent income, even if only the dole. If this is an accurate representation, then the young unemployed person is trapped between the worlds of childhood and adulthood.

Unemployment in the young, then, may be viewed as a transition problem. It occurs in the context of many other physical, political and social changes. As such it is perhaps best viewed from a developmental perspective. Erikson's (1959) fifth stage which regards healthy ego development as dependent upon a satisfactory occupational identity seems particularly appropriate. Such a perspective is consistent with most of the findings reported from our study.

While the satisfactorily employed young person continues to develop and gain in self-esteem and general well-being, the young unemployed person is denied this opportunity. This may well be one of the more important differences between the young job seeker and the redundant older worker.

The individual response

The questions arise as to what practical advice can be given to young people to enable them to avoid unemployment or, should they become unemployed, how best to cope with the experience.

In Chapter 7 we drew attention to factors that are relevant in predicting who is most likely to become unemployed. This sort of information, unfortunately, is unlikely to be of much help to the individual, since most of the predictors of unemployment are not controllable. For example, low socio-economic status, a non-English-speaking background and having an unemployed member of the immediate family are not factors that the individual normally has much influence over. It might be advocated that the length of education be extended, but even that recommendation presupposes the necessary intellectual ability to succeed. It is entirely possible that individuals of low academic ability who choose to prolong their schooling beyond the minimum level required by law, may actually damage rather than improve their chances of getting a job. We discuss this approach further in the next section.

Unfortunately, if, as seems to be the case, the economy is only able to sustain a fixed, insufficient number of jobs, individuals who take steps to strengthen their own chances must inevitably weaken the chances of others. Thus, courses designed to develop job-getting skills, such as interview techniques and grooming, are likely to result in a re-ordering of the queue, rather than more young people getting jobs. The disappearance of many entry-level jobs due to automation and restructuring of the workforce is not likely to be reversed in the foreseeable future.

In Chapter 4, we attempted to identify successful strategies for coping with unemployment. We found that those young people who had access to friends and confidants (social support), whose financial situation was secure and who used their time in constructive activities involving other people, coped best.

On the basis of these observations, we would advise unemployed young people to try to maintain a social support network of friends. As well as taking steps to maintain and develop social contacts, they should try to engage in activities with other people, such as sport, political lobby groups, crafts, voluntary work and so on. Parents who do not encourage their unemployed sons and daughters to engage in these sorts of activities, or who actively discourage them from doing so, may be doing them a great disservice. Socially structured, purposeful activity seems to be the most effective way of coping successfully with both unemployment and unsatisfactory employment.

The school response

It is clear that the educational system is by no means to blame for the current high level of youth unemployment. Employers and others who blame lowered literacy and numeracy standards overlook the fact that economic factors are the main reason, rather than the personal inadequacies of the job seekers. Nonetheless, the situation does focus renewed attention on educational policy. This section looks at some of the educational implications of our findings.

Until recent years, young people would move from high school to a job or else continue their education at a tertiary institution. The transition often presented difficulties of adjustment, but these were usually overcome. Now, many young people spend a period of time unemployed after leaving school, and some may never get jobs. Moreover, as the unemployment rate rises, so does the average unemployment duration and the longer someone has been unemployed, the more difficult it becomes to find work. Some join various government sponsored work experience schemes, or undertake courses in vocational training or courses to improve literacy and/or numeracy skills. The education system as a whole needs to be aware of these various possibilities. What is required is a responsible and flexible system designed to accommodate all young people. The diversity of economic, social, cultural and academic backgrounds of students must be recognised and, where appropriate, different learning models implemented. The prevailing economic and social context also needs to be taken into account. The ideal of developing the potential of every individual to the full is particularly important when economic conditions restrict job opportunities.

The fact that leaving school seems to produce such a marked improvement in psychological well-being, particularly for those getting jobs, suggests that some school environments might well be modified so as to promote greater responsibility, independence and autonomy in students. Similarly, it is no doubt desirable to instil into all students the notion that education is a life-long process, and that adult re-entry into formal education is feasible at any stage.

The treatment of senior high school students in a more adult way may also help to ameliorate one of the sad findings of our study. Students at school were shown to have relatively low self-esteem and to be relatively high in depression and negative mood. This was particularly evident in the girls. Any program that can improve this situation would clearly be desirable on a number of grounds. As well as improving the morale of the students themselves, it would no doubt also produce in them a more positive attitude towards school, and perhaps to education generally, as well as making the task of the teachers more pleasant. Also, it should improve the ability of students to cope, should they become unemployed after leaving school. (According to learned helplessness theory, prior experience of mastery over one's environment should provide immunisation against the potentially negative consequences of subsequent exposure to uncontrollable outcomes.)

A question that is sometimes raised is whether high school students should be offered education about unemployment. Courses could be made available that looked at economic and political structures, as well as the history of unemployment. Improving the understanding of the external causes of unemployment might well make it easier for the unemployed individual to reduce the amount of guilt experienced. On the other hand, it could also lead to social disruption. Illich (1978) argues for a redefinition, so that unemployment could be seen as 'a condition for autonomous, useful work' (Illich, 1978: 84). Windschuttle (1979), however, argues that such a redefinition of work is not feasible within modern capitalistic society, and suggests instead that, 'The most useful activity to end unemployment is to engage in political struggle to change the nature of the economic system that created it' (Windschuttle, 1979: 275). Although Windschuttle does not advocate the overthrow of capitalist institutions, educating young people about the economic causes of unemployment could well result in them developing radical, even militant, political attitudes.

Another possible strategy that has sometimes been suggested, is to try to educate students for unemployment. This notion has been resisted by teachers on the ground that they perceive their role as to educate for employment rather than for unemployment. Also, they fear that to acknowledge that some students will become unemployed may produce an attitude of resignation and thus weaken ambition and determination to succeed. A possible solution might be to teach basic survival skills which are generally acquired by all adults without being specifically taught: interpersonal and parenting skills; knowledge about legal, medical and welfare systems; how to rent houses; where to buy cheap clothes; how to buy and cook cheap nutritious food, etc. Such information would be useful to many young people, and of particular value to those who are not affluent and to the unemployed.

Unemployed people are deprived not only financially, but also of various other benefits usually provided by a job. Some of the negative consequences, as we have shown, can be mitigated by engaging in appropriate forms of unpaid activity. Students could be taught and encouraged to develop an interest in such activities. Moreover, they could also be taught that an individual's worth depends not only on occupational status and wealth but also on the intrinsic value of what he or she does – the extent to which it benefits other people. Such a change of attitude may take a long time to achieve, but, if successful could benefit not only the unemployed, but others who are engaged in productive but unpaid work, such as housewives.

These suggestions all have political and emotional overtones that are likely to frighten some people. Probably one of the greatest fears is that there may be a decline in the work ethic. A recent study by Shamir (1986b) produced some reassuring results in this context. Shamir proposed that the general commitment to work is represented by two related, but not identical concepts: work involvement and the Protestant work ethic, defining the former as 'a normative belief in the value of work in one's life' (Shamir, 1986b: 27) and the latter as 'a belief in the value of hard work and frugality which acts as a defence against sloth, sensuality, sexual temptation and religious doubt' (Shamir, 1986b: 27).

Analysis of cross-sectional and longitudinal data from 432 unemployed people showed that individuals with high work involvement were likely to suffer more from unemployment and to gain more from finding employment than low work-involved individuals. Protestant work ethic endorsement, on the other hand, did not moderate the relationship between employment status and psychological state. These results suggest that it may be possible to modify young people's commitment to work, without at the same time changing their adherence to the work ethic, and that such a change could help them to cope with unemployment.

The societal response

Governments and employers can choose to respond to the problem of unemployment in a number of ways. The introduction of structural changes such as job-sharing, shorter working hours or job creation could remove the problem. However, the economic costs of such solutions are likely to make them unacceptable.

Assuming the inevitability of a large number of young people being out of work, what is required are organisational structures designed to enable them to cope with a minimum of personal distress and social alienation. We have suggested that unemployment seems to retard normal psycho-social development in the young school leaver. If this is so, an important goal must be to provide alternative means which will foster this development. In a number of countries, including Australia, governments have introduced short-term work experience schemes designed to help the young unemployed school leaver. As yet there have been few evaluation studies aimed at assessing the psychological effects of such programs. Understandably, the main question of interest has been whether they improve the participants' chances of obtaining regular employment. However, several such evaluation studies have been reported from Britain on the psychological impact of the Youth Opportunities Program (YOP) which was introduced in 1978 in order to provide work experience for 16–18-year-olds. In general, the results have not been encouraging. The first psychological evaluation study was carried out by Stafford (1982). She compared three groups of youngsters: YOP participants, employed and unemployed, and used the General Health Questionnaire (GHQ-12) as her measure of well-being. Her results led her to conclude that 'YOP only acts as a temporary buffer against the detrimental psychological effects of unemployment, and that on leaving YOP this effect is replaced by the psychological impact of unemployment' (Stafford, 1982: 19).

Even more pessimistic conclusions have been expressed by other researchers. Oddy, Donovan and Pardoe (1984), for example, are sceptical about even the ongoing psychological benefits of participation in YOP. They found that in general YOP participants occupied an intermediate position between employed and unemployed youngsters on a range of measures of psychological well-being. However, more disturbingly, they also found that in a number of respects the YOP participants resembled the unemployed more than the employed. For example, they were very much aware that they had not succeeded in obtaining a 'proper' job, and expressed much less optimism about the future than those with permanent jobs. Moreover, they expressed less perceived control over their lives than either the employed or unemployed groups as measured by Rotter's Locus of Control Scale (Rotter, 1966).

Branthwaite and Garcia (1985) also question the psychological benefits of YOP and similar schemes. They compared four groups of youngsters on the Beck Depression Inventory (Beck, Ward, Mendelson, Mock and Erbaugh, 1961), finding significant differences between them such that the employed were less depressed than the other groups. However, the two groups on Youth Opportunities Schemes were intermediate, but did not differ significantly from the unemployed. The findings from this study, however, need to be treated with caution because it suffered from a number of methodological flaws. For example, the groups were not matched for sex, even though girls are known to score higher than boys on depression inventories. Also the groups were very small.

Since the early 1980s, the YOP in Britain has been replaced by an extended two-year apprenticeship program, the Youth Training Scheme (YTS), which unlike its predecessor requires no qualifying period of unemployment for entry. Although there is evidence that the YTS confers some ongoing psychological benefits to those engaged upon it (Hendry and Raymond, 1986), its overall value has been called into question:

> Economic and social changes portend a number of paradoxes for young people. First, the present position of youth in society has been structured by government policy. Instead of developing a potentially flexible, innovatively-minded future workforce training schemes offer low status, relatively poorly rewarded two-year 'apprenticeships' with no guarantees of full worker status on completion of training. Second, it is now law that adolescents *must* join a Youth Training Scheme to enable them to claim social benefits, yet prospective employers need not be involved in this arrangement. Hence, in some areas of the country there are insufficient places for young people to join schemes: Thus YTS opportunities are extremely restricted in some regions.
>
> (Coleman and Hendry, 1990: 190)

Just as temporary work experience schemes may be no real substitute for a 'proper' job, some low level jobs that are seen as well below what the individual is capable of, or indeed qualified to perform, may be viewed in the same light. This raises the question which we have previously addressed, of whether any job is necessarily better than no job at all. The answer to this question, at least for young people, although not necessarily for mature workers with dependents and financial commitments, is undoubtedly negative. For the young person still living with parents, unemployment seems to be no worse than being employed in an unsatisfactory job, even though the latter may pay better.

Policy implications

Government policy varies somewhat from country to country, but in all countries the main emphasis seems to be to improve the skills of the unemployed so as to make them employable. In the case of young people, this takes the form of encouraging them to stay on at school beyond the minimum leaving age, encouraging schools to offer more vocationally oriented, as opposed to academic courses, as well as initiating job creation and work experience programs of the kind described in the previous section.

There are two potential problems associated with increasing the number who stay on at school. The first is that those who are not academically capable may fail to improve their qualifications even with additional schooling. This may well involve a financial penalty in that while they were at school they did not receive any social security benefits or other financial payment. Second, even if they do succeed in improving their qualifications they still may not get a job. Nevertheless, following an analysis of national cohort data in Britain, Payne concluded:

> continuing full-time education can offer benefits even to those of relatively low academic potential, and perhaps more attention should be paid to the role that school and college can play in the vocational education of a generation for whom there are very few jobs.
>
> (Payne, 1987: 444)

A more pessimistic view about the long-term benefits of improving the vocational skills of the unemployed has been expressed recently by Dooley and Catalano (1988):

> A striking similarity among the programs on both sides of the Atlantic is the emphasis on improving the job skills of the unemployed . . . such an approach assumes that the labor market can absorb persons whose skills have been enhanced. Yet . . . the number of secure jobs is decreasing in most of the Western democracies. It is, we believe, reasonable to assume that the effectiveness of skill-enhancement programs will decline with increasing competition for a decreasing number of stable jobs. This assumption raises the troubling possibility that efforts to improve coping skills could become a means of social control that encourages resignation to lower standards of living. This is possible because the alternative coping strategy is to pursue political action that would redistribute wealth. Since many of the institutions that sponsor programs for the unemployed are controlled by those who benefit from the status quo, there is likely to be little support for teaching coping strategies that encourage political action.
>
> (Dooley and Catalano, 1988: 10)

A recent paper by Kieselbach and Svensson (1988) has argued that the psychological damage caused by unemployment is recognised in some European countries better than it is in Britain and North America. For example, they point out that Swedish studies have demonstrated considerable psychological and health strains caused by unemployment, even though in Sweden the unemployed receive a benefit of 90% of their previous net income during the first year of unemployment, so that unemployment does not lead to a dramatic fall in living standards.

Two opposing views concerning the effects of unemployment on health have been expressed recently by Kagan (1987) and Smith (1991). According to Kagan:

> Poverty and the psycho-social stressors that cause ill health in unemployment are not its inevitable consequence. Unemployment in the absence of such stressors can occur and then it is a zealously guarded privilege.
>
> (Kagan, 1987: 218)

Smith (1991) takes a radically different view. According to him: 'The evidence that unemployment kills – particularly the middle aged – now verges on the irrefutable' (Smith, 1991: 606). How can such seemingly contradictory statements be reconciled? First, it appears that Kagan's notion of unemployment is rather more akin to lack of employment. It is hard otherwise, to accept his suggestion that unemployment could conceivably be 'a thoroughly enjoyable experience'. The unemployed are usually defined as people who are seeking full-time employment, and the fact that they are seeking it unsuccessfully must mean that they are frustrated.

Most writers seem to be agreed that one of the main, if not the main, sources of unemployment distress is poverty, particularly in the middle-aged. Some have urged that unemployment benefits should be increased (Smith, 1991); others have argued for a guaranteed 'basic income' for all (Watts, 1987). The dilemma facing politicians and other policy makers is that if the unemployed are paid enough to live satisfactory and fulfilling lives they may well choose to remain unemployed. Moreover, such a situation would be unsustainable unless sufficient wealth could be generated by those who are employed.

Although poverty did not appear to be a major source of stress in our sample of young unemployed people, because of attrition bias (relatively more of the unemployed and dissatisfied employed dropped out), we may well have under-estimated its importance. Certainly, financial resources emerged as an important factor moderating the psychological effects of unemployment on psychological well-being. We do not believe that improving the financial situation of young unemployed people would be likely to reduce their desire for a good job, and would enable them to cope better with being unemployed. On the other hand, measures that worsen their financial situation are likely to have adverse effects, and some of the measures introduced in recent years in Australia fall into this category.

In the past year, for example, young unemployed Australians (under 21) have had their unemployment benefits cut, now only have access to extensive (more than 3–4 weeks) additional training schemes provided that they are over 18 and have been unemployed for more than a year and are increasingly coerced to take any offer of employment and are allowed to undertake no more than 20 days of voluntary work per year.

Methodological strengths and weaknesses

We have drawn attention to the potential advantages of a prospective longitudinal research design in studying the psychological impact of unemployment on school leavers. Unlike cross-sectional studies that can only identify the psychological correlates of employment status, longitudinal studies can suggest causal connections, and hopefully distinguish between antecedents (or predisposing factors) and consequences.

Our prospective longitudinal study, because of its size, because it was not confined to academic under-achievers and because the occupational groups were well matched on at-school baseline measures, allows us to draw more definite conclusions about the causal link between employment status and psychological well-being than is the case with many other similar studies.

As we pointed out in earlier chapters, the fact that unemployed youngsters show lower self-esteem and are more depressed than those in jobs does not in itself imply a definite causal link. People who are depressed and whose self-esteem is low are likely to project a poor self-image that makes them unattractive to prospective employers. Another possibility is that youngsters who fail to get jobs lose self-esteem and become depressed, whereas the ones who get jobs maintain the same levels of self-esteem and depressive affect.

Although both of these scenarios are perfectly plausible neither was supported by our findings. It was those who got jobs (at least satisfactory jobs) who showed the change in well-being and not the others. Of course, this conclusion itself depends on the fact that the comparison groups were well matched initially. Had they not been matched while they were at school, any later difference would have been difficult to interpret. We claim no credit for this matching. In non-experimental research, any matching of this kind is purely fortuitous. Nevertheless, the initial matching was one of the main strengths of the study.

We must also acknowledge some shortcomings associated with the study. We have drawn attention to the problem of selective attrition. As in most longitudinal studies of young people, those who drop out tend to differ systematically from those who stay in. This means that the eventual sample must differ from the original sample and may no longer be representative. We found, for example, that the drop outs tended to be of lower academic ability, lower socio-economic status and from non-English-speaking backgrounds. They also exhibited greater externality in locus of control, and were more likely to smoke, drink alcohol and use drugs, both prescribed and illicit (Winefield, Winefield and Tiggemann, 1990). Most of the differences were slight, however, and did not seriously compromise the external validity of the study (Hansen, Collins, Malotte, Johnson and Fielding, 1985). Our findings were similar to those that have been reported in North American longitudinal studies of young people by Brook, Cohen and Gordon (1983), Hansen, Collins, Malotte, Johnson and Fielding (1985), Jessor and Jessor (1977), Josephson and Rosen (1978), McAlister and Gordon (1986), Newcomb (1986) and Newcomb and Bentler (1988).

On the other hand, we also found that the drop out rate was higher amongst the unemployed and dissatisfied employed groups than amongst the satisfied employed and tertiary students (Winefield, Tiggemann and Winefield, 1991a). However, these status-related differences in attrition were not related to pre-test scores on our dependent measures or to background characteristics. We conclude therefore, that although the internal validity of our study is partially compromised by attrition bias, this is unlikely to distort our main conclusions.

A more serious weakness of our study concerns our classification of individuals. First, we classified people into groups on the basis of their responses at single points in time, a procedure that does not allow us to distinguish those who were employed intermittently. Second, we did not control for possible effects of repeated testing of the same individuals. Third, we did not study in detail specific aspects of employment and unemployment that might have produced the observed effects. These shortcomings all point the way to methodological improvements in future research.

FINAL COMMENTS

In many ways our study has raised more questions than it has answered. The whole issue of unemployment is complex and must be viewed within its social context. Future technological advances seem likely to reduce still further the number of available jobs. Thus, without major structural changes the prospect of large numbers of permanently unemployed people is a very real one. In turn, while we continue to accept gaining a job as a marker of adult identity, unemployment seems likely to have negative consequences for psychological well-being. The resultant problems for both the individual and for society cross disciplinary boundaries and need to be addressed by social scientists from a variety of fields.

The overall conclusion that seems to have emerged from our own study is that psychological well-being in young people depends on having a satisfactory job. Even tertiary students, although better off than the unemployed and the dissatisfied employed, suffered by comparison with the satisfied employed. However, these differences in well-being arose through an improvement shown by the satisfied employed (and, to a lesser extent, the tertiary students) rather than to a deterioration by the other groups. To some extent, merely leaving school, particularly for girls, was beneficial to well-being. Our initial sample of high school students displayed very positive work attitudes. Although a high commitment to work, as well as a high level of job satisfaction, was also exhibited after they had left school, the later results could well have been distorted by selective attrition. We found that the factors that seemed most important in helping our young people to cope with both unemployment and unsatisfactory employment were social support, financial security and using their time in constructive activities involving other people. We hope that future policies addressing the problem of youth unemployment will be informed by these findings.

Appendix

Table 4.1 Means (and standard deviations) on four psychological scales, 1980–1981

		At-school N = 1120 (594 M, 526 F)	Employed N = 617 (310 M, 307 F)	Unemployed N = 144 (58 M, 86 F)	Tertiary students N = 251 (129 M, 122 F)
Scale					
Self-esteem					
1980	Males	8.19 (1.96)	8.20 (1.90)	7.42 (2.17)	8.47 (1.75)
	Females	7.54 (2.15)	7.25 (2.14)	7.27 (2.24)	7.75 (2.13)
	Combined	7.89 (2.08)	7.56 (2.29)	7.26 (2.31)	8.12 (1.97)
1981	Males	8.41 (1.81)	8.61 (1.91)	7.86 (2.13)	8.30 (2.36)
	Females	7.80 (2.13)	8.36 (1.93)	7.88 (2.22)	8.40 (2.12)
	Combined	8.12 (1.99)	8.29 (2.28)	7.59 (2.55)	8.35 (2.24)
Depressive affect					
1980	Males	1.23 (1.16)	1.27 (1.24)	1.55 (1.40)	1.29 (1.30)
	Females	1.38 (1.23)	1.55 (1.32)	1.57 (1.41)	1.34 (1.18)
	Combined	1.30 (1.19)	1.40 (1.28)	1.56 (1.40)	1.31 (1.24)
1981	Males	1.12 (1.18)	1.11 (1.33)	1.79 (1.56)	1.29 (1.39)
	Females	1.25 (1.21)	1.05 (1.23)	1.38 (1.51)	1.10 (1.18)
	Combined	1.18 (1.20)	1.08 (1.28)	1.55 (1.54)	1.20 (1.29)
Locus of control					
1980	Males	13.04 (5.02)	13.25 (5.13)	15.27 (5.44)	11.42 (4.48)
	Females	13.92 (5.23)	14.46 (5.14)	13.85 (5.63)	12.48 (4.62)
	Combined	13.45 (5.14)	13.59 (5.48)	14.06 (5.94)	11.93 (4.57)
1981	Males	12.50 (5.18)	11.95 (5.14)	13.16 (4.83)	10.12 (4.28)
	Females	12.50 (5.11)	12.66 (5.03)	12.10 (5.44)	10.16 (4.71)
	Combined	12.50 (5.14)	12.12 (5.27)	12.35 (5.45)	10.14 (4.48)
Negative mood					
1980	Males	12.55 (2.57)	12.77 (2.91)	12.98 (3.37)	13.21 (2.82)
	Females	13.25 (2.77)	13.49 (2.80)	13.46 (3.31)	13.38 (2.47)
	Combined	12.88 (2.69)	13.13 (2.88)	13.27 (3.33)	13.29 (2.65)
1981	Males	12.71 (2.77)	12.21 (2.84)	13.35 (3.43)	12.47 (2.46)
	Females	13.13 (2.86)	12.41 (2.76)	14.04 (3.47)	12.23 (2.41)
	Combined	12.91 (2.82)	12.31 (2.80)	13.76 (3.46)	12.36 (2.43)

Group

Table 4.2 Means (and standard deviations) on four psychological scales, 1980–1982

Scale		At-school N = 374 (182 M, 192 F)	Employed N = 803 (402 M, 401 F)	Unemployed N = 121 (61 M, 60 F)	Tertiary students N = 338 (187 M, 151 F)
Self-esteem					
1980	Males	8.30 (1.74)	8.21 (1.82)	7.49 (2.29)	8.59 (1.47)
	Females	7.66 (2.02)	7.32 (2.05)	7.57 (2.41)	7.72 (2.04)
	Combined	7.97 (2.03)	7.77 (2.21)	7.53 (2.45)	8.17 (1.88)
1982	Males	8.57 (1.47)	8.84 (1.64)	8.47 (2.00)	8.81 (1.63)
	Females	8.13 (1.89)	8.61 (1.74)	8.42 (1.96)	8.65 (1.75)
	Combined	8.33 (1.76)	8.73 (2.01)	8.45 (2.46)	8.75 (2.02)
Depressive affect					
1980	Males	1.25 (1.13)	1.29 (1.24)	1.71 (1.31)	1.23 (1.18)
	Females	1.35 (1.21)	1.58 (1.24)	1.53 (1.42)	1.35 (1.22)
	Combined	1.30 (1.73)	1.44 (1.26)	1.62 (1.37)	1.27 (1.21)
1982	Males	1.16 (1.27)	0.94 (1.19)	1.25 (1.58)	1.05 (1.28)
	Females	1.37 (1.20)	1.01 (1.13)	1.40 (1.38)	0.98 (1.12)
	Combined	1.26 (1.23)	0.98 (1.16)	1.33 (1.47)	1.02 (1.22)
Locus of control					
1980	Males	12.83 (4.60)	12.96 (4.79)	15.03 (6.16)	11.90 (4.55)
	Females	14.12 (4.62)	14.67 (4.93)	14.32 (5.25)	12.88 (4.87)
	Combined	13.47 (4.84)	13.82 (5.25)	14.68 (5.81)	12.36 (4.96)
1982	Males	10.28 (4.70)	10.07 (4.38)	11.59 (4.71)	8.85 (4.23)
	Females	10.90 (4.56)	11.14 (4.88)	11.01 (4.55)	9.32 (4.16)
	Combined	10.58 (4.70)	10.61 (4.90)	11.30 (4.70)	9.06 (4.34)
Negative mood					
1980	Males	12.40 (2.42)	12.72 (2.76)	13.79 (3.27)	12.85 (2.75)
	Females	12.89 (2.71)	13.50 (2.79)	13.48 (2.94)	13.45 (2.83)
	Combined	12.65 (2.58)	13.11 (2.80)	13.63 (3.10)	13.12 (2.80)
1982	Males	12.52 (2.80)	11.82 (2.75)	13.13 (3.55)	12.35 (2.61)
	Females	13.19 (3.01)	12.16 (2.71)	13.31 (3.44)	11.93 (2.54)
	Combined	12.86 (2.92)	11.99 (2.73)	13.22 (3.48)	12.16 (2.58)

Table 4.3 Means (and standard deviations) on four psychological scales, 1980–1983

		Group		
Scale		Employed N = 813 (386 M, 427 F)	Unemployed N = 138 (70 M, 68 F)	Tertiary students N = 375 (196 M, 179 F)
Self-esteem				
1980	Males	8.00 (2.15)	8.07 (1.86)	8.46 (1.73)
	Females	7.36 (2.23)	6.83 (2.27)	7.79 (1.91)
	Combined	7.66 (2.21)	7.46 (2.16)	8.14 (1.84)
1983	Males	8.81 (1.76)	7.77 (2.47)	8.75 (1.74)
	Females	8.71 (1.98)	7.44 (2.72)	8.80 (1.99)
	Combined	8.76 (1.88)	7.61 (2.60)	8.78 (1.86)
Depressive affect				
1980	Males	1.30 (1.27)	1.39 (1.21)	1.30 (1.20)
	Females	1.46 (1.24)	1.77 (1.42)	1.30 (1.21)
	Combined	1.39 (1.27)	1.58 (1.21)	1.30 (1.20)
1983	Males	0.88 (1.23)	1.61 (1.64)	1.09 (1.33)
	Females	0.90 (1.11)	1.58 (1.46)	1.10 (1.23)
	Combined	0.89 (1.23)	1.60 (1.64)	1.09 (1.33)
Locus of control				
1980	Males	12.88 (5.42)	14.20 (4.89)	11.84 (4.85)
	Females	14.37 (5.15)	14.91 (6.16)	12.25 (4.42)
	Combined	13.66 (5.33)	14.55 (5.54)	12.03 (4.64)
1983	Males	9.59 (5.01)	11.76 (4.58)	8.68 (4.31)
	Females	10.32 (4.83)	10.98 (5.77)	8.57 (4.27)
	Combined	9.97 (4.93)	11.38 (5.21)	8.63 (4.28)
Negative mood				
1980	Males	12.74 (2.67)	13.26 (2.97)	12.90 (2.64)
	Females	13.34 (2.78)	13.62 (3.21)	13.16 (2.52)
	Combined	13.06 (2.74)	13.44 (3.09)	13.02 (2.61)
1983	Males	12.00 (2.55)	13.47 (3.41)	12.22 (2.66)
	Females	12.11 (2.73)	13.72 (3.12)	12.22 (2.45)
	Combined	12.06 (2.64)	13.60 (3.26)	12.22 (2.56)

Table 4.4 Means (and standard deviations) on four psychological scales, 1980–1984

	Group			
Scale	Satisfied employed N = 588 (263 M, 325 F)	Dissatisfied employed N = 76 (37 M, 39 F)	Unemployed N = 78 (41 M, 37 F)	Tertiary students N = 228 (128 M, 100 F)
Self-esteem				
1980 Males	8.25 (1.93)	8.19 (1.89)	7.76 (1.93)	8.45 (1.77)
Females	7.47 (2.04)	6.54 (2.43)	7.09 (2.20)	8.21 (1.81)
Combined	7.82 (2.03)	7.33 (2.33)	7.44 (2.08)	8.34 (1.78)
1984 Males	9.11 (1.35)	8.14 (2.26)	8.17 (2.15)	8.65 (1.76)
Females	8.78 (1.71)	8.03 (1.75)	7.98 (2.23)	9.08 (1.40)
Combined	8.93 (1.57)	8.08 (2.00)	8.08 (2.18)	8.84 (1.62)
Depressive affect				
1980 Males	1.28 (1.29)	1.31 (1.17)	1.68 (1.35)	1.17 (1.07)
Females	1.49 (1.31)	1.46 (1.27)	1.11 (1.07)	1.33 (1.22)
Combined	1.40 (1.31)	1.39 (1.22)	1.41 (1.25)	1.24 (1.14)
1984 Males	0.67 (0.95)	1.52 (1.72)	1.67 (1.51)	1.10 (1.23)
Females	0.78 (0.96)	1.28 (1.09)	1.46 (1.41)	0.94 (1.24)
Combined	0.73 (0.96)	1.39 (1.42)	1.57 (1.45)	1.03 (1.23)
Locus of control				
1980 Males	12.65 (5.45)	12.64 (4.78)	13.18 (5.10)	11.67 (4.77)
Females	14.16 (5.17)	14.70 (4.36)	13.70 (5.18)	11.53 (4.60)
Combined	13.48 (5.35)	13.71 (4.65)	13.43 (5.11)	11.61 (4.68)
1984 Males	9.17 (5.41)	10.29 (5.36)	11.49 (5.76)	8.03 (4.86)
Females	10.26 (5.26)	11.39 (5.37)	11.64 (5.52)	7.66 (4.32)
Combined	9.76 (5.35)	10.86 (5.36)	11.56 (5.61)	7.87 (4.62)
Negative mood				
1980 Males	12.62 (2.63)	13.86 (2.95)	13.08 (3.68)	12.62 (2.19)
Females	13.31 (2.72)	14.44 (3.00)	12.89 (3.16)	12.80 (2.74)
Combined	13.00 (2.70)	14.16 (2.97)	12.99 (3.42)	12.70 (2.45)
1984 Males	11.90 (2.69)	14.31 (4.00)	13.66 (3.50)	12.24 (2.91)
Females	11.85 (2.45)	13.41 (2.93)	13.70 (3.22)	12.05 (3.27)
Combined	11.88 (2.55)	13.85 (3.50)	13.68 (3.34)	12.16 (3.06)

Source: Winefield, Tiggemann and Goldney (1988)

Table 4.5 Means (and standard deviations) on four psychological scales, 1980–1985

	Group			
Scale	Satisfied employed N = 463 (214 M, 249 F)	Dissatisfied employed N = 47 (22 M, 25 F)	Unemployed N = 39 (16 M, 23 F)	Tertiary students N = 143 (78 M, 65F)
Self-esteem				
1980 Males	8.36 (1.79)	8.23 (2.00)	7.75 (2.41)	8.30 (1.77)
Females	7.40 (2.11)	7.16 (2.59)	6.46 (2.86)	7.94 (1.83)
Combined	7.84 (2.02)	7.66 (2.37)	6.99 (2.72)	8.14 (1.80)
1985 Males	9.25 (1.22)	8.44 (2.49)	7.86 (2.32)	8.61 (1.63)
Females	8.97 (1.51)	9.16 (1.25)	8.61 (2.44)	9.20 (1.39)
Combined	9.10 (1.39)	8.82 (1.94)	8.32 (2.37)	8.80 (1.55)
Depressive affect				
1980 Males	1.17 (1.24)	1.45 (1.30)	1.56 (1.41)	1.15 (1.02)
Females	1.43 (1.28)	1.72 (1.46)	1.39 (1.23)	1.37 (1.26)
Combined	1.31 (1.27)	1.60 (1.38)	1.46 (1.29)	1.25 (1.14)
1985 Males	0.63 (0.91)	1.32 (1.81)	1.44 (1.41)	1.17 (1.32)
Females	0.71 (0.83)	1.04 (1.30)	1.04 (1.43)	0.87 (1.12)
Combined	0.67 (0.87)	1.17 (1.55)	1.21 (1.42)	1.04 (1.24)
Locus of control				
1980 Males	11.86 (5.18)	13.59 (4.89)	15.97 (5.73)	11.38 (4.73)
Females	13.90 (5.28)	15.58 (5.23)	14.25 (5.89)	12.44 (4.77)
Combined	12.96 (5.33)	14.65 (5.12)	14.95 (5.81)	11.86 (4.76)
1985 Males	8.08 (4.69)	10.17 (4.74)	11.85 (5.94)	7.71 (4.52)
Females	9.70 (4.48)	9.36 (5.09)	12.06 (5.43)	8.27 (4.56)
Combined	8.95 (4.65)	9.74 (4.89)	11.98 (5.57)	7.97 (4.53)
Negative mood				
1980 Males	12.43 (2.40)	13.00 (2.69)	13.94 (3.38)	12.45 (2.09)
Females	13.32 (2.71)	14.44 (3.61)	13.09 (3.48)	12.83 (2.58)
Combined	12.91 (2.61)	13.78 (3.27)	13.44 (3.42)	12.63 (2.33)
1985 Males	11.44 (2.44)	12.86 (3.98)	13.92 (3.03)	12.29 (2.93)
Females	11.61 (2.43)	12.26 (2.22)	12.96 (3.72)	11.52 (2.22)
Combined	11.53 (2.43)	12.56 (3.18)	13.29 (3.49)	11.94 (2.65)

Table 4.6 Means (and standard deviations) on four psychological scales, 1980–1986

Scale		*Group*			
		Satisfied employed N = 501 (229 M, 272 F)	*Dissatisfied employed N = 39 (24 M, 15 F)*	*Unemployed N = 42 (29 M, 13 F)*	*Tertiary students N = 84 (50 M, 34 F)*
Self-esteem					
1980	Males	8.34 (1.86)	7.63 (2.22)	7.69 (2.24)	8.12 (1.90)
	Females	7.52 (1.99)	6.77 (2.56)	6.62 (2.99)	7.44 (2.26)
	Combined	7.89 (1.97)	7.30 (2.36)	7.36 (2.51)	7.84 (2.07)
1986	Males	9.25 (1.32)	8.04 (2.48)	8.28 (1.79)	8.88 (1.70)
	Females	9.17 (1.55)	8.67 (2.16)	8.34 (2.50)	9.15 (1.33)
	Combined	9.21 (1.45)	8.29 (2.35)	8.30 (2.01)	8.99 (1.56)
Depressive affect					
1980	Males	1.24 (1.20)	1.45 (1.32)	1.31 (1.07)	1.40 (1.28)
	Females	1.44 (1.23)	1.73 (1.53)	1.69 (1.60)	1.68 (1.61)
	Combined	1.35 (1.22)	1.56 (1.39)	1.43 (1.25)	1.51 (1.42)
1986	Males	0.69 (0.97)	1.42 (1.62)	1.31 (1.32)	0.98 (1.30)
	Females	0.71 (0.96)	1.15 (0.99)	1.33 (1.50)	0.91 (1.13)
	Combined	0.70 (0.96)	1.31 (1.41)	1.32 (1.36)	0.95 (1.22)
Locus of control					
1980	Males	11.84 (5.31)	14.11 (5.65)	14.75 (5.67)	11.71 (4.45)
	Females	14.18 (4.94)	13.67 (6.95)	14.08 (6.21)	12.10 (5.18)
	Combined	13.11 (5.24)	13.94 (6.09)	14.54 (5.71)	11.87 (4.73)
1986	Males	7.56 (4.65)	8.78 (4.82)	11.16 (5.75)	6.97 (3.48)
	Females	9.38 (4.79)	10.59 (6.52)	12.83 (7.63)	8.69 (5.23)
	Combined	8.54 (4.81)	9.49 (5.54)	11.65 (6.30)	7.68 (4.44)
Negative mood					
1980	Males	12.71 (2.72)	13.70 (2.95)	12.85 (2.03)	12.44 (2.77)
	Females	13.44 (2.84)	13.36 (3.20)	13.15 (4.04)	12.71 (3.06)
	Combined	13.11 (2.81)	13.57 (3.01)	12.95 (2.79)	12.55 (2.88)
1986	Males	11.47 (2.66)	13.70 (2.98)	13.34 (2.04)	11.92 (2.68)
	Females	11.51 (2.30)	12.57 (3.30)	12.77 (4.73)	11.24 (2.90)
	Combined	11.49 (2.47)	13.27 (3.11)	13.17 (3.08)	11.64 (2.77)

Table 4.7 Means (and standard deviations) on four psychological scales, 1980–1987

		Group			
Scale		Satisfied employed N = 417 (202 M, 215 F)	Dissatisfied employed N = 45 (27 M, 18 F)	Unemployed N = 40 (23 M, 17 F)	Tertiary students N = 52 (25 M, 27 F)
Self-esteem					
1980	Males	8.47 (1.50)	7.52 (2.47)	7.70 (2.48)	8.19 (1.53)
	Females	7.68 (1.88)	7.86 (1.72)	7.18 (2.96)	8.01 (1.91)
	Combined	8.06 (1.75)	7.66 (2.19)	7.47 (2.67)	8.10 (1.72)
1987	Males	9.24 (1.20)	9.19 (1.59)	8.70 (1.52)	9.08 (1.25)
	Females	9.18 (1.58)	8.56 (1.65)	9.07 (1.03)	9.30 (1.27)
	Combined	9.21 (1.40)	8.93 (1.63)	8.84 (1.35)	9.20 (1.25)
Depressive affect					
1980	Males	1.19 (1.21)	1.44 (1.34)	1.42 (1.12)	1.20 (1.12)
	Females	1.33 (1.13)	1.39 (1.14)	2.18 (1.85)	1.41 (1.25)
	Combined	1.26 (1.17)	1.42 (1.25)	1.75 (1.50)	1.31 (1.18)
1987	Males	0.65 (1.03)	0.81 (1.30)	1.64 (1.59)	0.96 (1.16)
	Females	0.74 (1.06)	2.00 (1.57)	1.27 (1.22)	1.04 (1.51)
	Combined	0.70 (1.05)	1.30 (1.52)	1.49 (1.45)	1.00 (1.34)
Locus of control					
1980	Males	11.48 (4.98)	12.79 (5.32)	13.24 (5.38)	12.74 (4.59)
	Females	13.65 (5.04)	12.08 (5.04)	14.65 (6.55)	11.47 (3.86)
	Combined	12.60 (5.12)	12.51 (5.16)	13.84 (5.86)	12.08 (4.23)
1987	Males	7.60 (4.59)	7.70 (4.08)	9.76 (4.20)	7.59 (5.59)
	Females	8.76 (4.58)	10.43 (6.69)	11.00 (5.46)	7.02 (3.97)
	Combined	8.20 (4.62)	8.80 (5.38)	10.29 (4.75)	7.29 (4.76)
Negative mood					
1980	Males	12.47 (2.69)	12.92 (2.13)	13.50 (2.74)	12.43 (1.78)
	Females	13.30 (2.76)	13.53 (3.08)	12.71 (3.87)	13.07 (2.50)
	Combined	12.90 (2.75)	13.16 (2.53)	13.14 (3.28)	12.78 (2.20)
1987	Males	11.27 (2.47)	11.84 (3.04)	13.74 (3.15)	11.92 (3.01)
	Females	11.52 (2.58)	14.11 (2.25)	12.21 (2.12)	11.54 (2.42)
	Combined	11.40 (2.53)	12.79 (2.93)	13.16 (3.18)	11.73 (2.71)

Source: Winefield, Tiggemann and Winefield (1991b)

Table 4.8 Means (and standard deviations) on four psychological scales,
1980–1988

		Group			
Scale		Satisfied employed N = 353 (175 M, 178 F)	Dissatisfied employed N = 31 (14 M, 17 F)	Unemployed N = 22 (13 M, 9F)	Tertiary students N = 36 (14 M, 22 F)
Self-esteem					
1980	Males	8.35 (1.61)	8.07 (2.79)	7.85 (2.27)	7.48 (2.59)
	Females	7.55 (1.97)	7.99 (1.50)	7.32 (3.16)	7.38 (2.47)
	Combined	7.95 (1.84)	8.03 (2.14)	7.63 (2.61)	7.42 (2.48)
1988	Males	9.12 (1.50)	8.43 (2.38)	8.62 (1.71)	9.00 (1.36)
	Females	9.25 (1.28)	8.88 (1.32)	8.33 (2.06)	9.50 (0.86)
	Combined	9.19 (1.39)	8.68 (1.85)	8.50 (1.82)	9.31 (1.09)
Depressive affect					
1980	Males	1.21 (1.23)	1.21 (1.31)	1.31 (0.85)	1.07 (1.00)
	Females	1.40 (1.12)	1.71 (1.49)	1.11 (1.76)	1.77 (1.57)
	Combined	1.31 (1.18)	1.48 (1.41)	1.23 (1.27)	1.50 (1.40)
1988	Males	0.71 (1.10)	2.43 (1.87)	1.54 (1.51)	0.77 (0.83)
	Females	0.61 (0.98)	1.38 (1.36)	1.44 (1.24)	1.05 (1.28)
	Combined	0.66 (1.04)	1.87 (1.68)	1.50 (1.37)	0.94 (1.13)
Locus of control					
1980	Males	11.29 (4.67)	11.06 (5.97)	13.50 (6.13)	13.21 (4.62)
	Females	13.62 (5.13)	12.40 (5.77)	11.72 (6.38)	13.10 (4.74)
	Combined	12.46 (5.04)	11.79 (5.80)	12.77 (6.14)	13.09 (4.70)
1988	Males	7.37 (4.55)	8.19 (4.03)	9.75 (5.45)	8.37 (5.70)
	Females	8.18 (4.19)	9.45 (5.27)	15.00 (6.00)	7.67 (3.23)
	Combined	7.77 (4.38)	8.88 (4.72)	12.00 (6.15)	7.94 (4.27)
Negative mood					
1980	Males	12.47 (2.77)	12.92 (2.02)	13.38 (1.89)	13.00 (2.19)
	Females	13.37 (2.57)	13.31 (3.18)	10.89 (3.86)	13.68 (3.03)
	Combined	12.93 (2.71)	13.14 (2.68)	12.36 (3.05)	13.45 (2.76)
1988	Males	11.41 (2.84)	14.23 (4.00)	13.46 (3.76)	12.36 (2.56)
	Females	11.18 (2.38)	12.06 (2.50)	12.63 (3.62)	12.23 (2.67)
	Combined	11.29 (2.62)	13.00 (3.26)	13.14 (3.64)	12.28 (2.59)

Source: Winefield, Winefield, Tiggemann and Goldney (1991)

Table 4.9 Means (and standard deviations) on depressive affect scale, 1980–1989

	Group		
Scale	Satisfied employed N = 292 (155 M, 137 F)	Dissatisfied employed and unemployed N = 40 (18 M, 22 F)	Tertiary students N = 20 (8 M, 12 F)
Depressive affect			
1980 Males	1.14 (1.64)	2.17 (1.38)	1.00 (1.41)
Females	1.47 (1.23)	1.27 (1.08)	1.75 (1.42)
Combined	1.29 (1.21)	1.67 (1.29)	1.45 (1.43)
1989 Males	0.54 (0.87)	1.67 (1.53)	1.25 (0.89)
Females	0.57 (0.93)	1.00 (1.20)	1.18 (1.68)
Combined	0.55 (0.90)	1.30 (1.38)	1.21 (1.03)

Table 4.10 Means (and standard deviations) for GHQ, 1984–1989

		Group			
Year		Satisfied employed	Dissatisfied employed	Unemployed	Tertiary students
1984	Males	9.49 (4.27)	12.11 (5.04)	12.37 (5.04)	11.77 (4.58)
	Females	9.92 (4.33)	12.48 (5.45)	12.03 (5.53)	12.36 (5.58)
	Combined	9.73 (4.30)	12.28 (5.21)	12.21 (5.24)	12.03 (5.02)
1985	Males	9.00 (4.01)	11.57 (4.46)	11.31 (3.74)	10.41 (4.57)
	Females	9.17 (4.43)	12.08 (6.23)	12.41 (7.05)	10.30 (4.40)
	Combined	9.09 (4.24)	11.84 (5.42)	11.95 (5.84)	10.36 (4.48)
1986	Males	8.38 (3.46)	11.74 (5.07)	10.66 (3.91)	8.92 (3.48)
	Females	9.39 (4.52)	11.93 (5.76)	11.92 (8.18)	10.38 (4.13)
	Combined	8.93 (4.09)	11.81 (5.26)	11.05 (5.51)	9.52 (3.81)
1987	Males	9.05 (3.75)	9.40 (5.85)	11.13 (6.51)	10.88 (4.01)
	Females	9.47 (4.27)	15.00 (6.32)	12.00 (6.22)	10.88 (6.51)
	Combined	9.27 (4.03)	11.74 (6.59)	11.49 (6.32)	10.88 (5.40)
1988	Males	9.52 (3.61)	16.57 (6.22)	12.30 (6.78)	10.93 (4.23)
	Females	9.91 (4.85)	11.47 (4.78)	12.44 (8.38)	11.14 (5.21)
	Combined	9.72 (4.28)	13.77 (5.97)	12.32 (7.29)	11.06 (4.97)

		Satisfied employed	Dissatisfied and unemployed	Tertiary students
1989	Males	8.73 (3.03)	12.64 (4.95)	10.13 (2.10)
	Females	8.75 (3.72)	11.20 (5.75)	11.17 (6.91)
	Combined	8.74 (3.36)	11.87 (5.38)	10.75 (5.44)

Table 4.11 Means (and standard deviations) for hopelessness, 1984–1988

Year		Satisfied employed	Dissatisfied employed	Unemployed	Tertiary students
1984	Males	2.83 (2.67)	5.54 (4.78)	4.82 (4.69)	3.54 (3.31)
	Females	3.12 (2.69)	4.09 (3.31)	4.01 (3.82)	3.12 (3.04)
	Combined	2.99 (2.68)	4.78 (4.11)	4.43 (4.28)	3.36 (3.19)
1985	Males	2.62 (2.45)	4.74 (4.46)	5.90 (3.60)	2.97 (2.71)
	Females	2.69 (2.19)	2.63 (2.80)	3.80 (3.80)	2.73 (2.58)
	Combined	2.66 (2.31)	3.62 (3.78)	4.66 (3.82)	2.86 (2.65)
1986	Males	2.40 (2.67)	4.01 (2.38)	4.16 (3.12)	2.75 (2.76)
	Females	2.46 (2.17)	4.41 (4.67)	4.78 (5.27)	2.57 (2.06)
	Combined	2.44 (2.42)	4.16 (3.35)	4.35 (3.86)	2.68 (2.48)
1987	Males	2.50 (2.36)	3.03 (3.73)	3.71 (3.16)	3.67 (3.07)
	Females	2.58 (2.52)	4.54 (3.70)	3.09 (2.88)	2.48 (3.06)
	Combined	2.54 (2.44)	3.62 (3.75)	3.43 (3.02)	3.04 (3.09)
1988	Males	2.09 (2.58)	4.36 (4.05)	4.38 (3.73)	3.12 (3.47)
	Females	2.34 (2.76)	3.41 (3.19)	5.01 (4.83)	2.33 (1.93)
	Combined	2.21 (2.67)	3.84 (3.57)	4.62 (4.08)	2.62 (2.59)

Table 4.12 Means (and standard deviations) for anomie, 1984–1988*

Year		Satisfied employed	Dissatisfied employed	Unemployed	Tertiary students
1984	Males	1.78 (1.47)	2.37 (1.61)	2.38 (1.71)	1.44 (1.33)
	Females	1.93 (1.50)	2.39 (1.50)	2.47 (1.52)	1.51 (1.42)
	Combined	1.86 (1.49)	2.38 (1.54)	2.42 (1.61)	1.47 (1.37)
1985	Males	1.69 (1.36)	2.48 (1.72)	2.57 (1.55)	1.49 (1.25)
	Females	1.87 (1.59)	1.72 (1.57)	2.37 (1.80)	1.22 (1.28)
	Combined	1.79 (1.49)	2.07 (1.67)	2.39 (1.70)	1.37 (1.26)
1986	Males	1.65 (1.36)	2.19 (1.53)	2.57 (1.53)	1.72 (1.23)
	Females	1.92 (1.47)	2.00 (1.24)	2.58 (1.78)	1.29 (1.49)
	Combined	1.80 (1.43)	2.11 (1.41)	2.58 (1.58)	1.54 (1.35)
1987	Males	1.58 (1.46)	2.23 (1.73)	1.86 (1.28)	1.43 (1.25)
	Females	1.67 (1.44)	1.83 (1.69)	2.20 (1.52)	0.96 (1.29)
	Combined	1.62 (1.45)	2.07 (1.70)	2.00 (1.37)	1.17 (1.28)
1988	Males	2.41 (2.12)	2.64 (2.53)	3.82 (2.44)	3.00 (2.55)
	Females	2.40 (2.13)	2.73 (2.05)	4.67 (2.96)	2.50 (1.65)
	Combined	2.41 (2.12)	2.69 (2.25)	4.20 (2.65)	2.69 (2.01)

* 1984–1987 based on 5-item scale (Srole, 1956), 1988 based on 9-item scale (Dodder and Astle, 1980)

Table 5.1 Multiple regression analyses for younger sample

Dependent variable	Predictor variable	Beta	t	P	R^2
Satisfied employed (N = 586)					
Self-esteem	Sex	−0.14	3.03	0.005	0.04
	Number of friends	0.12	2.34	0.05	
	Years of schooling	0.10	2.25	0.05	
Depressive affect	Number of friends	−0.22	4.72	0.0001	0.09
	Borrowing ability	−0.12	2.62	0.01	
	Confidants	−0.10	2.26	0.05	
	Sex	0.10	2.25	0.05	
	Age	0.09	2.03	0.05	
GHQ–12	Financial hardship	0.15	3.10	0.005	0.08
	Confidants	−0.12	2.65	0.05	
	Borrowing ability	−0.11	2.39	0.05	
	Number of friends	−0.11	2.39	0.05	
	Sex	0.10	2.08	0.05	
Hopelessness	Financial hardship	0.15	3.04	0.001	0.07
	Employment commitment	−0.12	2.52	0.05	
	Unhealthy attributional style	0.12	2.49	0.05	
	Sex	0.10	2.27	0.05	
	Socio-economic status	−0.10	2.19	0.05	
Dissatisfied employed (N = 75)					
Self-esteem	Number of friends	0.32	2.47	0.05	0.18
	Borrowing ability	0.27	2.05	0.05	
Depressive affect	Employment commitment	−0.37	2.98	0.005	0.36
	Borrowing ability	−0.36	2.96	0.005	
	Number of friends	−0.31	2.51	0.05	
Hopelessness	Confidants	−0.28	2.14	0.05	0.17
	Borrowing ability	−0.28	2.14	0.05	
Unemployed (N = 78)					
Self-esteem	Number of friends	0.41	3.32	0.005	0.24
	Academic potential	0.27	2.13	0.05	
Depressive affect	Socio-economic status	−0.42	3.32	0.005	0.34
	Number of friends	−0.41	3.30	0.005	
	Years of schooling	0.35	2.67	0.05	
Hopelessness	Borrowing ability	−0.34	2.54	0.05	0.20
	Confidants	−0.27	2.05	0.05	

NB Sex was coded 1 for male and 2 for female
Source: Winefield, Tiggemann and Winefield (1990)

Table 5.2 Multiple regression analyses for older sample

Dependent variable	Predictor variable	Beta	t	P	R^2
Satisfied employed (N = 417)					
Self-esteem	Number of friends	0.14	2.51	0.05	0.04
	Confidants	0.13	2.26	0.05	
Depressive affect	Number of friends	–0.29	5.44	0.0001	0.11
	Unhealthy attributional style	0.12	2.35	0.05	
	Financial hardship	–0.11	2.01	0.05	
GHQ–12	Number of friends	–0.20	3.74	0.0005	0.09
	Unhealthy attributional style	0.17	3.24	0.005	
	Years of schooling	0.12	2.32	0.05	
Hopelessness	Unhealthy attributional style	0.21	4.01	0.0001	0.10
	Number of friends	–0.18	3.29	0.001	
	Employment commitment	–0.14	2.54	0.05	
Dissatisfied employed (N = 45)					
Self-esteem	Financial hardship	–0.40	2.36	0.05	0.16
Depressive affect	Financial hardship	0.46	3.09	0.005	0.40
	Number of friends	–0.33	2.20	0.05	
GHQ–12	Confidants	–0.41	2.70	0.05	0.46
	Number of friends	–0.40	2.69	0.05	
Unemployed (N = 40)					
Self-esteem	Ethnic origin	0.56	2.86	0.05	0.31
Hopelessness	Number of friends	–0.51	3.11	0.01	0.58
	Unhealthy attributional style	–0.44	2.67	0.05	
	Academic potential	–0.40	2.41	0.05	

NB Ethnic origin was coded 1 for non-English-speaking and 2 for English-speaking
Source: Winefield, Tiggemann and Winefield (1990)

Table 5.3 Correlations between activities and measures: unemployed group, 1981–1983

			Activity			
Year	Measure		Doing nothing	Watching TV	Solitary activities	Gregarious activities
1981	Depressive affect	F	0.46			
	Negative mood	F	0.48			
1982	Depressive affect	C				−0.44
		M				−0.45
		F	0.45			−0.46
	Negative mood	C	0.39			
		M	0.46	0.44		−0.48
1983	Depressive affect	M				−0.43

NB C refers to males and females combined, M refers to males, F refers to females
Only statistically significant correlations of 0.39 or more are given

Table 5.4 Correlations between activities and measures: unemployed group,
1984–1988

			Activity			
Year	Measure		Doing nothing	Watching TV	Solitary activities	Gregarious activities
1984	Self-esteem	M	–0.40			
	Negative mood	M	0.45			
1985	Negative mood	M	0.53			
	Hopelessness	C	0.52	0.53		
		M	0.62	0.46		
		F	0.44	0.59		
	Anomie	M		0.49		
	GHQ	M	0.66			
1986	Self-esteem	F		–0.53		0.52
	Depressive affect	C			–0.42	
		M			–0.40	–0.39
		F		0.60		–0.67
	Negative mood	C	0.47			
		M	0.42			
		F	0.53	0.50	–0.51	–0.76
	Hopelessness	M		0.44		
	Anomie	F		0.47		–0.72
	GHQ	C	0.47		–0.56	
		F			–0.76	–0.72
1987	Self-esteem	C	–0.51	–0.42		
		M	–0.48			
		F	–0.52			0.56
	Depressive affect	C				–0.63
		M				–0.68
		F				–0.66
	Negative mood	C	0.54			–0.55
		M	0.61			–0.55
		F				–0.69
	Hopelessness	F	0.47			–0.81
	Anomie	C	0.43			–0.51
		M		0.52		–0.53
		F	0.45			–0.66
	GHQ	C		0.40		–0.56
		M		0.43		–0.49
		F	0.45			–0.80
1988	Self-esteem	C			0.45	
		M			0.54	0.65
		F	–0.56	–0.75	0.66	
	Depressive affect	M				–0.49
		F	0.60	0.88		

Table 5.4 Continued

			Activity			
Year	Measure		Doing nothing	Watching TV	Solitary activities	Gregarious activities
[1988]	Negative mood	M	0.49			−0.51
		F			−0.92	
	Hopelessness	C		0.45		−0.55
		M				−0.74
		F		0.81		
	Anomie	C		0.59		−0.45
		M			−0.55	−0.54
		F		0.85		
	GHQ	M	0.55			
		F			−0.95	

NB C refers to males and females combined, M refers to males, F refers to females
Only statistically significant correlations of 0.39 or more are given

Table 5.5 Correlations between activities and measures: dissatisfied employed group, 1984–1988

Year	Measure		Doing nothing	Watching TV	Solitary activities	Gregarious activities
1984	Self-esteem	C	−0.45			
		M	−0.45			
		F	−0.46			
	Depressive affect	C	0.45			
		M	0.51			−0.46
	Negative mood	C	0.52			
		M	0.72			
	Hopelessness	C	0.45			
		M	0.52			
	Anomie	C	0.46			
		M	0.53			
1985	Self-esteem	C	−0.61			0.40
		M	−0.72		−0.51	0.59
		F	−0.52		−0.44	
	Depressive affect	C	0.57			
		M	0.85			−0.69
	Negative mood	C	0.62			−0.48
		M	0.75			−0.65
	Hopelessness	F		−0.43		
	Anomie	C	0.67			
		M	0.81			−0.55
		F			−0.41	
	GHQ	C	0.41			
		M	0.80			−0.59
1986	Self-esteem	F	−0.52		−0.44	
	Depressive affect	C				−0.46
		M				−0.61
		F	0.50	0.70		
	Negative mood	C	0.54			
		M	0.47			−0.47
		F	0.62			
	Hopelessness	C	0.39			
		F	0.75	0.51		
1987	Self-esteem	F			0.50	
	Depressive affect	M				−0.39
		F		0.55		
	Negative mood	M	0.49			−0.40
	Hopelessness	M			0.40	
	Anomie	F				−0.52

Table 5.5 Continued

Year	Measure		Doing nothing	Watching TV	Solitary activities	Gregarious activities
					Activity	
1988	Self-esteem	M		−0.45	−0.52	
	Depressive affect	C				−0.51
		M				−0.59
		F	0.47			−0.48
	Negative mood	C	0.47	0.44		
		M			−0.62	−0.55
		F	0.66	0.42		
	Anomie	C		0.39		
		M		0.52		
	GHQ	C		0.50		
		F		0.76		

NB C refers to males and females combined, M refers to males, F refers to females
Only statistically significant correlations of 0.39 or more are given

Table 5.6 Means and standard deviations at pre-test and later for four affective scales: combined years

Scale	Time	3 months or less		4–8 months		9 months or more	
		Mean	*SD*	*Mean*	*SD*	*Mean*	*SD*
Self-esteem	Pre-test	7.95	1.98	7.92	1.77	6.80	2.58
	Later	8.57	1.68	8.69	1.81	7.99	2.40
Depressive affect	Pre-test	1.47	1.23	1.28	1.23	1.62	1.43
	Later	1.11	1.21	1.18	1.39	1.98	1.66
Negative mood	Pre-test	13.26	3.05	13.00	3.33	13.48	3.85
	Later	12.82	3.04	12.88	3.27	14.55	3.56
Locus of control	Pre-test	13.30	5.36	13.47	5.10	15.32	4.93
	Later	8.45	3.63	9.73	4.96	14.16	5.51

Table 5.7 Means and standard deviations on four scales: combined years

Scale	3 months or less		4–8 months		9 months or more	
	Mean	SD	Mean	SD	Mean	SD
Work involvement	24.56	6.19	24.92	5.65	21.74	7.11
Social alienation	1.91	1.43	2.08	1.43	3.17	1.36
Hopelessness	3.26	2.74	3.10	3.03	5.90	4.90
GHQ	10.51	6.44	11.74	4.90	13.05	6.20

Source: Winefield and Tiggemann (1990b)

Table 8.1 Other studies of GHQ and youth unemployment

Author	Instrument	Subjects	Results
Banks *et al.* (1980)	12-item	Unemployed 16-year-olds	Unemployed scored 14.06 and the employed scored 8.67
Stafford *et al.* (1980)	12-item	647 'less qualified' school leavers	'Unemployed displaying significantly higher scores'
Finlay-Jones and Eckhardt (1981)	30-item	Unemployed 16–24-year-olds	56% of unemployed scored as 'probable cases of psychiatric disorder'
McPherson and Hall (1983)	12-item	Unemployed men under 25 years	48% 'psychiatric case rate'
Donovan *et al.* (1986)	12-item	16-year-old school leavers	Unemployed scored 11.00 and the employed scored 6.45

Table 8.2 Mean psychometric values (and standard deviations) for those who acknowledged ever having had thoughts of killing themselves, 1988

Scale	Satisfied employed (N = 69)	Dissatisfied employed (N = 15)	Unemployed (N = 8)	Tertiary students (N = 13)	F-ratio	P
Negative mood	13.68 (2.90)	14.86 (4.05)	15.62 (2.83)	14.69 (1.65)	1.597	0.195
Self-esteem	8.46 (1.99)	8.00 (2.17)	7.88 (2.03)	8.61 (1.44)	0.459	0.712
Depressive affect	1.12 (1.23)	2.40 (1.59)	1.63 (0.92)	1.38 (0.77)	4.614	0.005
GHQ (12-item)	11.21 (5.14)	16.00 (6.56)	13.00 (6.59)	13.08 (4.25)	3.435	0.020
Hopelessness	3.22 (3.51)	4.88 (4.04)	5.75 (4.83)	3.89 (3.22)	1.750	0.162
Locus of control	8.74 (4.66)	10.63 (5.27)	12.38 (4.17)	11.45 (4.06)	2.560	0.060
Anomie	3.21 (2.36)	3.23 (2.65)	4.38 (2.07)	3.85 (2.15)	0.782	0.507

Table 8.3 Mean psychometric values (and standard deviations) for those in the revised employment groups who acknowledged ever having had thoughts of killing themselves, 1988

Scale	Full-time satisfied employed (N = 55)	Full-time dissatisfied employed (N = 11)	Unemployed longer than six months (N = 13)	F-ratio	P
Negative mood	13.32 (3.10)	14.91 (4.35)	14.33 (2.31)	0.588	0.558
Self-esteem	8.36 (2.08)	8.18 (2.48)	8.46 (1.51)	0.057	0.945
Depressive affect	1.21 (1.32)	2.36 (1.50)	1.23 (0.93)	3.745	0.028
GHQ (12-item)	11.33 (4.63)	15.36 (5.70)	12.23 (8.24)	2.455	0.093
Hopelessness	3.54 (3.82)	4.75 (3.54)	2.92 (2.84)	0.776	0.464
Locus of control	8.86 (4.93)	10.20 (6.05)	10.17 (4.70)	0.560	0.574
Anomie	3.34 (2.37)	3.11 (2.98)	2.77 (1.64)	0.319	0.728

References

Abramson, L.Y., Metalsky, G.L. and Alloy, L.B. (1989) Hopelessness depression: a theory-based subtype of depression. *Psychological Review, 96*, 358–72.

Abramson, L.Y., Seligman, M.E.P. and Teasdale, J.D. (1978) Learned helplessness in humans: critique and reformulation. *Journal of Abnormal Psychology, 87*, 49–74.

Adams, A.V. and Mangum, G.C. (1978) *The Lingering Crisis of Youth Unemployment*. Kalamazoo: Upjohn.

American Psychiatric Association (1980) *Diagnostic and Statistical Manual of Mental Disorders, Third Edition*. Washington: APA.

Ary, D.V. and Biglan, A. (1988) Longitudinal changes in adolescent cigarette smoking behavior: onset and cessation. *Journal of Behavioral Medicine, 11*, 361–81.

Aubrey, T., Tefft, B. and Kingsbury, N. (1990) Behavioral and psychological consequences of unemployment in blue-collar couples. *Journal of Community Psychology, 18*, 99–109.

Australian Industries Development Association (1978) *Understanding Unemployment*. Melbourne: Australian Industries Development Association.

Bakke, E.W. (1933) *The Unemployed Man*. London: Nisbet.

Banks, M.H. and Jackson, P.R. (1982) Unemployment and risk of minor psychiatric disorder in young people. *Psychological Medicine, 12*, 789–98.

Banks, M.H. and Ullah, P. (1988) *Youth Unemployment in the 1980s: Its Psychological Effects*. London: Croom Helm.

Banks, M.H., Clegg, C.W., Jackson, P.R., Kemp, N.J., Stafford, E.M. and Wall, T.D. (1980) The use of the General Health Questionnaire as an indicator of mental health in occupational studies. *Journal of Occupational Psychology, 53*, 187–94.

Barnett, R.C. and Baruch, G.K. (1978) *The Competent Woman: Perspectives on Development*. New York: Halstead Press.

Bartlett, F. (1933) *Remembering*. Cambridge: Cambridge University Press.

Beale, N.R. and Nethercott, S. (1985) Job loss and family morbidity. A factory closure study in general practice. *Journal of the Royal College of General Practitioners, 35*, 510–14.

Beck, A.T., Weisman, A., Lester, D. and Trexler, L. (1974) The measurement of pessimism: the hopelessness scale. *Journal of Consulting and Clinical Psychology, 42*, 861–5.

Beck, A.T., Ward, C.H., Mendelson, M., Mock, J. and Erbaugh, J. (1961) An inventory for measuring depression. *Archives of General Psychiatry, 4,* 561–71.

Beehr, T.A. (1986) The process of retirement: a review and recommendations for future investigation. *Personnel Psychology, 39,* 31–55.

Blakers, C. (1984) The effects of unemployment: a summary of the research. *Youth Studies Bulletin, 3,* 71–101.

Bland, R.C., Stebelsky, G., Orn, H. and Newman, S.C. (1988) Psychiatric disorders and unemployment in Edmonton. *Acta Psychiatrica Scandinavica, 77,* 72–80.

Bolton, W. and Oatley, K. (1987) A longitudinal study of social support and depression in unemployed men. *Psychological Medicine, 17,* 453–60.

Boor, M. (1980) Relationships between unemployment rates and suicide rates in eight countries, 1962–1976. *Psychological Reports, 47,* 1095–101.

Braithwaite, J. and Biles, D. (1979) On being unemployed and being a victim of crime. *Australian Journal of Social Issues, 14,* 192–200.

Branthwaite, A. and Garcia, S. (1985) Depression in the young unemployed and those on youth opportunities schemes. *British Journal of Medical Psychology, 58,* 67–74.

Brenner, M.H. (1971) Economic changes and heart disease mortality. *American Journal of Public Health, 61,* 606–11.

Brenner, M.H. (1973) *Mental Illness and the Economy.* Cambridge: Harvard University Press.

Brenner, M.H. (1979a) Influence of the social environment on psychopathology: the historical perspective, in J.E. Barrett, R.M. Rose and G.L. Klerman (eds) *Stress and Mental Disorder.* New York: Raven Press.

Brenner, M.H. (1979b) Unemployment, economic growth and mortality. *Lancet, 1,* 672.

Brenner, M.H. (1987) Relation of economic change to Swedish health and social well-being, 1950–1980. *Social Science and Medicine, 25,* 183–96.

Brenner, M.H. and Mooney, A. (1983) Unemployment and health in the context of economic change. *Social Science and Medicine, 17,* 1125–38.

Brewer, G. (1975) *Workers without Jobs: A Study of a Group of Unemployed People.* Melbourne: Brotherhood of St Lawrence.

Brewin, C.R. (1985) Depression and causal attributions: what is their relation? *Psychological Bulletin, 98,* 297–309.

Brook, J.S., Cohen, P. and Gordon, A.S. (1983) Impact of attrition in a sample in a longitudinal study of adolescent drug use. *Psychological Reports, 53,* 375–8.

Broom, L. and Jones, F. (1969) Career mobility in three societies: Australia, Italy and the United States. *American Sociological Review, 34,* 650–8.

Broomhall, H.S. and Winefield, A.H. (1990) A comparison of the affective well-being of young and middle-aged unemployed men matched for length of unemployment. *British Journal of Medical Psychology, 63,* 43–52.

Carr-Hill, R.A. and Stern, N.H. (1983) Unemployment and crime: a comment. *Journal of Social Policy, 12,* 341.

Casson, M. (1979) *Youth Unemployment.* London: Macmillan.

Catalano, R. and Dooley, D. (1977) The economic predictors of depressed mood and stressful life events in a metropolitan community. *Journal of Health and Social Behavior, 18,* 292–307.

Catalano, R. and Dooley, D. (1983) Health effects of economic instability: a test of economic stress hypothesis. *Journal of Health and Social Behavior, 24,* 46–60.

Charlton, A. and Blair, V. (1989) Predicting the onset of smoking in boys and girls. *Social Science and Medicine, 29,* 813–18.

Cohen, J. (1977) *Statistical Power Analysis for the Behavioral Sciences.* New York: Academic Press.

Cohen, S. and Wills, T.A. (1985) Stress, social support and the buffering hypothesis. *Psychological Bulletin, 98,* 310–57.

Coleman, J.C. (1980) Friendship and the peer group in adolescence, in J. Adelson (ed.) *Handbook of Adolescent Psychology.* New York: Wiley.

Coleman, J.C. and Hendry, L.B. (1990) *The Nature of Adolescence.* London: Routledge.

Constantinople, A. (1969) An Eriksonian measure of personality development in college students. *Developmental Psychology, 1,* 357–72.

Cook, D.G., Bartley, M.J., Cummins, R.O. and Shaper, A.G. (1982) Health of unemployed middle-aged men in Great Britain. *Lancet, 1,* 1290–4.

Corti, B. and Ibrahim, J. (1990) Women and alcohol – trends in Australia. *Medical Journal of Australia, 152,* 625–32.

Costello, C.G. (1978) A critical review of Seligman's laboratory experiments on learned helplessness and depression in humans. *Journal of Abnormal Psychology, 87,* 21–31.

Coyne, J.C. and Gotlib, I.H. (1983) The role of cognition in depression: a critical appraisal. *Psychological Bulletin, 94,* 472–505.

Crombie, I.K. (1989) Trends in suicide and unemployment in Scotland, 1976–86. *British Medical Journal, 298,* 782–4.

Cullen, J.H., Ryan, G.M., Cullen K.M., Ronayne, T. and Wynne, R.F. (1987) Unemployed youth and health: findings from the pilot phase of a longitudinal study. *Social Science and Medicine, 25,* 133–46.

Daley, M. (1983) *Employment, Unemployment, and Young People: A South Australian Perspective.* Adelaide: Department of Technical and Further Education.

Dillman, D.A. (1978) *Mail and Telephone Surveys.* New York: Wiley.

Dodder, R.A. and Astle, D.J. (1980) A methodological analysis of Srole's nine-item anomia scale. *Multivariate Behavioral Research, 15,* 329–34.

Donovan, A. and Oddy, M. (1982) Psychological aspects of unemployment: an investigation into the emotional and social adjustment of school leavers. *Journal of Adolescence, 5,* 15–30.

Donovan, A., Oddy, M., Pardoe, R. and Ades, A. (1986) Employment status and psychological well-being: a longitudinal study of 16-year-old school leavers. *Journal of Child Psychology and Psychiatry, 27,* 65–76.

Dooley, D. and Catalano, R. (1980) Economic change as a cause of behavioral disorder. *Psychological Bulletin, 87,* 450–68.

Dooley, D. and Catalano, R. (1988) Recent research on the psychological effects of unemployment. *Journal of Social Issues, 44,* 1–12.

Dooley, D., Catalano, R. and Rook, K.S. (1988) Personal and aggregate unemployment and psychological symptoms. *Journal of Social Issues, 44,* 107–23.

Dooley, D., Rook, K. and Catalano, R. (1987) Job and non-job stressors and their moderators. *Journal of Occupational Psychology, 60,* 115–32.

Dooley, D., Catalano, R., Rook, K. and Serxner, S. (1989) Economic stress and suicide: multilevel analyses part 1: aggregate time-series analyses of economic stress and suicide. *Suicide and Life-threatening Behavior, 19,* 321–36.

Dumont, M.P. (1989) Effects of unemployment on mental health. *Current Opinion in Psychiatry, 2,* 287–90.

Edwards, W. (1954) The theory of decision making. *Psychological Bulletin, 51,* 380–417.

Eisenberg, P. and Lazarsfeld, P.F. (1938) The psychological effects of unemployment. *Psychological Bulletin, 35,* 358–90.

Endicott, J., Spitzer, R.I., Fleiss, J.I. and Cohen, J. (1976) The Global Assessment Scale: a procedure for measuring the overall severity of psychiatric disturbance. *Archives of General Psychiatry, 76,* 766–71.

Ensminger, M.E. and Celentano, D.D. (1990) Gender differences in the effect of unemployment on psychological distress. *Social Science and Medicine, 30,* 469–77.

Erikson, E.H. (1956) The problem of ego identity. *Journal of the American Psychoanalytic Association, 4,* 56–121.

Erikson, E.H. (1959) Identity and the life cycle. *Psychological Issues, 1,* 50–100.

Erikson, E.H. (1971) *Identity: Youth and Crisis.* London: Faber & Faber.

Fagin, L. (1983) Physical and psychological aspects of unemployment. *Update,* 15 April, 1353–60.

Feather, N.T. (1959) Subjective probability and decision under uncertainty. *Psychological Review, 66,* 150–64.

Feather, N.T. (1982) Expectancy-value approaches: present status and future directions, in N.T. Feather (ed.) *Expectations and Actions: Expectancy-value Models in Psychology* (pp. 395–420). Hillsdale, N.J.: Erlbaum.

Feather, N.T. (1985) The psychological impact of unemployment: empirical findings and theoretical approaches, in N.T. Feather (ed.) *Australian Psychology: Review of Research.* Sydney: Allen & Unwin.

Feather, N.T. (1990) *The Psychological Impact of Unemployment.* New York: Springer.

Feather, N.T. and Barber, J.G. (1983) Depressive reactions and unemployment. *Journal of Abnormal Psychology, 92,* 185–95.

Feather, N.T. and Bond, M.J. (1983) Time structure and purposeful activity among employed and unemployed university graduates. *Journal of Occupational Psychology, 56,* 241–54.

Feather, N.T. and Davenport, P.R. (1981) Unemployment and depressive affect: a motivational and attributional analysis. *Journal of Personality and Social Psychology, 41,* 422–36.

Feather, N.T. and O'Brien, G.E. (1986a) A longitudinal analysis of the effects of employment, different patterns of employment and unemployment on school-leavers. *British Journal of Psychology, 77,* 459–79.

Feather, N.T. and O'Brien, G.E. (1986b) A longitudinal study of the effects of employment and unemployment on school-leavers. *Journal of Occupational Psychology, 59,* 121–44.

Feather, N.T. and O'Brien, G.E. (1987) Looking for employment: an expectancy-valence analysis of job-seeking behaviour among young people. *Journal of Occupational Psychology, 78,* 251–72.

Ferrara, S.D. (1987) Alcohol, drugs and traffic safety. *British Journal of Addiction, 82,* 871–83.

Festinger, L. (1957) *A Theory of Cognitive Dissonance.* Evanston: Row Peterson.

Finlay-Jones, R. and Eckhardt, B. (1981) Psychiatric disorder among the young unemployed. *Australian and New Zealand Journal of Psychiatry, 15,* 265–70.

Finlay-Jones, R. and Eckhardt, B. (1984) A social and psychiatric survey of unemployment among young people. *Australian and New Zealand Journal of Psychiatry, 18*, 135–43.

Fitts, W.H. (1965) *The Experience of Psychotherapy*. Princeton: Van Nostrand.

Freud, S. (1930) *Civilisation and its Discontents*. London: Hogarth.

Fryer, D.M. (1985) Stages in the psychological response to unemployment: a (dis)integrative review. *Current Psychological Research and Reviews, Fall*, 257–73.

Fryer, D.M. (1986) Employment deprivation and personal agency during unemployment: a critical discussion of Jahoda's explanation of the psychological effects of unemployment. *Social Behaviour, 1*, 3–23.

Fryer, D.M. and McKenna, S.P. (1987) The laying off of hands – unemployment and the experience of time, in S. Fineman (ed.) *Unemployment: Personal and Social Consequences* (pp. 47–73). London: Tavistock.

Fryer, D.M. and Payne, R.L. (1984) Pro-active behaviour in unemployment: findings and implications. *Leisure Studies, 3*, 273–95.

Furness, J.A., Khan, M.C. and Pickens, P.T. (1985) Unemployment and parasuicide in Hartlepool 1974–83. *Health Trends, 17*, 21–4.

Furnham, A. and Stacey, B. (1991) *Young People's Understanding of Society*. London: Routledge.

Gallatin, J.E. (1975) *Adolescence and Individuality*. New York: Harper & Row.

Gergen, K.J. and Gergen, M.M. (1982) Explaining human conduct: form and function, in P. Secord (ed.) *Explaining Human Behavior: Consciousness, Human Action, and Social Structure* (pp. 127–54). Beverly Hills, CA: Sage.

Goldberg, D.P. (1972) *The Detection of Psychiatric Illness by Questionnaire*. London: Oxford University Press.

Goldberg, D.P. (1978) *Manual of the General Health Questionnaire*. Windsor: NFER.

Goldney, R.D. (1981) Parental loss and reported childhood stress in young women who attempt suicide. *Acta Psychiatrica Scandinavica, 64*, 34–9.

Goldney, R.D. and Spence, N.D. (1987) Is suicide predictable? *Australian and New Zealand Journal of Psychiatry, 21*, 3–4.

Goldney, R.D., Winefield, A.H, Tiggemann, M. and Winefield, H.R. (1992) Unemployment and suicidal ideation. Unpublished manuscript.

Goldney, R.D., Smith, S., Winefield, A.H., Tiggemann, M. and Winefield, H.R. (1991) Suicidal ideation: its enduring nature and associated morbidity. *Acta Psychiatrica Scandinavica, 83*, 115–20.

Goldney, R.D., Winefield, A.H., Tiggemann, M., Winefield, H.R. and Smith, S. (1989) Suicidal ideation in a young adult population. *Acta Psychiatrica Scandinavica, 79*, 481–9.

Gore, S. (1978) The effect of social support in moderating the health consequences of unemployment. *Journal of Health and Social Behavior, 19*, 157–65.

Graham, H. (1987) Women's smoking and family health. *Social Science and Medicine, 25*, 47–56.

Gurney, R.M. (1980a) Does unemployment affect the self-esteem of school leavers? *Australian Journal of Psychology, 32*, 175–82.

Gurney, R.M. (1980b) The effects of unemployment on the psycho-social development of school leavers. *Journal of Occupational Psychology, 53*, 205–13.

Gurney, R.M. (1981) Leaving school, facing unemployment, and making attributions about the causes of unemployment. *Journal of Vocational Behavior, 18*, 79–91.

Halford, W.K. and Learner, E. (1984) Correlates of coping with unemployment in young Australians. *Australian Psychologist, 19*, 333–44.

Hansen, W.B., Collins, L.M., Malotte, C.K., Johnson, C.A. and Fielding, J.E. (1985) Attrition in prevention research. *Journal of Behavioral Medicine, 8*, 261–75.

Harrison, R. (1976) The demoralizing effect of prolonged unemployment. *Department of Education Gazette, 84*, 339–48.

Hartley, J.F. (1980) The impact of unemployment on the self-esteem of managers. *Journal of Occupational Psychology, 53*, 147–55.

Hartley, J.F. and Fryer, D.M. (1984) The psychology of unemployment: a critical appraisal, in G.M. Stephenson and J.H. Davis (eds) *Progess in Applied Social Psychology*, Vol. 2. Chichester: Wiley.

Hawton, K. and Rose, N. (1986) Unemployment and attempted suicide among men in Oxford. *Health Trends, 18*, 29–32.

Hawton, K., Fagg, J. and Simkin, S. (1988) Female unemployment and attempted suicide. *British Journal of Psychiatry, 152*, 632–7.

Hayes, J. and Nutman, P. (1981) *Understanding the Unemployed*. London: Tavistock.

Heider, F. (1958) *The Psychology of Interpersonal Relations*. New York: Wiley.

Henderson, S., Byrne, D.G. and Duncan-Jones, P. (1981) *Neurosis and the Social Environment*. Sydney: Academic Press.

Hendry, L.B. and Raymond, M. (1986) Psychological/sociological aspects of youth unemployment: an interpretative theoretical model. *Journal of Adolescence, 9*, 355–66.

Hepworth, S.J. (1980) Moderating effects of the psychological impact of unemployment. *Journal of Occupational Psychology, 53*, 139–45.

Hill, D.J., White, V.M. and Gray, N.J. (1988) Measures of tobacco smoking in Australia 1974–1986 by means of a standard method. *Medical Journal of Australia, 149*, 10–12.

Hill, D.J., White, V.M., Pain, M.D. and Gardner, G.J. (1990) Tobacco and alcohol use among Australian secondary schoolchildren in 1987. *Medical Journal of Australia, 152*, 124–30.

Hyman, H.H. (1979) The effects of unemployment: a neglected problem in modern social research, in R.K. Merton, J.S. Coleman, and P.H. Rossi (eds) *Qualitative and Quantitative Social Research*. New York: The Free Press.

Illich, I. (1978) *The Right to Useful Unemployment*. London: Marion Boyars.

Isralowitz, R.E. and Singer, M. (1986) Unemployment and its impact on adolescent work values. *Adolescence, 21*, 145–58.

Isralowitz, R.E. and Singer, M. (1987) Long-term unemployment and its impact on black adolescent work values. *Journal of Social Psychology, 127*, 227–36.

Iversen, L., Sabroe, S. and Damsgaard, M.T. (1989) Hospital admissions before and after a shipyard closure. *British Medical Journal, 299*, 1073–6.

Jackson, P.R., Stafford, E.M., Banks, M.H. and Warr, P.B. (1983) Unemployment and psychological distress: the moderating role of employment commitment. *Journal of Applied Psychology, 68*, 525–35.

Jahoda, M. (1979) The impact of unemployment in the thirties and seventies. *Bulletin of the British Psychological Society, 32*, 309–14.

Jahoda, M. (1981) Work, employment and unemployment: values, theories and approaches in social research. *American Psychologist, 36*, 184–91.

Jahoda, M. (1982) *Employment and Unemployment: A Social-psychological Analysis*. London: Cambridge University Press.

186   *Growing up with unemployment*

Jahoda, M. (1986) In defence of a non-reductionist social psychology. *Social Behaviour, 1*, 25–9.

Jahoda, M. (1988) Economic recession and mental health: some conceptual issues. *Journal of Social Issues, 44*, 13–23.

Jahoda, M., Lazarsfeld, P.F. and Zeisel, H. (1933) *Marienthal: The Sociography of an Unemployed Community.* (English translation, 1971, Chicago: Aldine Atherton).

Jardine, E. and Winefield, A.H. (1981) Achievement motivation, psychological reactance, and learned helplessness. *Motivation and Emotion, 5*, 99–113.

Jessor, R. and Jessor, S.L. (1977) *Problem Behavior and Psychosocial Development: A Longitudinal Study of Youth.* New York: Academic Press.

Jones, S.C., Forster, D.P. and Hassanyeh, F. (1991) The role of unemployment in parasuicide. *Psychological Medicine, 21*, 169–76.

Josephson, P. and Rosen, M.A. (1978) Panel loss in a high school drug study, in D. Kandel (ed.) *Longitudinal Research on Drug Use: Empirical Findings and Methodological Issues.* Washington, D.C.: Hemisphere.

Kagan, A.R. (1987) Unemployment causes ill health: the wrong track. *Social Science and Medicine, 25*, 217–18.

Kalachek, E. (1980) Longitudinal surveys and the youth labour market. Annex 1 to *Youth Unemployment: The Causes and Consequences.* Paris: OECD.

Kasl, S.V. and Cobb, S. (1979) Some mental health consequences of plant closing and job loss, in L.A. Ferman and J.P. Gordus (eds) *Mental Health and the Economy.* Kalamazoo: Upjohn.

Kasl, S.V. and Cobb, S. (1980) The experience of losing a job: some effects on cardiovascular functioning. *Psychotherapy and Psychosomatics, 34*, 88–109.

Kasl, S.V., Gore, S. and Cobb, S. (1975) The experience of losing a job: reported changes in health, symptoms, and illness behavior. *Psychosomatic Medicine, 37*, 106–22.

Kaufman, H.G. (1982) *Professionals in Search of Work: Coping with the Stress of Job Loss and Unemployment.* New York: Wiley.

Kelley, H.H. (1967) Attribution theory in social psychology, in D. Levine (ed.) *Nebraska Symposium on Motivation.* Lincoln: University of Nebraska Press.

Kelly, J.A. and Worell, L. (1976) Parent behaviors related to masculine, feminine, and androgynous sex role orientations. *Journal of Consulting and Clinical Psychology, 44*, 843–51.

Kelvin, P. (1980) Social psychology 2001: the social psychological bases and implications of structural unemployment, in R. Gilmour and S.W. Duck (eds) *The Development of Social Psychology.* London: Academic Press.

Kelvin, P. and Jarrett, J.E. (1985) *Unemployment: Its Social Psychological Effects.* Cambridge: Cambridge University Press.

Kemp, N.J. and Mercer, A. (1983) Unemployment, disability, and rehabilitation centres and their effects on mental health. *Journal of Occupational Psychology, 56*, 37–48.

Kessler, R.C., Turner, J.B. and House, J.S. (1987) Intervening processes in the relationship between unemployment and health. *Psychological Medicine, 17*, 959–61.

Kessler, R.C., Turner, J.B. and House, J.S. (1988) Effects of unemployment on health in a community survey: main modifying and mediating effects. *Journal of Social Issues, 44*, 69–85.

Kieselbach, T. and Svensson, P.G. (1988) Health and social policy responses to unemployment in Europe. *Journal of Social Issues, 44*, 173–191.

Kilpatrick, R. and Trew, K. (1985) Life-styles and psychological well-being among unemployed men in Northern Ireland. *Journal of Occupational Psychology, 58,* 207–16.

Kline, R.B., Canter, W.A. and Robin, A. (1987) Parameters of teenage alcohol use: a path analytic conceptual model. *Journal of Consulting and Clinical Psychology, 55,* 521–8.

Kreitman, N. (1988) The British anomaly: suicide, domestic gas and unemployment in the United Kingdom, in H.J. Moller, A. Schmidtke and R. Welz (eds) *Current Issues of Suicidology* (pp. 364–71). Berlin and New York: Springer-Verlag.

Lancet (1984) Unemployment and health, *ii.* 1018–19.

Lang, M. and Tisher, M. (1978) *Children's Depression Scale – Research Edition.* Hawthorn, Victoria: Australian Council for Educational Research.

Lazarus, R. and Folkman, S. (1984) *Stress, Appraisal, and Coping.* New York: Springer.

Lee, A.J., Crombie, I.K., Smith, W.C.S. and Tunstall-Pedoe, H.D. (1991) Cigarette smoking and employment status. *Social Science and Medicine, 33,* 1309–12.

Lewis, A. (1935) Neurosis and unemployment. *Lancet, ii,* 293–7.

Liem, R. and Liem, J.H. (1988) Psychological effects of unemployment on workers and their families. *Journal of Social Issues, 44,* 87–106.

Lippman, S.A. and McCall, J.J. (1976) The economics of job search: a survey. *Economic Inquiry, 14,* 155–89.

Little, C.B. (1976) Technical-professional unemployment: middle-class adaptability to personal crisis. *Sociological Quarterly, 17,* 262–74.

Little, C.R., Villemez, W.J. and Smith, D.A. (1982) One step forward, two steps back: more on the class/criminality controversy. *American Sociological Review, 47,* 435–8.

McAlister, A. and Gordon, N.P. (1986) Attrition bias in a cohort study of substance abuse onset and prevention. *Evaluation Review, 10,* 853–9.

McAllister, I., Moore, R. and Makkai, T. (1991) *Drugs in Australian Society: Patterns, Attitudes and Policies.* Melbourne: Longman Cheshire.

McClelland, D.C., Atkinson, J.W., Clark, R.A. and Lowell, E.L. (1953) *The Achievement Motive.* New York: Appleton-Century-Crofts.

McKenna, S.P. and Fryer, D.M. (1984) Perceived health during lay-off and early unemployment. *Occupational Health, 36,* 201–6

McPherson, A. and Hall, W. (1983) Psychiatric impairment, physical health and work values among unemployed and apprenticed young men. *Australian and New Zealand Journal of Psychiatry, 17,* 335–40.

Maizels, J. (1970) *Adolescent Needs and the Transition from School to Work.* London: Athlone Press.

Mandler, G. and Sarason, S.B. (1952) A study of anxiety and learning. *Journal of Abnormal and Social Psychology, 47,* 166–73

Marjoribanks, K.A. (1986) A longitudinal study of adolescents' aspirations as assessed by Seginer's model. *Merrill-Palmer Quarterly, 32,* 211–30.

Marsden, D. (1982) *Workless.* London: Croom Helm.

Marsden, D. and Duff, E. (1975) *Workless: Some Unemployed Men and their Families.* Harmondsworth: Penguin.

Martikainen, P.T. (1990) Unemployment and mortality among Finnish men, 1981–5. *British Medical Journal, 301,* 407–11.

Mehrabian, A. (1968) Male and female scales of the tendency to achieve. *Educational Psychology and Measurement, 28,* 493–502.

Moos, R.H. (1986) *Coping with Life Crises*. New York: Plenum.

Murray, C. (1978) *Youth Unemployment*. Slough: NFER.

Murray, H.A. (1938) *Explorations in Personality*. New York: Oxford University Press.

National Health and Medical Research Council. (1987) *Is There a Safe Level of Daily Consumption of Alcohol for Men and Women? Recommendations Regarding Responsible Drinking*. Canberra: Australian Government Publishing Service.

Neuling, S.J. and Winefield, H.R. (1988) Social support and recovery after surgery for breast cancer: frequency and correlates of supportive behaviours by family, friends, and surgeons. *Social Science and Medicine, 27*, 385–92.

Newcomb, M.D. (1986) Nuclear attitudes and reactions: associations with depression, drug use and quality of life. *Journal of Personality and Social Psychology, 50*, 906–20.

Newcomb, M.D. and Bentler, P.M. (1988) Impact of adolescent drug use and social support in problems of young adolescents: a longitudinal study. *Journal of Abnormal Psychology, 97*, 64–75.

Nisbett, R.W. and Wilson, T.D. (1977) Telling more than we know: verbal reports on mental processes. *Psychological Review, 84*, 231–59.

Nowicki, S. and Duke, M.P. (1974) A locus of control scale for noncollege as well as college adults. *Journal of Personality Assessment, 38*, 136–7.

O'Brien, G.E. (1986) *Psychology of Work and Unemployment*. Chichester: Wiley.

O'Brien, G.E. and Feather, N.T. (1990) The relative effects of unemployment and quality of employment on the affect, work values and personal control of adolescents. *Journal of Occupational Psychology, 63*, 151–65.

O'Brien, G.E. and Kabanoff, B. (1979) Comparison of unemployed and employed workers on values, locus of control, and health variables. *Australian Psychologist, 14*, 143–54.

Oakes, W.F. and Curtis, N. (1982) Learned helplessness: not dependent upon cognitions, attributions, or other such phenomenal experiences. *Journal of Personality, 50*, 387–408.

Oddy, M., Donovan, A. and Pardoe, R. (1984) Do government training schemes for unemployed school leavers achieve their objectives? A psychological perspective. *Journal of Adolescence, 7*, 377–86.

OECD (1991a) *Economic Outlook*, December 1991.

OECD (1991b) *Labour Force Statistics 1969–1989*. Paris: OECD Department of Economics and Statistics.

Offer, D., Ostrov, E. and Howard, K.I. (1982) *The Offer Self-Image Questionnaire for Adolescents: A Manual*. Chicago: Michael Reese Hospital.

Ostell, A. and Divers, P. (1987) Attributional style, unemployment and mental health. *Journal of Occupational Psychology, 60*, 333–7.

Parkes, C.M. (1971) Psycho-social transitions: a field for study. *Social Science and Medicine, 5*, 101–15.

Parnes, H.S. (1982) *Unemployment Experiences of Individuals over a Decade*. Kalamazoo: Upjohn Institute.

Parry, G. and Brewin, C.R. (1988) Cognitive style and depression: symptom-related, event-related or independent provoking factor? *British Journal of Clinical Psychology, 27*, 23–35.

Patton, W. and Noller, P. (1984) Unemployment and youth: a longitudinal study. *Australian Journal of Psychology, 36*, 399–413.

Patton, W. and Noller, P. (1990) Adolescent self-concept: effects of being employed, unemployed or returning to school. *Australian Journal of Psychology*, 42, 247–59.

Payne, J. (1987) Unemployment, apprenticeships and training: does it pay to stay on at school? *British Journal of Sociology of Education*, 8, 425–45.

Payne, R.L. and Hartley, J. (1987) A test of a model for explaining the affective experience of unemployed men. *Journal of Occupational Psychology*, 60, 31–47.

Payne, R.L., Warr, P.B. and Hartley, J. (1984) Social class and psychological ill-health during unemployment. *Sociology of Health and Illness*, 6, 152–74.

Perris, C., Jacobsson, L., Lindström, H., von Knorring, L. and Perris, H. (1980) Development of a new inventory for assessing memories of parental rearing behavior. *Acta Psychiatrica Scandinavica*, 61, 265–74.

Peterson, C. and Seligman, M.E.P. (1984) Causal explanations as a risk factor for depression: theory and evidence. *Psychological Review*, 91, 347–74.

Peterson, C., Semmel, A., von Baeyer, C., Abramson, L.Y., Metalsky, G.I. and Seligman, M.E.P. (1982) The attributional style questionnaire. *Cognitive Therapy and Research*, 6, 287–99.

Platt, S. (1984) Unemployment and suicidal behaviour: review of the literature. *Social Science and Medicine*, 19, 93–115.

Platt, S. (1986a) Parasuicide and unemployment. *British Journal of Psychiatry*, 149, 401–5.

Platt, S. (1986b) Clinical and social characteristics of male parasuicides: variation by employment status and duration of employment. *Acta Psychiatrica Scandinavica*, 74, 24–31.

Platt, S. and Duffy, J.C. (1986) Social and clinical correlates of unemployment in two cohorts of male parasuicides. *Social Psychiatry*, 21, 17–24.

Platt, S. and Kreitman, N. (1984) Trends in parasuicide and unemployment among men in Edinburgh, 1968–82. *British Medical Journal*, 289, 1029–32.

Platt, S. and Kreitman, N. (1985) Parasuicide and unemployment among men in Edinburgh. *Psychological Medicine*, 15, 113–23.

Platt, S. and Kreitman, N. (1990) Long-term trends in parasuicide and unemployment in Edinburgh, 1968–87. *Social Psychiatry and Psychiatric Epidemiology*, 25, 56–61.

Pokorny, A.D. (1983) Prediction of suicide in psychiatric patients. *Archives of General Psychiatry*, 40, 249–57.

Poole, M. (1983) *Youth: Expectations and Transitions*. London: Routledge & Kegan Paul.

Rabkin, J.G. and Klein, D.F. (1987) The clinical measurement of depressive disorders, in A.J. Marsella, R.M.A. Hirschfield and M.M. Katz (eds) *The Measurement of Depression*. Chichester: Wiley.

Rao, V.V. (1975) Suicide in India, in N.C. Farberow (ed.) *Suicide in Different Cultures* (pp. 231–8). Baltimore: University Park Press.

Robins, L.N. and Regier, D.A. (eds) (1991) *Psychiatric Disorders in America*. New York: The Free Press.

Rosenberg, M. (1965) *Society and the Adolescent Self-image*. Princeton: Princeton University Press.

Ross, M.W., Campbell, R.L. and Clayer, J.R. (1982) New inventory for measurement of parental rearing patterns: an English form of the EMBU. *Acta Psychiatrica Scandinavica*, 66, 499–507.

Rotter, J.B. (1966) Generalised expectancies for internal versus external control of reinforcement. *Psychological Monographs, 80* (1, Whole No. 609).

Rowley, K.M. and Feather, N.T. (1987) The impact of unemployment in relation to age and length of unemployment. *Journal of Occupational Psychology, 60*, 323–32.

Sainsbury, P. (1986) The epidemiology of suicide, in A. Roy (ed.) *Suicide* (pp. 17–40). Baltimore: Williams & Wilkins.

Seabrook, J. (1982) *Unemployment*. London: Quartet Books.

Seligman, M.E.P. (1975) *Helplessness*. San Francisco: Freeman.

Seligman, M.E.P. (1991) *Learned Optimism*. New York: Knopf.

Shamir, B. (1986a) Self-esteem and the psychological impact of unemployment. *Social Psychology Quarterly, 49*, 61–72.

Shamir, B. (1986b) Protestant work ethic, work involvement and the psychological impact of unemployment. *Journal of Occupational Behaviour, 7*, 25–38.

Shapiro, C.M. and Parry, M.R. (1984) Is unemployment a cause of parasuicide? *British Medical Journal, 289*, 1622.

Shore, E.S. and Batt, S. (1991) Contextual factors related to the drinking behaviors of American business and professional women. *British Journal of Addiction, 86*, 171–6.

Sinfield, A. (1980) *What Unemployment Means*. Oxford: Martin Robertson.

Smith, J.M. (1973) A quick measure of achievement motivation. *British Journal of Social and Clinical Psychology, 12*, 137–43.

Smith, P. (1981) *Work or the Want of It*. Sydney: Australian Council of Social Services.

Smith, R. (1987a) More evidence on unemployment and health. *British Medical Journal, 294*, 1047–8.

Smith, R. (1987b) *Unemployment and Health: A Disaster and a Challenge*. Oxford: Oxford University Press.

Smith, R. (1991) Unemployment: here we go again. *British Medical Journal, 302*, 606–7.

Srole, L. (1956) Social integration and certain corollaries: an exploratory study. *American Sociological Review, 21*, 709–16.

Stafford, E.M. (1982) The impact of the Youth Opportunities Programme on young people's employment prospects and psychological well-being. *British Journal of Guidance and Counselling, 10*, 12–21.

Stafford, E.M., Jackson, P.R. and Banks, M.H. (1980) Employment, work involvement and mental health in less qualified young people. *Journal of Occupational Psychology, 53*, 291–304.

Stokes, G. (1983) Work, unemployment, and leisure. *Leisure Studies, 2*, 269–86.

Tabachnik, B.G. and Fidell, L.S. (1983) *Using Multivariate Statistics*. New York: Harper & Row.

Talaga, J. and Beehr, T.A. (1989) Retirement: a psychological perspective, in C.L. Cooper and I.T. Robertson (eds) *International Review of Industrial and Organisational Psychology* (Chapter 6, pp. 185–211). Chichester: Wiley.

Taylor, K.F. and Gurney, R.M. (1984) So you're thinking of studying unemployment? in M.C. Nixon (ed.) *Issues in Psychological Practice*. Melbourne: Longman Cheshire.

Tiffany, D.W., Cowan, J.R. and Tiffany, P.M. (1970) *The Unemployed: A Socio-psychological Portrait*. Englewood Cliffs: Prentice-Hall.

Tiggemann, M. and Winefield, A.H. (1980) Some psychological effects of unemployment on school leavers. *Australian Journal of Social Issues, 15,* 269–76.

Tiggemann, M. and Winefield, A.H. (1984) The effects of unemployment on the mood, self-esteem, locus of control and depressive affect of school leavers. *Journal of Occupational Psychology, 57,* 33–42.

Tiggemann, M. and Winefield, A.H. (1989) Predictors of future employment, unemployment and further study in school leavers. *Journal of Occupational Psychology, 62,* 213–21.

Tiggemann, M., Winefield, A.H., Winefield, H.R. and Goldney, R.D. (1991a) The prediction of psychological distress from attributional style: a test of the hopelessness model of depression. *Australian Journal of Psychology, 43,* 125–7.

Tiggemann, M., Winefield, A.H., Winefield, H.R. and Goldney, R.D. (1991b) The stability of attributional style and its relation to psychological distress. *British Journal of Clinical Psychology, 30,* 247–55.

Tiggemann, M., Winefield, H.R., Goldney, R.D. and Winefield, A.H. (1992) Attributional style and parental rearing as predictors of psychological distress. *Personality and Individual Differences, 13,* 835–41.

Turner, M. (1983) *Stuck! Living Without Work.* Ringwood, Victoria: Penguin.

Ullah, P. and Osborn, P. (1991) Some correlates of psychological health among Australian school pupils. Unpublished manuscript.

Ullah, P., Banks, M.H. and Warr, P. (1985) Social support, social pressures and psychological distress during unemployment. *Psychological Medicine, 15,* 283–95.

Warr, P.B. (1983) Work, jobs, and unemployment. *Bulletin of the British Psychological Society, 36,* 305–11.

Warr, P.B. (1984) Economic recession and mental health: a review of research. *Tijdschrift voor Sociale Gezondheidszorg, 62,* 289–308.

Warr, P.B. (1987) *Work, Unemployment, and Mental Health.* Oxford: Clarendon Press.

Warr, P.B. and Jackson, P.R. (1984) Men without jobs: some correlates of age and length of unemployment. *Journal of Occupational Psychology, 57,* 77–85.

Warr, P.B. and Jackson, P.R. (1985) Factors influencing the psychological impact of prolonged unemployment and re-employment. *Psychological Medicine, 15,* 795–807.

Warr, P.B. and Jackson, P.R. (1987) Adapting to the unemployed role: a longitudinal investigation. *Social Science and Medicine, 24,* 1–6.

Warr, P.B. and Parry, G. (1982) Paid employment and women's psychological well-being. *Psychological Bulletin, 91,* 498–516.

Warr, P.B. and Payne, R.L. (1983) Social class and reported changes in behavior after job loss. *Journal of Applied Social Psychology, 13,* 206–22.

Warr, P.B., Banks, M.H. and Ullah, P. (1985) The experience of unemployment among black and white urban teenagers. *British Journal of Psychology, 76,* 75–87.

Warr, P.B., Cook, J. and Wall, T. (1979) Scales for the measurement of work attitudes and psychological well-being. *Journal of Occupational Psychology, 52,* 129–48.

Warr, P.B., Jackson, P.R. and Banks, M.H. (1982) Duration of unemployment and psychological well-being in young men and women. *Current Psychological Research, 2,* 207–14.

Watts, A.G. (1987) Beyond unemployment? Schools and the future of work. *British Journal of Educational Studies, 35*, 3–17.

Weiner, B. (1985) An attributional theory of achievement motivation and emotion. *Psychological Review, 92*, 548–73.

Wilks, J. and Callan, V.J. (1988) Expectations about appropriate drinking contexts: comparisons of parents, adolescents and best friends. *British Journal of Addiction, 83*, 1055–62.

Windschuttle, K. (1979) *Unemployment.* London: Penguin.

Winefield, A.H. (1989) A seven-year longitudinal study of school leavers, in B.J. Fallon, H.P. Pfister and J. Brebner (eds) *Proceedings of the XXIV International Congress of Psychology, Sydney, Vol. 5: Advances in Industrial Organisational Psychology* (pp. 211–19). Amsterdam: Elsevier.

Winefield, A.H. and Tiggemann, M. (1985) Psychological correlates of employment and unemployment: effects, predisposing factors, and sex differences. *Journal of Occupational Psychology, 58*, 229–42.

Winefield, A.H. and Tiggemann, M. (1989a) Job loss versus failure to find work as psychological stressors in the young unemployed. *Journal of Occupational Psychology, 62*, 79–85.

Winefield, A.H. and Tiggemann, M. (1989b) Unemployment duration and affective well-being in the young. *Journal of Occupational Psychology, 62*, 327–36.

Winefield, A.H. and Tiggemann, M. (1990a) Employment status and psychological well-being: a longitudinal study. *Journal of Applied Psychology, 75*, 455–9.

Winefield, A.H. and Tiggemann, M. (1990b) Length of unemployment and psychological distress: longitudinal and cross-sectional data. *Social Science and Medicine, 31*, 461–5.

Winefield, A.H. and Tiggemann, M. (1992) Affective reactions to employment and unemployment as a function of prior employment expectations and motivation: a longitudinal study. Unpublished manuscript.

Winefield, A.H. and Tiggemann, M. (1993) Psychological distress, work attitudes and intended year of leaving school. *Journal of Adolescence* (in press).

Winefield, A.H. and Winefield, H.R. (1987) Changing attitudes to unemployment in school leavers. *Psychological Reports, 60*, 478.

Winefield, A.H., Tiggemann, M. and Goldney, R.D. (1988) Psychological concomitants of satisfactory employment and unemployment in young people. *Social Psychiatry and Psychiatric Epidemiology, 23*, 149–57.

Winefield, A.H., Tiggemann, M. and Smith, S. (1987) Unemployment, attributional style, and psychological well-being. *Personality and Individual Differences, 8*, 659–66.

Winefield, A.H., Tiggemann, M. and Winefield, H.R. (1989) Socio-economic status and changing work attitudes in high school students. *Australian Journal of Social Issues, 24*, 303–12.

Winefield, A.H., Tiggemann, M. and Winefield, H.R. (1990) Factors moderating the psychological impact of unemployment at different ages. *Personality and Individual Differences, 11*, 45–52.

Winefield, A.H., Tiggemann, M. and Winefield, H.R. (1991a) Attrition bias and internal validity in a longitudinal study of youth unemployment. *Australian Journal of Psychology, 43*, 69–73.

Winefield, A.H., Tiggemann, M. and Winefield, H.R. (1991b) The psychological impact of unemployment and unsatisfactory employment in young men and women: longitudinal and cross-sectional data. *British Journal of Psychology,* *82,* 473–86.

Winefield, A.H., Tiggemann, M. and Winefield, H.R. (1992a) Unemployment distress, reasons for job loss and causal attributions for unemployment in young people. *Journal of Occupational and Organizational Psychology, 65,* 213–18.

Winefield, A.H., Tiggemann, M. and Winefield, H.R. (1992b) Spare time use and psychological well-being in employed and unemployed young people. *Journal of Occupational and Organizational Psychology, 65,* 307–13.

Winefield, A.H., Winefield, H.R. and Tiggemann, M. (1990) Sample attrition bias in a longitudinal study of young people. *Australian Journal of Psychology, 41,* 75–85.

Winefield, A.H., Tiggemann, M., Winefield, H.R. and Goldney, R.D. (1991) Social alienation and employment status in the young. *Journal of Organizational Behavior, 12,* 145–54.

Winefield, A.H., Winefield, H.R., Tiggemann, M. and Goldney, R.D. (1991) A longitudinal study of the psychological effects of unemployment and unsatisfactory employment on young adults. *Journal of Applied Psychology, 76,* 424–31.

Winefield, H.R. (1992) Work satisfaction and psychological distress in older university students. Unpublished manuscript.

Winefield, H.R. and Winefield, A.H. (1992) Psychological development in adolescence and youth: education, employment, and vocational identity, in P. Heaven (ed.) *Psychological Bases of Human Development* (pp. 140–66). Sydney: Harcourt Brace Jovanovich.

Winefield, H.R., Winefield, A.H. and Tiggemann, M. (1992a) Social support and psychological well-being in young adults: the multidimensional support scale. *Journal of Personality Assessment, 58,* 198–210.

Winefield, H.R., Winefield, A.H. and Tiggemann, M. (1992b) Psychological attributes of young adult smokers. *Psychological Reports, 70,* 675–81.

Winefield, H.R., Goldney, R.D., Tiggemann, M. and Winefield, A.H. (1989) Reported parental rearing patterns and psychological adjustment: a short form of the EMBU. *Personality and Individual Differences, 10,* 459–65.

Winefield, H.R., Goldney, R.D., Tiggemann, M. and Winefield, A.H. (1990) Parental rearing behaviors: stability of reports over time and their relation to adult interpersonal skills. *Journal of Genetic Psychology, 151,* 211–19.

Winefield, H.R., Goldney, R.D., Winefield, A.H. and Tiggemann, M. (1989) The General Health Questionnaire: reliability and validity for Australian youth. *Australian and New Zealand Journal of Psychiatry, 23,* 53–8.

Winefield, H.R., Goldney, R.D., Winefield, A.H. and Tiggemann, M. (1992) Psychological correlates of level of alcohol consumption in young adults. *Medical Journal of Australia, 156,* 755–9.

Winefield, H.R., Tiggemann, M., Goldney, R.D. and Winefield, A.H. (1992) Predictors and consequences of tertiary education: a nine-year followup of academically capable school leavers. *British Journal of Educational Psychology, 62,* 527–33.

Winefield, H.R., Winefield, A.H., Tiggemann, M. and Goldney, R.D. (1988) Psychological and demographic predictors of entry into tertiary education in young Australian females and males. *British Journal of Developmental Psychology, 6,* 183–90.

Winefield, H.R., Winefield, A.H., Tiggemann, M. and Goldney, R.D. (1989)

Psychological concomitants of tobacco and alcohol use in young Australian adults. *British Journal of Addiction, 84*, 1067–73.

Winefield, H.R., Winefield, A.H., Tiggemann, M. and Smith, S. (1988) Unemployment, drug use and health in late adolescence. *Psychotherapy and Psychosomatics, 47*, 204–10.

Wing, J.K. (1980) The use of the Present State Examination in general population surveys. *Acta Psychiatrica Scandinavica, 285*, 230–40.

World Health Organisation Constitution (1948) *World Health Organization Basic Documents*. Geneva: WHO.

Name index

Subject index